Operations Management in Context

Operations Management in Context

Les Galloway, Frank Rowbotham and Masoud Azhashemi

OXFORD AUCKLAND BOSTON JOHANNESBURG MELBOURNE NEW DELHI

Butterworth-Heinemann
Linacre House, Jordan Hill, Oxford OX2 8DP
225 Wildwood Avenue, Woburn, MA 01801-2041
A division of Reed Educational and Professional Publishing Ltd

A member of the Reed Elsevier plc group

First published 2000

British Library Cataloguing in Publication Data
Galloway, Les
    Operations management in context
    1. Production management
    I. Title   II. Rowbotham, Frank   III. Azhashemi, Masoud
    658.5

ISBN 0 7506 4280 7

Typeset by Florence Production Ltd, Stoodleigh, Devon
Printed and bound in Great Britain

FOR EVERY TITLE THAT WE PUBLISH, BUTTERWORTH-HEINEMANN
WILL PAY FOR BTCV TO PLANT AND CARE FOR A TREE.

Contents

Preface

Operations management is a component of the majority of under-graduate business and management courses. Although sometimes only introductory, it is frequently followed by deeper treatment through electives.

This book is aimed at such introductory programmes, although it goes into sufficient depth for those follow-up modules which do not specialize in particular aspects of operations management. The main objectives are to:

- cover the content of mainstream operations modules taught at the introductory level on undergraduate, Higher National Diploma and Higher National Certificate programmes
- cover the content in a structure which permits the reader to develop an appropriate study plan
- provide the reader with an easily understood text
- avoid a mathematical and technique driven approach to the subject
- provide a format which reinforces the learning process.

While the book follows a logical sequence, operations management can be approached in several different ways, so your course may not adopt the same topic sequence and may not include all topics. Since the book chapters do not make any great demands on prior knowledge this should not pose a problem, though we recommend that you read the entire book to develop a wider background understanding of the subject.

Operations management is essentially a practical subject, so its application is illustrated throughout the book with examples. These are all taken from the real world, though the organizations in question are not always identified.

There are also numerous small exercises and discussion topics. These are intended to promote classroom discussion, but can be used individually. Each chapter ends with a series of self-assessment questions intended to allow the reader to test their grasp of the basic issues. The book ends with a series of detailed case studies. These provide the reader with more extended illustrations of operations management situations and problems. They can be used for individual consideration or they can form the basis of extended group discussions in the classroom. While they are aimed in part at particular topics, the real world does not conform to chapter headings, so most overlap into several areas of the subject.

Les Galloway, Frank Rowbotham
and Masoud Azhashemi

Introduction

The operations function is probably less well understood than any other business function. In manufacturing industries it is generally taken to be 'production' and best left to specialists. In some service organizations the term is hardly recognized. It is certainly not as well recognized as the other business functions. A little thought, however, shows that the better identified disciplines, such as finance, marketing or personnel, are essentially support activities to the main value-adding activity of the organization. This core activity of any organization, the transformation of some input – material, information, customer – into an output of greater value – for example a computer, an insurance policy or a satisfied customer – is the operations function. Without this the other functions would be irrelevant. Operations management is concerned with any productive activity, whether manufacturing or service, public sector or private sector, profit-making or not for profit. It is concerned with ensuring that operations are carried out both efficiently and effectively.

All managers are operations managers since all functions within an organization are, presumably, productive activities. It goes without saying that all functions should be carried out efficiently and effectively. However, the operations function is at the heart of all manufacturing and service enterprises, and unless this core operation is carried out effectively, there is little hope that the organization as a whole will be effective.

An understanding of operations management principles can help any manager manage more effectively, whatever functional area they are concerned with, but it also leads to a greater understanding of the function of the organization as a whole, and a greater appreciation for the issues which affect overall organizational performance.

An important aim of the book is to reinforce the learning process. In order to achieve this it is suggested that the following approach be adopted. The content of the book should be compared with the syllabus being studied and the chapters should be read in the order of the syllabus. The chapters are probably best read after the taught syllabus sessions, as they can then be used to go over and extend the material covered. The exercises and discussion topics are placed where it is felt appropriate to stop reading and to engage the content from a more active perspective. Used in this way the questions have a clear context. When each chapter is completed the self-test question exercises should be used to test understanding of the content. The case studies can be used when the appropriate chapters have been completed and before progressing to the next topic. By following an approach such as this the role of the book in acquiring knowledge and understanding about operations management will be greatly enhanced.

Abbreviations

ATM	automated teller machine
BPR	business process re-engineering
CAD	computer-aided design
CAM	computer-aided manufacturing
CNC	computer numerical control
CPM	critical path method
EBQ	economic batch quantity
EDI	electronic data interchange
EFQM	European Foundation for Quality Management
EOQ	economic order quantity
ERP	enterprise resource planning
FMS	flexible manufacturing system
GDP	gross domestic product
GNP	gross national product
HRM	human resource management
ISO	International Standards Organization
IT	information technology
JIT	just in time
MRP	manufacturing resources planning
MRP 1	materials requirement planning
MRP 2	manufacturing resources planning
NC	numerical control
NVQ	National Vocational Qualification
O&M	organization and methods
OPT	optimized production technology
PERT	performance evaluation and review techniques
QMS	quality management systems
SPC	statistical process control
SQA	supplier quality assurance

TIM   Total integrated management
TPM   total productive maintenance
TQM   total quality management

Chapter 1

The operations function

The purpose of this first chapter is to introduce the reader to the area of study called operations management. As such it sets the scene for many of the subsequent chapters in the book. The specific objectives are outlined below:

Learning Objectives

1 *Defining operations management.* Some functional descriptions are readily understood to convey a sense of what their subject matter actually is. Finance and personnel fall into this category. The words operations management, however, do not appear to carry the same immediacy. One of the first aims of the chapter is to provide its readers with an understanding of what the term means, so that they can accurately describe the function in their own words.

2 *The importance of operations management.* Once understood, operations management can be seen as a vital part of any organization. It is this understanding which the chapter intends to convey. Without an operation an organization remains an abstract wish. Operations management is, therefore, a widespread activity embracing all sectors of the economy.

3 *Setting a context for the subject.* Much of the book necessarily breaks down operations management into discrete topics. At the outset it is intended to set the subject into an overall context, so that its history, current concerns and economic role can be readily absorbed. One aspect of this aim is to

also consider integrative ways of looking at operations that are not specifically drawn out by the individual topics.

4 *Focusing upon the environment.* In the past operations managers have been accused of being too insular. 'You can have any model T car as long as its black' and 'pile it high and sell it cheap' echo this view. One of the aims of the chapter is to bring home to the reader that this internal focus upon the operation is not viable. Modern operations management requires a strong grasp of the nature of the environment within which it functions.

5 *Operations is a practical subject.* At the end of the chapter it should be clear that operations is about real people working in the real world. Although the subject does involve concepts, techniques and principles of its own, ultimately operations management is about making things happen.

Definition of operations management

Operations management is concerned with managing the resources that directly produce the organization's service or product. The resources will usually consist of people, materials, technology and information but may go wider than this. These resources are brought together by a series of processes so that they are utilized to deliver the primary service or product of the organization. Thus, operations management is concerned with managing inputs (resources) through transformation processes to deliver outputs (service or products). This idea is explored further in Chapter 2. As an area of study operations management is essentially a practical subject.

Case Study

Education is an operation

In an educational setting the students are a primary input. The transformation process is the learning that takes place. The main output is the educated student. For this operation to take place there has to be timetabling, lecture facilities and management of the whole activity.

Expressed in this way it can be seen that the term 'operations' covers a wide range of organizations. Manufacturing, commercial service, public service and other not-for-profit sectors are all included within its scope. One way of defining the operations function of the organization is to define what the end service or product actually is. Once this is clear, the people who directly contribute to the delivery of the end service or product, and the people who closely support them in this task, can be said to be the operational personnel of the organization.

Case Study

Supermarkets are operations

Obtaining at least a partial view of operations in practice is not difficult. As consumers and users of products and services we gain insights into the function many times. Shopping at supermarkets reveals staff at the checkouts, staff stocking shelves and staff running specialist areas like delicatessens. To make the supermarket work there must be a chain of suppliers providing the many items on display. The computers, the buildings and the vehicles involved in the total operation have to function smoothly. To bring all these staff and all these physical resources together in a co-ordinated manner so that the operation is not chaotic requires planning and monitoring. The store itself has to be designed so that it functions to the benefit of both customers and staff. The term 'operations management' embraces all of this. Without operations, there would be no supermarket. This is not to say that the operation is the most important function. It is merely to point out that it is important.

Exercise

Who are the operational personnel of:

● a university
● a police force?

Unfortunately, people who actually perform operational roles under this definition are not always called operations managers. This makes identifying the operation more difficult than, say, identifying the financial, marketing or personnel functions. Job titles such as Hospital Manager, Technical Director and Store Manager do not have the word operations in them, yet they are all operations management roles. Identifying the operations function is an important task however. In many organizations it is the operations function that accounts for the bulk of the staff, most of the facilities and the major costs.

The people who receive the end service or product are usually referred to as customers, although this does not mean that there is necessarily a commercial relationship involved. Citizens reporting a burglary, patients receiving National Health Service treatment and students in state-funded education are all covered by the term 'customer'. Moreover, customers need not be external to the organization. The idea of internal customers has gained strong currency in recent years. Thus, the medical staff of a hospital can be seen as the customers of the patients' records section. Customer, therefore, has a wide meaning within operations management. When defined as an internal entity it leads to the view of organizations as a network of interlocking operations. Department A, for instance, can be visualized as a transformation process providing inputs to Department B. Department B is the customer in this relationship. Department B transforms these into its own outputs, which in turn become the inputs of Department C, the customer. If these departments are actually labelled as Finance, or some other functional description, it does not stop them being perceived as both customers and operations. Similarly, individual people can be thought of as customers and operations. Work requests arrive as inputs. The knowledge of the individual, the phone and the computer constitute the processes. Letters, memorandums and other forms of communication are the outputs. These then become the inputs for other people within the organization, i.e., internal customers.

The term 'stakeholder' may also be used to identify who an operation is intended to serve. Essentially, a stakeholder is any person or organization with an interest in the performance of the operation. External stakeholders might include customers, the government and the media. Like the term 'customers', there is also an internal aspect to the definition. Employees, trade unions and senior managers might be described as internal stakeholders.

The tasks of operations managers

An important feature of operations is that they are dynamic systems. In other words, the inputs, the processes and the outputs are all liable to change over time. It is the role of the operations manager to make sure that these changes are planned and controlled so that the output conforms to what is required. This role requires that the operations manager undertake a range of demanding tasks. Some of these tasks are outlined below:

1 The operations manager must understand what the overall objectives of the operation are. These objectives are usually the same general areas no matter what type of operation is concerned. They can be listed as:
(a) quality
(b) speed
(c) dependability
(d) flexibility
(e) cost.
Quality may be defined at this introductory point as performing the task to the required standard within the resources available. Improving quality can be key in improving performance against all the other objectives. Speed objectives refer to the time it takes the operation to deliver what is required of it. The dependability objective covers how reliable the organization must be in keeping its promises to its customers. Flexibility concerns how quickly the operation can change to meet new demands. These new demands might be in terms of changing the amount of service or product delivered, changing the balance of the current range of services or products or changing the type of product or service delivered. Cost refers to the level of finances consumed by the operation. An important task for operations managers, therefore, is to understand what each of these generic objectives means in their own particular external environments.

Exercise

What might the objectives of operations mean in the following contexts:

● a car factory
● a supermarket
● a police force?

2 The operations manager has to plan and control the operations function so that it can meet the objectives set for it. Even the simplest of operations usually requires a network of interdependent activities for it to function properly. Without adequate planning the result will be fairly chaotic. Imagine a hospital where admissions for operations were not planned. How would operating theatres, beds and staff be brought together in order to provide health care? To be most effective the operation should also plan strategically, showing what it intends to do over the medium and long terms as well as over the short term. Planning by itself, however, is not sufficient. The dynamic state of operations and the environments within which they function make it essential that there is feedback on progress against the plans. In this way plans can be amended accordingly and the operation altered in some way to reflect the new realities. This process of gaining feedback on performance and reacting to it is called control. Control is important not only in relation to the type of plans mentioned earlier, but also in relation to the daily performance of the operation. The operations manager needs to know what the operation is actually achieving in terms of quality, speed, cost and reliability. With this knowledge he or she can then alter the performance of the operation to remedy shortfalls. Planning and control therefore feature large in the role of operations management.

Case Study

The Paddington train crash

At the centre of the railway disaster that occurred close to London's Paddington station was the question of why the train driver of the local service train did not stop when the signal was red. There were two control systems to try to prevent a train proceeding through a red light. First, the train was equipped with a receiver to pick up a red or yellow light condition on a signal and to automatically warn the driver of potential danger by sounding hooters or bells inside the driver's cabin. This system, known as the Automatic Warning System, could be cancelled by the driver. Second, the driver was supposed to manually observe red lights and react by stopping the train. In this case, it seems that the warning system was cancelled by the driver and he did not react to the red light which was displayed on the signal. The control systems were designed with the possibility of failure built into them and when the failure happened in this instance the consequences were disastrous.

3 The operations manager has to undertake responsibility for being involved in the design of both the end service/product and the delivery processes. This means taking responsibility for: the way in which the end product functions, the organization of the transformation process, the technology used and the design of the jobs involved. In services the encounter between staff and users is key to success. Designing people's jobs so that they are well trained and motivated is thus vital. Without this involvement the operations manager will be placed in the position of having to deliver a service or product with a process that is not designed with the operations perspective taken into account. Being involved in design is not an easy role, as the operations perspective is usually concerned with the constraints of the operation, whilst the design perspective is focused upon creativity. As a result, the operations input into design can easily be construed as unduly negative. Bringing the creative and the operations perspectives together in a positive manner is one of the features of organizations that manage design well.

4 The operation has to be improved. Knowing what today's requirements are for quality, speed, dependability, flexibility and cost, and managing to meet them, is only part of the task. Superior operations also work hard to improve their performance in these areas over time. Continuous improvement is an essential aspect of modern operations management. The reasons for this emphasis are not too hard to find. The customers of operations have changing expectations in all the fields in which operations have to be good performers. Other operations which either compete directly or which set benchmark standards are also likely to be continuously improving. The net result of these two factors is that an operation that is not improving is probably actually opening up a negative gap between itself and its customers and between itself and other relevant operations. This will ultimately lead to dissatisfied customers and a poor reputation for the operation. One way of summarizing the implications of this trend is to say that operations managers must be continuously planning improvements, implementing them, checking on the results of improvements and taking action to reinforce what has gone well and to address what has not worked so well.

5 Operations exist in a wider organizational context. Marketing, personnel, finance and design functions have close links to operations. If they are all to work successfully to a common goal then good communication between operations and the other functions

of the organization is essential. Operations managers have to be able to explain to the other functions their own plans. In addition, the operational implications of what the other functions are trying to achieve need to be made clear. In essence, operations managers need to communicate the capabilities of the operation that they control. They must therefore be able to understand the different perspectives of these various functions and be able to communicate with them in an informed manner.

In performing all these tasks the overriding objective is for the operation to be managed in a way which is both effective and efficient. Being effective means making the operation work so that it successfully delivers the intended service or product. Efficiency means performing for the lowest feasible cost. Focusing upon one of these objectives is clearly easier than attempting to achieve both. However, today's operations have to strive to achieve both. This explains why the operations manager's job is increasingly a difficult one.

Case Study

Operations management job advertisements

The following are examples of operations jobs advertised nationally in the UK:

1 *Head of Operations.*
   Dealing in e-commerce, operations expand across the USA, the UK, Europe and Canada. Reporting to the Chief Executive (Europe) you will be responsible for the profitable development of order processing and distribution. You will head a team responsible for the European call centre, distribution operations, inventory procurement and inventory management.

2 *Customer Services Operations Manager.*
   The organization is a leading direct computer systems company. You will have a crucial role in ensuring that all functions are focused on how they contribute to enhancing the customers' experience. Liaising with manufacturing, sales, technical support and financial services, you will ensure that all customer concerns are driven to a satisfactory conclusion. You will champion the quality focus throughout the organization.

3 *Gas Exploration and Production Project Manager.*
   Working for a leading worldwide gas chain business you will report to the Vice-President, Project and Engineering Manage-

ment. Responsibilities include developing and maintaining international reporting procedures, and co-ordinating project performance appraisal and supply chain management. You will advise the Executive Committee on project performance across worldwide operations and against world-class benchmarks.

4 *Production Manager*.
A leading food industry company seeks a professional manager to run a team of twenty people. You will have responsibility for organizing shift patterns as well as day-to-day production and control.

5 *Operations Manager*. The company provides a specialist, same day, high street delivery service. The Operations Manager is responsible for all inventory management, customer service, warehousing and transport. This is a complex and demanding function where meeting customer service targets and controlling costs are critical.

Exercise

Having read the job adverts, list what you think are the important qualities for an operations manager.

The roots of operations management

The history of social and economic development is dominated by organizations being formed to pursue various objectives. Such organizations require active management if they are to survive. The roots of operations management therefore go back many years. In the sixteenth century the Venice arsenal used operations management principles to achieve extremely high efficiencies. It could, for instance, produce a war galley in twenty-four hours. This was the result of practices such as the standardization of parts, flowline process design and specialization of labour. These principles were jealously guarded and their unauthorized knowledge was punishable by death. As a management discipline, operations management is usually associated with the work of Frederick Taylor in the late nineteenth century. He studied the execution and organization of work in a manufacturing environment and was instrumental in founding the scientific school of management. Since then the body of techniques and principles which make up operations management has developed greatly.

The main focus of operations management was for many years the factory organization. As a result the discipline tended to be called manufacturing management. Later other bodies such as distributors came within the boundary of the subject and its name evolved into production management. During the 1960s the service sector was included as a focus of attention and the name of the subject continued to evolve into today's title: operations management.

The following are among the key factors currently driving the continued development of operations management.

Globalization of the economy

Increasing competition from foreign companies has stimulated organizations to strive for better ways of producing efficiently and effectively. One aspect of this fierce competition has been the steady decline in the importance of domestic manufacturing to the economy.

Case Study

Body Shop moves away from manufacturing
Anita Roddick's Body Shop pioneered the commercial development of natural and ethical cosmetics. The manufacturing operation suffered from competition based in low-cost areas of the world. Moreover, these manufacturers were capable of quickly copying successful products. As a result Body Shop's profit margins fell. The solution was to retrench from manufacturing and to concentrate on marketing and managing a contract supply chain.

The current battleground for marketplace dominance is being fought on the speed objective, described as time-based competition. This requires the quick provision of goods and services and rapid design-to-market lead times. These are major challenges for operations managers.

Total quality management

In the 1980s and 1990s total quality management ideas swept across all types of organizations. The approach was seen as embodying a unified way of managing operations for improved quality and productivity. Amongst other ideas, the movement emphasized the need to get all operational personnel involved in improvement activities, the idea of operations being part of a chain of linked operations and the necessity for operations managers to have an external orientation.

Empowerment

In the 1990s empowerment was viewed as the key to cost-effective operations. It challenged the way that work was designed and managed, attempting to place responsibility for decision-making with the people who actually performed the work. Currently the challenge is to make the workforce of the operation a source of knowledge and ideas.

Technology

The information technology revolution of the late twentieth century has posed new opportunities for the way in which operations function. Operations managers have to master all aspects of technology, from its design to its implementation and operation. The technology has vast potential to improve the way that operations work. On the downside, technology can also be poorly managed and lead to major organizational problems.

Case Study

Computer system causes passport chaos

The Home Office began a project in 1996 to switch from a paper-based to a computer-based passport processing system. The aim was to speed up decision-making in granting passports. It took three years to install the system at a cost to the taxpayer of £77 million. The technology led to a situation described in the media as chaotic. Among the results were:

- the volume of processed applications fell dramatically
- the backlog of asylum and refugee cases grew enormously
- the queues of personal callers to the offices stretched for hundreds of metres
- many telephone calls went unanswered
- sacks of letters were left unopened around the offices.

The company responsible for the computer system, Siemens, had its contract fee reduced by £4.5 million for the delays.

Improving public services

The desire to improve public services such as health, social security, justice and education is creating opportunities for the development of operations principles and practices in these fields.

Improving service sector productivity

As a major consumer of resources it is important to improve service sector productivity. In the private sector this will serve the dual purpose of increasing profit and making those sectors which are open to foreign competition more competitive. In the public sector it will yield a greater return for the public money which is invested.

Manufacturing and service-based organizations

From an operational point of view the distinction between manufacturing and service rests upon the nature of the output. Broadly, manufacturing delivers tangible outputs, whilst services produce intangible outputs. In both types of organization the efficient and effective use of resources is a primary concern, and the principles and practices of operations management are therefore highly relevant to both. This is not to say that all the techniques are equally applicable to all operations. Before considering the application of a particular approach, like statistical process control for example, the context of the operation and the scope of the technique must be fully understood.

It is rare to find an organization that is purely a producer of goods or purely a producer of services. Most operations are a mixture of the two. A factory will have a telephone call-handling service and will also take customers and prospective customers on factory tours in order to impress them. Some factories have showrooms and shops where they display their outputs. These are all service operations, even though the company may regard itself as predominantly a manufacturer. Moreover, the very product itself often has intangible benefits for its user. The motor car is a classic example of this. Beyond the physical characteristics of the car, purchasers may also want a sense of safety and a feeling of prestige. Hotels might regard themselves as service operations, and yet they have many tangible outputs. Brochures, reservation documents, food, the bedrooms and other facilities are all tangible outputs. Thus a hotel may view itself as in the business of providing service, but it is also in the business of producing tangible items.

This mix of product and service leads to the notion that organizations may be scaled from being 100 per cent tangible product to being 100 per cent intangible service. It is difficult to conceive of organizations occupying pure 100 per cent positions. It is far easier to accept that organizations may be defined as over 50 per cent of one type or the other. Figure 1.1 portrays the idea of organizations being part of a continuum ranging from pure manufacturing to pure service. The ratings, of course, are subjective

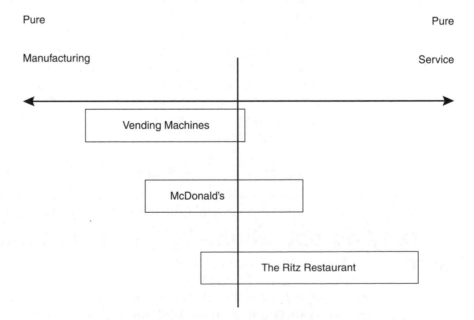

Figure 1.1 The organization as part of a continuum

Economic development seems to follow a pattern of initially being based upon agriculture, then developing into reliance upon manufacturing and, finally, becoming dominated by service activity. The role of services in modern economies is certainly very important and reaffirms this general pattern.

Case Study

The role of manufacturing and services in the economy

The pattern of the developed western economies has changed substantially over the last fifty years. There has been a shift away from manufacturing to services, especially to financial services and business services such as computer services, equipment hire and accountancy. Over this period other services have constantly remained as important areas of economic activity, including health, education and social services.

Today, services account for over half of the gross domestic product (GDP) in the UK, France, Germany and Italy. In these same countries, manufacturing provides around 20 per cent of the GDP. In the USA the role of the service sector is even greater.

In terms of contributing to export earnings, in the UK at least, manufacturing is still the dominant sector. Services account for around only 25 per cent of the total exports of goods and services.

Productivity performance across the two sectors shows marked differences. In manufacturing the UK's productivity lags that of the USA, France and Germany. The gap, however, has been steadily reducing. In the service sector, the overall productivity gap with other nations has not been closing. Thus, the increasingly important role of services as major sources of employment seems to be driven by the dual stimuli of increasing demand and stubbornly low productivity.

Classifying operations by key environmental factors

Identifying if the operation is a service- or manufacturing-orientated organization is an important step in analysing its performance. Another important criterion is the type of environment within which the operation functions. The key environmental variables for operations managers are:

● volume
● variation
● variety
● customer contact.

The key task is to design the operation so that it matches these features of its environment as closely as possible. If the planning and control of the well-designed operation is good, then the dual goals of efficiency and effectiveness are more likely to be achieved.

Volume

Volume refers to the number of times that an operation has to deliver a service or product. The usual descriptors for the volume dimension are high volume, medium volume and low volume. The distinctions between these three categories are usually drawn on a subjective basis. For example, McDonald's may be said to be high volume in comparison to a French restaurant. An operation dealing with high volumes should be designed to process the demands placed upon it more speedily than the operation meeting lower volumes. Higher volume operations can gain efficiency by breaking down the task into small units so the staff specialize in only a small part of the total work. The fact that the task is repeated many times makes it worthwhile to standardize ways of working, so that the same actions are followed time after time.

The combination of specialization, standardization and high volume also usually opens up the possibility of using technology to perform the task. The result is high output from an efficient process. Moreover, the higher volume allows the costs of the operation to be spread across more units of output, thereby reducing individual unit costs. In this way the higher level of demands will be met with greater efficiency, yielding lower costs per unit of service or product.

Variation

Variation describes the pattern of the volume demands. If there are many peaks and troughs in demand the situation is said to be one of high variation. The challenge in this case is to design an operation that can provide the correct level of capacity to meet this pattern. Carrying extra capacity in times of low demand is inherently expensive, involving underutilization of key resources such as staff, technology and facilities. Providing extra capacity at busy times can also be costly, possibly requiring recruitment, training and overtime costs. Managing a high variation operation is also more difficult and a drain on managerial resources. Low variation environments thus offer the potential for greater efficiency.

Variety

Variety is the term applied to the number of different types of service or product demanded. High variety environments require different services or products on a frequent basis, whereas low variety demands look for the same output for most of the time. An operation facing high variety has to be designed to provide the appropriate level of flexibility. This flexibility usually will be expensive compared to the costs of an operation designed to cope with low variety. In addition, coping with high variety is a more challenging managerial task than dealing with low variety. Planning and control and the other operations tasks will therefore be more difficult and involve more overhead costs.

Customer contact

The customer contact dimension is concerned with how much time the personnel of the operation have to spend with its customers. Customers are independent of the operation compared with its staff. The more that customers get involved, therefore, the greater is the challenge to the planning and control of the operations manager. Where the planning and control is weaker, the ability to be successful and low cost will be impaired. In the service sector the tension between the benefits of high control and the flexibility required to satisfy the customer can be particularly acute. One way of viewing service operations is to divide their activities into front office and back office. Front office activities involve high levels of customer contact, whereas back-office activities require little customer contact. In car service operations, the customer reception area is the front office, whilst the workshop is the back office. At McDonald's the front office is the counter and the seating area, the back office is the food preparation area. Clearly, it is in the back office where the efficiency and effectiveness gains of high degrees of planning and control can best be obtained. The front office/back office split is an important factor to be borne in mind when operational activities are being designed.

Generally, the four factors covered above influence both efficiency and effectiveness by determining how complex the task of managing the operation is. The more complex the situation, the greater will be the challenge to get both efficient and effective delivery. In broad terms, the low volume, high variation, high variety and high customer contact operation is the greatest managerial challenge.

Exercise

What are the implications for the McDonald's operation if its customers move towards low volume, high variation, high variety and high customer contact features?

Changes caused by the environment can clearly be difficult for operations managers to cope with. The temptation is to try to insulate the operation so that it can continue to run smoothly. In manufacturing this desire manifests itself in large inventory stores. The rationale for this approach is that any interruptions in supply or sudden peaks in demand can be covered by the large stock. Large stocks, however, also mean large financial costs. In the service sector the desire to protect the operation from the environment may lead to creating long queues of customers, so that the operation performs at one continuous level. The cost of this strategy is that of dissatisfying customers who have to wait for their service. Both manufacturing and service sectors operations may try to retain their insularity from the environment by making the management of the required changes the responsibility of some other function, such as marketing or purchasing. The overall drawback of these approaches is that the operations become very difficult to change. The modern emphasis, therefore, is upon removing such barriers to the environment so that operations become more responsive.

Frameworks for analysing operations

Analysing operations can be a difficult task. Many techniques have been developed to aid this process and many of these are covered in this book. What follows is a brief overview of two 'integrative' ways of analysing operations that have become influential in recent years.

The value chain

Activities may be analysed in terms of how much they cost compared with how much revenue (value) they add. Activities that add more cost than they add in revenue are not value-adding and should therefore be designed out of the operation. The essential question for operations managers, therefore, is to understand how all their activities fit into this calculation for the organization as a whole. This requires several layers of analysis:

1 The operations managers have to know how the operation's activities fare under this calculation.
2 The ways in which inbound logistics affect the value structure of operations have to be analysed.
3 The effects of the supporting activities of the company structure, human resource management, technology development and purchasing have to be assessed.
4 The effects of operational activities on the value calculations of the downstream functions of outbound logistics, marketing and sales and customer service have to be evaluated.

The net result of this analysis is a clearer view of which activities do not add value and how value is actually created.

The notion of value as expressed so far is clearly a commercial concept. It can be transferred to non-commercial organizations, however, to support the same type of analysis. In this context value is defined not as revenue but as some benefit delivered to the customers of the operation. The costs of all activities contributing to this benefit can be identified and compared with a subjective assessment of their contribution to the end benefit delivered. The costs must be outweighed by their perceived contribution to the benefit to make them worth incurring.

Using the notion of value in this broad sense to include both commercial and non-commercial meanings, value can clearly be made up of many aspects. Operations can provide these different aspects of value in differing ways:

1 Operations can change the state of some input. Manufacturing is a classic example of adding value in this way. Basic inputs, such

as vehicle components, engines and car bodies, can be changed to produce a car that is then valued highly enough to generate revenue. In the service sector the changes might be of a more personal nature. Consider the changes made by a surgeon or a hairdresser for example!

2 Operations can create value by transporting inputs. Public transport is a good example of this, where the passengers are the inputs moved to a new location.

3 Storage may also add value in certain situations. The whole warehousing industry is structured on the premise that people will pay to have their goods dealt with in a protected environment.

4 Inspections may be perceived as adding value. We place a value upon the medical inspections carried out by our doctors for instance.

Exercise   What does value mean in the education process?

The systems approach

Since the Second World War a body of knowledge called systems thinking has been developed. It emphasizes that operations should be seen as systems consisting of individual elements which are linked together and which have a purpose or goal. What happens in any one element, therefore, has an effect upon the elements to which it is linked. Thus, education can be seen as a system of individual elements such as students, academic staff and administrative staff. The purpose is to provide a positive educational experience. The primary link between these elements is information. Take away any one of these elements and the system will behave in a very different way.

Systems thinking has contributed at least three key ideas. First, the notion of operations as a series of inputs–processes–outputs open to environmental influences. This is explored in more detail in Chapter 2. It is the foundation of the view that what matters most is to identify the processes of the operation and then to design these in the most optimum manner. Business process re-engineering is a development of this perspective.

Second is the concept of control. The basic idea of control is that information on the performance of the operation is obtained and

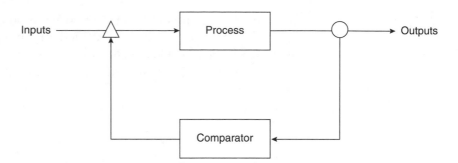

Figure 1.2 Feedback control model

compared with some agreed standard. If the performance does not meet the standard then the operation is corrected until it does. In this way operations can be proactively managed rather than being left simply to run their own course.

The idea of control reoccurs throughout the book. Feedback control is the more usual method of measuring and correcting operations. Figure 1.2 shows in outline the basic feedback control model.

A measurement of the operation's performance is made, in Figure 1.2 on the outputs. The information so obtained is then fed back to a comparator. The comparator may be a person or a machine. At this stage the results of the measurement are compared with some predetermined standard. If the results do not match this standard then the comparator requests changes, in this case to the inputs. The changes are then made and the effects are measured so that the whole loop is repeated again. The output measurement might show, for instance, that the level of demand is not being met. In this instance the comparator might call for extra inputs in the form of more staff hours paid for at overtime rates. The results of this action would then be measured again to see if they were successful. Feed-forward control models are less frequent. The basic feed-forward system is shown in outline in Figure 1.3.

The essential elements are the same as in the feedback model, except that in this case the change action is effected downstream from where the measurement is taken.

Third, systems thinking emphasizes the need for a structured approach towards decision-making. Broadly, the structures for decision-making fall into two categories: hard systems and soft systems. The hard systems methodology should be followed when there is clear agreement about the nature of the problem to be solved. For example, it could be that the operations team all agree that the level of current quality performance is unacceptable and needs to be

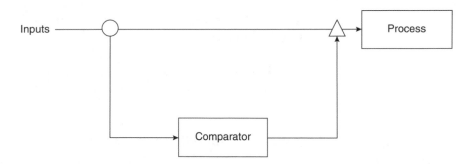

Figure 1.3 Feed-forward control model

improved. The hard systems methodology in such cases is to take the following steps:

1 Define the problem.
2 Analyse the existing situation and the relevant systems.
3 Identify the objectives and the constraints in relation to them.
4 Generate feasible options to achieve the objectives.
5 Formulate measures that will indicate how well the objectives are being achieved.
6 Develop in detail the preferred options.
7 Test the preferred options.
8 Choose the best option.
9 Implement the solution.
10 Monitor the success of the solution.

In contrast, the soft systems methodology is applied when there is a contentious issue with little or no agreement about what the problem is. In a hospital, for instance, there might be intractable views about whether the real problem is a long waiting list or a budget deficit. The aim of the soft methodology is not to provide a solution. The purpose is to get the parties to agree on what the problem really is. The steps of the soft systems approach are:

1 Gather information about the situation.
2 Analyse the situation for the key contentious issues and the key tasks.
3 Identify the relevant systems and state their primary purposes.
4 Construct a conceptual model of what is needed to achieve the primary purposes.
5 Compare stage 4 with stage 2 in order to provide topics for discussion with the parties.

6 Review the process with the parties and explore the topics if they agree to do so.

The end point for the soft systems approach is to ask if the parties want to change the situation or not.

Definition of operations management

The key to understanding what the term 'operations management' means is the simple idea that it is concerned with the management of the processes which actually deliver the products or services of the organization. The processes are ways of working and what they work on are the inputs of the operation. As an activity, operations management is therefore very broad. It can be found in all sectors of the economy, those dedicated to profit and those not so dedicated. Not all jobs that are operations actually have the term in their descriptions. This makes identifying the role less than straightforward.

The people or organizations that receive the outputs of operations are usually called customers. Customer, however, is very broadly defined to include both internal and external people. It does not mean that there has to be payment for the product or service. The term 'stakeholder' is sometimes used instead of customer. A stakeholder is anyone who has an interest in the operation. Stakeholders, too, can be internal or external.

The tasks of operations managers

The role of managing operations involves many tasks. Five specific tasks have been identified.

1 Managers have to understand what their operation has to be good at in their particular environment. What operations has to be good at is usually delivering to the right quality, at the right speed, keeping its promises, providing appropriate flexibility and incurring the lowest feasible costs.
2 Planning and control are major activities. Planning involves arranging for the orderly flow of resources so that the objectives can be met. Control means checking the performance of the operation against the standards expected of it. If performance is not satisfactory then taking the appropriate action to change the inputs, the processes or the outputs completes the control loop.
3 Simply accepting the output and the process as factors designed by someone else and trying to manage them as well as can be

expected is not acceptable. Operations managers have to take responsibility for being involved in these design activities too.

4 Managing the operation to hit today's targets is important, but it is not sufficient. Customer expectations change and the best operations continue to get better. This means that modern operations managers have to seek continuous improvement in everything that their operation does.

5 Operations is an important part of any organization. Good communication between it and the other functions will help to make the organization function smoothly. Operations managers, therefore, have to be able to communicate across the functional boundaries. In this way the capabilities of the operation and the expectations placed upon it stand a better chance of being properly understood by all.

In performing these tasks the goal is to make the operation both efficient and effective. Efficiency focuses upon the costs of the operation, whilst effectiveness concerns success in meeting the other objectives.

The roots of operations management

References to operations management go back many years. As a discipline, operations management is usually taken to have started with the work of Frederick Taylor at the end of the nineteenth century. Today, some of the main forces shaping the development of the area are as follows:

1 Globalization.
2 Total quality management.
3 Empowerment.
4 Technology.
5 Improving public services.
6 Improving service sector productivity.

Manufacturing and service-based organizations

The distinction between manufacturing and service is that the former produces tangible goods, whereas the latter produces intangible benefits. Most organizations, in fact, produce a mix of the two. In terms of the economy, the service sector has grown in importance over the last fifty years. Over half of the gross domestic product of advanced economies is accounted for by services. In terms of productivity improvement, manufacturing's performance is better than that of services and manufacturing continues to be the major export-earning sector.

Classifying operations by key environmental factors

The way that an operation performs, and the way that it should be designed to best achieve its objectives, is greatly influenced by its environment. Four variables in particular are important. Volume refers to the number of services or products to be produced. Variation concerns the pattern of peaks and troughs in demand. Variety covers the range of tasks that an operation is asked to undertake. Customer contact reflects the amount of time staff have to allocate to dealing directly with customers. These factors influence the complexity of the managerial challenge. The greatest challenge is posed by low volume, high variation, high variety and high customer contact.

Frameworks for analysing operations

Two integrative ways of looking at operations are especially influential.

The value chain

Value is defined in the commercial environment as the amount of revenue less the amount of cost. In the not-for-profit sector value is defined as the benefit delivered to the user. The purpose of defining the value added by operational activities is to reveal those that appear to add negative or little positive value and to make people aware of where value really comes from. With this awareness operations can be designed to achieve the most feasible value.

The systems approach

Systems thinking has contributed at least three key ideas for analysing operations:

1 Operations can be conceived as a series of inputs–processes–outputs which is open to influence from the environment.
2 Operations have to be controlled, and control means gaining information on the performance of the operation and then changing the operation if it is not meeting some predefined standard.
3 Problems should be solved by following structured methodologies. The hard systems methodology applies where there is agreement on what the problem is. In situations of conflict the soft systems methodology is used.

1 Insert the missing words in this definition of operations management: 'Operations is concerned with managing _____ through transformation _____ to deliver _____.'

2 Operations covers a narrow range of organizations. True or false?

3 Which of the following are operations management roles?
(a) Hospital Manager
(b) Technical Director
(c) Store Manager
(d) all of the above.

4 Customers must be external to the organization. True or false?

5 There are five overall objectives for operations. List at least three of them.

6 Planning by itself is not sufficient to manage processes. What other major element is needed?

7 Operations managers have to undertake all of the following, except:
(a) operational strategic planning
(b) meeting today's operational objectives
(c) liaising with the design function
(d) marketing the product
(e) improving the operation.

8 Being effective means:
(a) delivering the very best product or service
(b) successfully delivering the required product or service
(c) keeping costs as low as possible.

9 Operations management was developed in the 1950s. True or false?

10 Operations management refers to:
(a) manufacturing
(b) service
(c) distribution
(d) all of the above.

11 Manufacturing is the dominant contributor to gross domestic product. True or false?

12 The implementation of technology generally:
(a) requires little preparation
(b) requires careful planning and control
(c) is of no importance to operations managers
(d) is important to operations managers.

13 Identify three reasons why improving service sector productivity is important.

14 Which of the following is not a tangible output:

    (a) food
    (b) chairs
    (c) comfort
    (d) documents
    (e) cars.

15 Insert the missing words in the following statement: 'Economic development seems to follow a pattern of initially being based upon _____, developing into reliance upon _____ and finally becoming dominated by _____ activity.'

16 The term 'volume' refers to:
    (a) the peaks and troughs of demand
    (b) the number of times a product or service has to be produced
    (c) the number of different types of product or service offered.

17 The type of environment which presents the greater challenge to operations managers is characterized by low volume, high variation, high variety and high customer contact. True or false?

18 Operations can add value by:
    (a) changing the state of an input
    (b) transporting an input
    (c) storing items
    (d) inspections
    (e) all of the above.

19 In your own words describe the concept of control.

20 The systems approach to operations management emphasizes two methodologies for resolving problems and using opportunities. Name them both.

Further reading

Barnett, H. (1996). *Operations Management*. Macmillan.
D'Netto, B. and Sohal, A. S. (1999). Changes in the production manager's job: past, present and future trends. *International Journal of Operations and Production Management*, **19** (2), 157–81.
Slack, N., Chambers, S., Harland, C., Harrison, A. and Johnston, R. (1998). *Operations Management*. Pitman.

Chapter 2

The context of operations management

Chapter 1 has shown the important role played by operations management and operational managers in implementing and achieving organizational goals and objectives. The aim of this chapter is to view operations as micro and macro operating systems, examine their interrelationships and strategic and tactical implications on the performance of the operations management function. Amongst the topics considered are:

Learning Objectives

1 *What is an operating system?* An operating system can be either a micro or a macro system. An understanding of the difference between the two will help to see the link between operational efficiency and business performance.
2 *What are the internal relationships and their influences on operations?* There are different functions within a business that can enhance or reduce performance of the operations function. These internal links are identified and investigated.
3 *What are the external relationships and their impact on operations?* The results achieved by the operations function can be influenced by the external factors affecting the operations. These are identified and their implications considered.

Internal influences on the operations function

This section considers the operations function interface with other internal functions within an organization.

Human resources

The personnel function is responsible for recruiting and developing the workforce required by various internal functions. As such it can influence the performance of the operations function by having the right recruitment strategy and selecting and training the right people for the right jobs. Personnel is also responsible for the health and safety of all employees. Therefore, beside being in touch with legislation such as the Employment and Equal Opportunity Acts, this function should be aware of any changes to the health and safety rules and regulations in order to avoid any future inconveniences that may be caused by employees and Health and Safety Executives/Officers, leading to disruptions and reduced productivity. Furthermore, operations activities can be influenced by the trade union laws and agreements. Union policies may lead to industrial disputes and strikes, which in turn can affect employee productivity and company profitability.

Sales

The relationship between sales and operations functions is an important one. Today, there are still companies where sales people dominate the production function. This means that they go out filling the order book without checking with production people whether they have the internal skills and capacity to satisfy customers specification and delivery requirements. The absence or lack of communication and interaction between these functions creates interruptions in production activities and results in loss of output and productivity.

Marketing

The marketing function has an important role to play both in manufacturing and service operations. In the 1960s, when there was less competition between firms, manufacturing tended to be the dominating function. A company could virtually sell everything that it produced, as demand for products exceeded their supply. Today, because of competition, the marketing function has become a major driving force in many types of organization. This means that to be successful all departments in a firm should be market led or customer orientated, and there should be integration between all functions, especially between marketing and operations/production functions.

Case Study

Imperial Decor International (IDI) is the export division of Imperial House Decor Group (UK). The company's attention to individual customer requirements and market trends have led to a threefold increase in turnover in six years and the NatWest-Financial Times award for export. The company consults closely with its customer to understand and identify individual trends and tastes. It then tailors its products to meet those tastes in order to maximize sales. The company also determines which are the key markets and focuses resources on them. Its recruitment strategy is to employ the right people for the job required, taking into consideration that exporting to a wide variety of different markets needs a diverse workforce that is multilingual, multi-ethnic and comfortable in changing environments.

Exercise

Describe the difference between a 'production' and a 'marketing' orientated organization.

Finance

Financial and accounting people are responsible for budgets, labour costs, inventory levels, purchase decisions for raw materials and capital equipment. By accepting or rejecting the departmental budget, the finance function can influence the performance of the operations function in meeting the targets set periodically by the marketing forecast.

Purchasing

The role of the purchasing function is to make materials and parts of the right quality, and quantity available for use by operations at the right time and at the right price. If any of these conditions are not met by the chosen suppliers then the operations performance will be affected. Therefore, effective communication between purchasing and operations people is essential in order to establish the correct materials specifications and source the right supplier who can reliably meet the purchasing requirements.

External influences on the operations function

External factors that can influence the performance of the operations function include the following:

Political and legal impact

Political instability and the government's overall attitudes towards an organization can affect its performance. Legislation on pollution and noise control as well as procurement policies will have implications on operations activities. A firm's overall performance can also be influenced by intergovernment relations (for example, the recent European Union directive on maximum weekly working hour of forty-eight hours per employee).

Economic conditions

Changes in the economic conditions both at the national and international levels can have implications for operations activities. If there is a growth in the world economy then the demand for goods and services increases. In the case of economic contraction, the export level will suffer. If there is an increase in interest rates then it will be difficult for a firm to raise finances, whilst a reduction in the rate of interest makes it easier for a company to invest in new resources. All these issues will affect the performance of the operations function.

Competitors

If a firm's competitors can produce products of similar or better design, cheaper, faster and of better quality, it will soon make the company out of date and capture its present markets. This can have a significant impact on the activities of the operations function. A company should watch its competitors closely and benchmark against their products, processes and business strategies in order to implement the necessary changes which will reduce the overall operating costs, and improve performance of the operations function.

Case Study

TNT UK generates an annual turnover of almost £500 million through its transport, distribution and logistics operations. Everyone in the company believes that they have got to be better than the rest. The business world is divided into companies that like to compete. From TNT's point of view, competing makes them better at serving customers in their very competitive situations. The competition is ruthless. Senior management at TNT believe that loyalty in business seems to be disappearing. The company has to give customers compelling reasons why they should not go elsewhere.

Labour market

Variability in skills and performance of the workforce can influence the activities of the operations function. A firm having access to the right labour market, which can supply the company with the required labour force of the right skills and capabilities, can increase the performance of its operations.

Customers

Today, customers can put a lot of pressure on the operations function. They can ask for faster delivery, better quality, lower price, more variety etc. A firm needs to change or improve its methods of production, type of technology and other related practices in order to accommodate changes expected in customers requirements year on year.

Case Study

One of the major reasons for Jaguar cars' sales revival in recent years is the lesson learnt by its management that the 'voice of the customer' is the only one worth listening to. Step-by-step improvements have been achieved in various business areas when the entire Jaguar workforce started listening and fed back the results into the production process. The company created its best sales force by trusting its people to talk to customers and act on what they hear.

Exercise

Explain the difference between a firm that is mainly taking care of its own interests and the firm that is taking care of its customers' needs and wants.

Suppliers

A firm's relationship with its suppliers can affect the performance of the operations function. Lack of communication and partnership with suppliers can lead to delays and errors by them, which in turn will disrupt operations activities.

Technological development

Performance of the operations function can be influenced by developments in technology and the firm's willingness to take advantage of this advancement. A company which hesitates to invest in new technology will not be able to compete with those who welcome technological development and are committed to fully exploit it.

Case Study

London Ambulance Service (LAS) responds to all '999' emergency calls for medical assistance in the capital. Staffed twenty-four hours a day in three eight-hour watches, its central room takes an average of 2000 calls a day and co-ordinates the dispatch of vehicles from its fleets of 395 ambulances, ten motor cycles and an air ambulance. Five years ago the LAS was an object of anger when its attempt to introduce a computer-aided dispatch system went terribly wrong. It has recently won an award for information system management that may not be matched for years. The cost of the new control room including construction, computers and conversion was £2.5 million of which £300 000 was accounted for by the computer system. The company believes that the new technology should be presented to people as a better tool to achieve their objectives and not as a threat or challenge to their abilities. It should serve their needs and those of the business, not vice versa.

Capital and money markets

The extent to which a company is able to raise money from banks and stock markets to support investments in its people, resources, processes and new technology will also affect the performance of its operations function.

Operations management as a transformation process

All types of operations take inputs such as people, materials and capital and convert them into the desired outputs such as products and services. Hence, operations management can be viewed as a transformation process. The key components of this process are:

1 *Inputs*. These are main resources that are used by the operating system. According to Slack et al. (1998), there are two categories of inputs. Those resources such as information and materials whose status will change as the result of the conversion process are called the transformed resources. On the other hand, input

resources such as staff, equipment and buildings, that are used to help the transformation process but their status does not change as the result of the conversion process, are called the transforming resources. Usually, one of the transformed resources in an operation tends to be the dominant one, for example, information in a bank and material in a manufacturing operation.

2 *Conversion process.* This is concerned with the design of the operation system, planning and control and improvement activities that are needed for the manufacture and supply of goods and services to customers.

3 *Outputs.* These are products and services produced by the operation to satisfy the customers' requirements and the operation and business strategic objectives in order for it to remain competitive in the marketplace.

The transformation model shown in Figure 2.1 can be used as a vehicle to evaluate the appropriateness of the operation's input

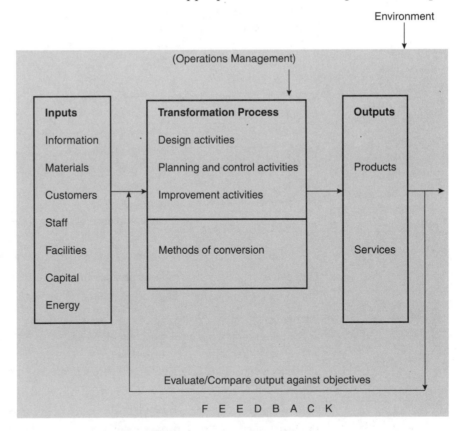

Figure 2.1 The transformation process

resources, the effectiveness of its conversion processes and the quality or standards of the resultant outputs. This information can further assist in identifying areas in need of improvement together with management decisions and corrective actions to overcome them.

We should also note that all types of operations could be influenced by the environmental elements such as changes in the law, innovation by competitors, supplier problems etc.

The conceptual framework in Figure 2.1 can be applied to every type of organization in order to identify its strength and weaknesses. Tables 2.1–2.3 illustrate broad examples from manufacturing, service, and not-for-profits operations.

Exercise

Apply the above operating system approach to the following:

- a brewery operation
- a hospital operation.

Table 2.1 Example of the operating system approach as applied to a manufacturing operation

Inputs	Conversion process	Outputs
People		
• Labour	Operate plant	End product
• Managers	Devise and control plans	Meet department's objectives
• Technicians	Provide support services	Usable resources
Materials	Spares and consumable	Final assembly
Equipment/machines	Process materials	Finished goods
Information		
• Customer requirements	Production plans and schedules	Efficient use of resources
• Technical drawings		Finished product
• Political/legal input	Health and safety rules	Safer environment in which to work
Capital	Budgeting	New resources
Energy	Heating, lighting	Better working conditions

Table 2.2 Example of the operating system approach as applied to the police force

Inputs	Conversion process	Outputs
Labour	Beat duties	Public tranquillity
	Traffic duties	Maintenance of peace
	Riot control	
	Special situations	
'Special labour'	Administrative duties	Public confidence
• Civilian employee	Documentation for courts,	
• Traffic wardens	councils, etc.	
Materials/equipment	Used for: Prevention of crime	
• Cars	Demonstration control	Public confidence
• Radio	Processions control	
• Firearms	Sport functions	
Information	Filing, interviewing, vetting	arrests

Table 2.3 Example of the operating system approach as applied to an Environmental Health Department

Inputs	Conversion process	Outputs
Staff	Promoting environmental health	Better environment for the area
Equipment/materials	Pest control	Satisfy public expectations
Capital	Budget allocation	Health education
Information		
• Legal requirements	Housing inspection	Compliance with statutory requirements
• Political input	Food hygiene and health and safety	Higher standards

Benefits of the transformation model

Developing an operating system model as shown in Tables 2.1–2.3 can be a useful means of identifying and evaluating the key inputs, conversion processes and the output elements for an operation. Amongst the benefits are the identification of:

- the range of inputs and an indication of the more dominating one
- the mismatches and areas for adjustment and improvement
- the alternative methods or processes available
- the labour skills and determination of training needs
- the organizational factors and breakdown of responsibilities.

However, we must bear in mind that any improvement in the operating system components depends on how effective is our feedback mechanism. Therefore, people and instruments that are used to collect data must be adequate. Also, supervisors and managers who compare the results against objectives should be those with the right skills in order to make the right decisions for adjusting relevant inputs and replacing or improving existing processes so that the desired outputs or standards can be achieved.

Exercise

Outline actions that you may take if:

- the budget target for your product or service is not being achieved
- the quality or standard of your product or service is not adequate.

The strategic importance of operations

As we mentioned earlier, improvement decisions made by operations management after evaluating elements of the operation's transformation model should be in line with the strategic objectives of the total business. The remainder of this section deals with the link between the strategic decisions and the operations objectives in organizations.

What is strategy?

In order to understand the strategic role of operations in manufacturing and services we need to first understand the meaning of the word 'strategy' and its different forms in organizations.

Strategy is a course of action together with decisions on the specification and deployment of resources required to attain a stated objective. Depending on the size and type of organizations there are three forms of strategy: corporate, business and operational or functional.

Corporate strategy

This relates to the organization as a whole. How should the business fulfil its long-term objectives and satisfy its mission. A mission here means a statement of the purpose or the main reason for the organization's existence. For example, a business school's mission statement could be: 'To be amongst the top ten business schools in Europe providing programmes at undergraduate, postgraduate and executive levels.' Similarly, a mission for a construction firm may be: 'To provide quality dam and highway bridges both at home and overseas.'

Exercise

What do you think could be the mission statement for:

● an automobile company
● a hotel?

Case Study

British Airways is the third largest airline in the world. The company's main corporate objectives are:

● To have inspired people who are continually motivated and able to learn.
● To have satisfied customers – customer choice is paramount in the service offered by the airline.
● To be truly global – to have international presence by choosing the right partners for joint ventures overseas.
● To be strongly profitable through efficient and cost-effective operations.

Business strategy

This relates to how an organization intends to compete in the marketplace. It sets the strategic objectives for various functions in the business, such as marketing, finance, operations, and so on. For example, a firm's competitive strategy may include:

- produce at lowest cost (cost leadership)
- make products different (differentiation)
- focus on one group of customers (focus).

The business strategy usually covers plans for three- to five-years ahead and is reviewed annually. It should specify what needs to be done over the next year or so in order to achieve the long-term goals of the business.

 Exercise | What do you think would be the strategic objectives of a non-profit-making organization?

Operational or functional strategies

These are concerned with how the individual business functions such as personnel, marketing and production can contribute to the achievement of a firm's corporate and business strategies.

What is operations strategy?

Operations strategy is the pattern of decisions and the course of action taken either by the individual functions within a business (micro operations) or the whole organization (macro operation), in order to create goods and services that will satisfy the organization's business strategy. This means that operation's resources must be selected, deployed and managed in the most effective manner using the right technology, workforce, systems and procedures to meet the strategic goals of the organization.

Pizza Hut is a US company that produces and markets pizzas nationally and in overseas markets. It consists of many outlets or stores in the USA, UK and in other countries worldwide. The operations strategy for this company exists at individual store level. This means that each outlet at micro level should plan effectively to deploy its resources efficiently in order for the organization at the macro level to achieve its corporate objectives.

An operations strategy has two main components, the content and the process. These elements and the main strategies in operations management decision areas are explained below.

Process and content of operations strategy

The content of operations strategy refers to the policies, plans and principles that guide the operation's activities. It prioritizes the performance objectives for operation's products or services and identifies the strategies to be pursued by the operation in each of the design, planning and control, and improvement decision areas. The process of operations strategy explores the way in which operation's policies, plans and principles are decided and developed.

Performance characteristics of operations

The contribution made by an operations function is crucial to the long-term success of a manufacturing or service organization. The operations function makes this vital contribution to a firm's competitiveness through the following five performance objectives.

Quality

Doing things right. Striving to satisfy customers by providing goods and services that are fit for their purpose. The quality advantage in manufacturing and service operations can be achieved through a skilled workforce, adequate technology and effective communication of quality standards and job specifications. For example, in a bank operation quality could mean that services are provided correctly, customers are kept informed of changes and staff are courteous, friendly and helpful. Quality in a car plant could mean that all parts and assembly conform to specifications and the end product is both attractive and reliable.

Case Study

Unique Images is Europe's market leader in private label festive products such as cards, gift-wrap and Christmas accessories. The company has a culture of continuous improvement and has developed a senior team committed to change and achieving a high quality environment. The top management team started to ensure that it understood what the company's customers wanted and the changes needed to satisfy their requirements. This was achieved through regular meetings with customers to discuss their specific 'own label' requirements. The company also made a commitment to change its autocratic management style in favour of a team-working approach that would better tap into the enthusiasm and talents of its 650-strong workforce, which it had identified as the key to significant improvement. The company rejected the traditional vision/mission statement in favour of: 'We always want to be the first choice for our customers' through:

- our unique package of highly innovative products and fully integrated services
- our honest commitment to do better
- the way we manage relationships and share the rewards of success
- our energy, enthusiasm and drive.

Speed

Doing things quickly. This involves delivering goods and services to customers as fast as they want them. Speed can be achieved through spare capacity, rapid suppliers, effective control of workflow, etc.

Exercise

What do you think that the term speed means to:

● a television manufacturer
● a building society operation?

Dependability

Doing things on time. This means keeping the delivery schedule that has been promised to the customer. This can be achieved through an efficient scheduling system, reliable equipment and the motivation and commitment of personnel (low absenteeism, turn-over, etc.). For example, in a car plant 'dependability' means on time delivery of cars and spare parts to dealers and part centres. Dependability in a supermarket could mean keeping the number of goods that are out of stock to a minimum.

Flexibility

This is being able to change what you do to respond to changes in customer requirements in terms of products and services design, volume, mix and delivery times. Flexibility can be achieved through dependable suppliers, mobility of multiskilled labour, and versatile equipment, etc.

Exercise

What do you believe to mean by the term 'flexibility' in the following operations:

● a dental surgery
● a car plant?

Cost

Doing things cheaply involves aiming to get the right mix of resources and facilities to provide good value products and services at low cost. Cost-efficiency can be achieved through increased capacity utilization, reduced overheads, multipurpose equipment and facilities, and higher productivity.

Case Study

In order to reduce overhead costs and manage the personnel levels, Morrison Construction Group (UK), have developed the term 'Target Zero'. This is the aggregate time behind or ahead of schedule for all the company's construction projects. Traditionally the target for management has been to keep this figure at zero – indicating an average of all projects that are exactly on schedule.

Prioritizing operations performance objectives

An operations function can prioritize the five performance objectives by deciding on their relative importance to the operation. This depends on the following factors:

- The needs of the organization's customers.
- The influence of the company's competitors.
- The stage of the firm's products and services in their life cycle.

Order-winning and order-qualifying criteria

In today's volatile market there are certain characteristics that a firm's products should possess before it can be considered by potential customers. These characteristics are called order-qualifying criteria and may include factors such as delivery, quality, cost and so on. Order-winning criteria are those characteristics that can exist beyond the order qualifiers, such as design ability and customization, that a firm can offer to its customers to win their orders.

Decision areas in operations strategy

In order to maintain and improve the performance of the operations function, the operations strategy needs to set the direction for each of the operation's main decision areas. These areas are related both to operation's structural and infrastructure decisions. The structural decisions determine the operating environment, while the infrastructure decisions are those which are concerned with day-to-day planning, control and improvement activities.

Structural decision areas

Facilities strategy

This refers to decisions as to the size, number of sites and location of the operation. What activities should be allocated to the operation and where the operation's facilities should be located.

Technology strategy

This involves decisions on the range of equipment, type of technology and systems that should be used by the operation in order to make the required contribution to meet its quality, speed, cost, delivery and flexibility requirements.

Integration strategy

This relates to decisions as to how much of the operation's activities should be undertaken by its own, and how much should be done by acquiring its external, suppliers or customers.

Process strategy

This involves decisions on the design of the production or service delivery system and the organization of operation's resources for updating and developing new products and services.

Organization strategy

This involves decisions on the structure of the operation and the role and responsibilities of people in its management, and what type of control and rewards systems should be used.

Infrastructure decision areas

Capacity strategy

This relates to decisions as to how the capacity of the operation should be adjusted in response to changes in the forecast or in the market demand for its products and services.

Supplier strategy

This involves decisions on how suppliers for the operation are selected and the relationships with them are developed. It also is concerned with how the operation monitors and improves suppliers' performance.

Case Study

Bella Pasta with eighty-four outlets is one of the largest pasta restaurant chains in the UK. Before it was acquired by Whitbread, in 1996, the company was forced to accept contracts with suppliers who were chosen for their price benefits rather than the quality of service, reducing the potential value to the final consumer. In the restaurant business a guaranteed supply of fresh high quality food is crucial to maintain a chain's reputation. Whitbread has given Bella Pasta the financial resources it needs to persuade suppliers into producing higher quality products and services. Quality has become the focus rather than cost. The company deals with its suppliers on a fair and consistent basis aiming to forge and foster some very long-term relationships.

The saving made by managing their suppliers better has been translated into better food without an increase in price. This means better products, better quality meals for the same price. Furthermore, employees have been empowered to reject goods or services that they feel do not match up to the minimum standard demanded by Bella Pasta. On taking delivery of a consignment of perishable goods, staff are encouraged to check the state of the food as well as the regularity of on-time delivery as a further test of the quality of the supplier. The result has been to force suppliers to raise their standards in line with those expected by the company.

4 *What is a transformation model?* In the context of operations management, a transformation model is the framework used by the operation to convert its resources into the outputs desired by customers. The key elements of the model are identified and its application to both service and manufacturing industries are investigated.

5 *What role is played by the operations strategy in meeting the strategic goals of an organization?* To be successful an organization needs to clearly define and implement its corporate, business and functional objectives. The strategies to set and achieve these objectives are defined and the distinction and links between them highlighted.

6 *What are the main elements of an operations strategy?* The process and content of an operations strategy can contribute to the operation's efficiency and effectiveness. These elements and their relevance to the performance objectives of operations are discussed. The type and nature of decision areas in operations management are also explored.

Macro and micro operating systems

Manufacturing or service operations are number of interrelated functions designed to produce or provide a predetermined range of products or services. They can be considered as part of a macro (large) operating system which include the firm's internal organization and external environment, or a micro system at the operating level. For example, various departments at a university can be viewed as micro systems, all part of the total university organization at macro operating level.

Operations function like any other major function in an organization such as marketing, finance, and so on is in charge of its own set of distinct activities, but at the same time is part of the 'total organization'. This means that any internal and external factor that can influence performance of the organization as a whole can also affect the performance of the operations function.

Inventory strategy

This involves decisions on how much inventory the operation should hold and where it is to be located, and what should be the sourcing policies and the material control systems used.

Human resource strategy

This relates to decisions as to how the staff of the operation are selected, organized, and developed, and what role and mix of skills they should provide in order to contribute to the management of the operation.

Tesco is the UK's largest supermarket chain. As part of its human resource strategy, the company believes that any investment in customer service hinges on looking after and motivating those employees who have most contact with customers. The aim here is to encourage multiskilling and specialization, offer a variety of challenging tasks and opportunities for promotion.

Planning and control strategy

This relates to decisions as to how the operation should plan its future activities, and decide, allocate and control its resources in order to meet its demand expectation.

Over the years, British Airways (BA) management has learnt that in a global market companies must be aware of the cultural differences in order to serve its customers effectively. Hence, as part of its planning and control strategy, BA decided that overseas key management positions should be filled by home-country nationals to get the necessary degree of market understanding and knowledge. The company ensures that all its managers should be conscious of cross-cultural differences, preferably instilled through international assignments. British Airways believes that customer satisfaction indices can be positively influenced by providing a culturally and linguistically specific service.

Performance measurement and improvement strategy

This relates to decisions as to how the operation's performance should be measured and improved, and who should be involved in the improvement process and how the process should be managed. It also deals with the way the operation organizes its resources in order to prevent failure and cope with disruption if failure does occur.

Hewlett Packard Ltd is the UK sales region unit of the Hewlett Packard, a California-based high technology equipment and service provider. The company is a market leader in office and home computer printers. Behind the smooth, empowered and informal organization lies a rigorous performance measurement system. Hewlett Packard uses the business excellence model and quality management systems (QMS) tools (see Chapter 11). Individuals in the company set many of their own goals at the start of the year, with self-determined improvement targets. A 'reality' check will take place with the relevant functional manager to ensure that targets are appropriate, but the objective is ownership, not imposition of outside goals.

Macro and micro operations

Organizations, large and small, are either viewed as macro operations (the total business), or as micro operations which are the individual functions within the 'total organization' such as marketing, finance, operations, and so on. The efficiency and effectiveness of these micro operations has a profound influence on the performance of the whole business. On the other hand, factors affecting the total business performance (macro operation) will influence the performance of individual micro operations.

Internal influences on the operations function

This relates to relationships between the operations function and other internal departments in the business. Some of the key functions that can influence the performance of the operations function include:

● Sales Department
● Human Resources Department
● Finance Department
● Marketing Department
● Purchasing Department.

External influences on the operations functions

This relates to the effect of the external factors on the performance of the operations function in the organization. These factors include:

● political and legal
● economic condition
● competition
● labour market
● customers
● suppliers
● technological development
● capital and money market.

Operations management as a transformation process

All operations use their resources as inputs to the operating systems and, through management decision-taking and actions, convert these inputs into the desired outputs. Hence an operation can be viewed as a 'transformation model'. The model has three distinct components:

1 *Input elements*. These are either the operation's 'transforming resources' such as people and facilities, or the 'transformed resources' such as information and materials.
2 *Conversion process*. This refers to the operations management activities that takes place during the transformation process.
3 *Outputs elements*. These are the outcomes of the contribution made by the input resources and the relevant conversion processes.

The transformation model can be used as a framework to evaluate the strength and weaknesses of an operation.

Strategic importance of operations

Decisions made in operations management must be in harmony with the organization's corporate and business strategic objectives. This will help the total business to maintain its competitive position in the marketplace. Depending on the type and size of organization there are three forms or levels of strategies:

1 *Corporate strategy*. How should the organization as a whole fulfil its long-term objectives?
2 *Business strategy*. How should the individual functions in the business such as marketing, finance, operations, and so on, compete in the marketplace?
3 *Functional strategy*. How should the individual business functions manage their resources in order to contribute to the fulfilment of a firm's corporate and business objectives?

Process and content of operations strategy

An operations strategy consists of two parts. The first component is the 'content' of the operations strategy, which is an outline of the operation's policies and principles. The second component is the 'process' of the operations strategy, which shows the way in which these policies and plans are decided.

Performance characteristics of operations

Operations can have five performance objectives. They usually prioritize these objectives according to the needs of their immediate markets, the actions of their competitors, and the stage of their organization's products and services in their life cycles. These performance objectives are:

1 Quality – doing things right.
2 Speed – doing things quickly.
3 Dependability – doing things on time.
4 Flexibility – being able to change what you do.
5 Cost – doing things cheaply.

Decision areas in operations management

Operations strategy needs to set the direction for the operation's structural and infrastructure decisions. Structural decisions are those which are related to the operating environment. These type of decisions relate to the following areas:

- facilities strategy
- technology strategy
- integration strategy
- organization strategy.

Infrastructure decisions are those that are concerned with the day to day planning, control and improvement activities. These include:

- capacity strategy
- supplier strategy
- inventory strategy
- human resource strategy
- planning and control strategy
- performance measurement and improvement strategy.

Self Assessment

1 Differentiate between a macro and micro operating system.
2 List four examples of micro operations.
3 List three examples of macro operating systems.
4 The following have internal influences on the operations function, except:
   (a) sales
   (b) finance
   (c) human resource
   (d) suppliers
   (e) purchasing.
5 The following have external influences on the operations function, except:
   (a) competition
   (b) technological innovation
   (c) economic condition
   (d) labour market
   (e) research and development.
6 Personnel function is responsible for the health and safety of the staff working in the operations function. True or false?
7 For a firm to be successful, only its marketing function should be customer orientated. True or false?
8 A marketing-led organization is a firm which gives importance to:
   (a) sales figures
   (b) customers' needs
   (c) product research
   (d) production output

(e) only (a)?

9 Which of the following creates a perfect integration in a company:
(a) personnel
(b) operations
(c) suppliers
(d) marketing
(e) finance?

10 The following are the main elements of the purchasing mix, except :
(a) promotion
(b) quality
(c) quantity
(d) price
(e) delivery.

11 List three economic related factors which can influence the ability of a firm to invest.

12 Differentiate between an operation's 'transformed resources' and 'transforming resources'.

13 The following are inputs to an operation, except:
(a) finished products
(b) labour
(c) equipment
(d) buildings
(e) information.

14 Outputs from an operation are:
(a) information
(b) products
(c) services
(d) all of the above
(e) only (b) and (c)?

15 List three environmental issues which can influence activities of the operations function.

16 Give four benefits of developing a transformation model for an operation.

17 List three factors that can make an operation's control system more effective.

18 Improvement decisions made by the operations function should be in line with:
(a) capital available
(b) skills available
(c) capacity available
(d) only (a)

(e) strategic goals of the organization?

19 Differentiate between three forms of strategies in an organization.

20 Operations strategy can be described by one of the following:
(a) deciding a firm's long-term objectives
(b) deciding the organization's business strategy
(c) deciding the firm's functional strategy
(d) deciding the firm's marketing strategy
(e) deciding the firm's corporate strategy?

21 Differentiate between the 'content' and the 'process' of an operations strategy.

22 List five performance objectives for an operation.

23 An operation is dependable if it is capable of doing things quickly. True or false?

24 An operation is flexible if it is capable of changing what it can do in response to changes in the customer requirements. True or false?

25 An operation decides on its performance objectives based on the:
(a) customer needs
(b) influence of its competitors
(c) the stage of its products in their life cycle
(d) all of the above
(e) only (a)?

26 Differentiate between an operation's structural and infrastructure decisions.

27 An operations process strategy refers to the design of its production or service delivery system. True or false?

28 An operation's integration strategy is the way in which it is integrated with the the firm's internal functions. True or false?

29 The following strategies are related to an operation's structural decisions, except:
(a) facilities strategy
(b) improvement strategy
(c) technology strategy
(d) integration strategy
(e) process strategy.

30 The following strategies are related to the operation's infrastructure decisions, except:
(a) organization strategy
(b) capacity strategy
(c) supplier strategy
(d) inventory strategy
(e) planning and control strategy.

References and further reading

Dilworth, J. (1989). Production and Operations Management. McGraw-Hill.

Gilgeous, V. (1997). Operations Management of Change. Pitman.

Hill, T. (1991). *Production and Operations Management*. Prentice Hall.

Lockyer et al. (1983). *Production and Operations Management*. Pitman.

Schroeder, R. (1989). *Operations Management*. McGraw-Hill.

Slack, N., Chambers, S., Harland, C., Harrison, A. and Johnston, R. (1998). *Operations Management*. Pitman.

Waller, D. (1999). *Operations Management*. Thomson International.

Chapter 3

Organization of the operations process

Chapter 2 has shown how operations is a complex function which interacts with all other functions within the organization. At its heart, however, is the idea of transformation. Inputs are acquired, and the operations process converts them into outputs. This is the core activity of the whole organization, and organizational success, or even survival, depends upon how well this is carried out. Without an effective and efficient operations process an organization will only succeed for as long as the competition is even less competent. This chapter considers the major factors and choices involved in the design of the operation. In particular it addresses:

Learning Objectives

1 *Objectives.* What are we seeking to achieve in the design of the process? What are the constraints and trade-offs involved? Issues of effectiveness, efficiency and flexibility are considered.
2 *Process organization.* A number of alternative ways of organizing the process have evolved in response to different conditions. These are described and their suitability considered.
3 *Manufacturing and service operations.* While there is a great deal of common ground between manufacturing and service

operations, the nature of services imposes constraints and demands upon the operation which are unique. The most important of these are identified and their implications considered.

4 *Location*. One of the most important operations decisions is the location of the operation. In many operations, location is a capital-intensive decision, and relatively difficult to change. The factors to be taken into account in arriving at a location decision are discussed. The use of a single location is increasingly rare in all but the smallest of operations, and the arguments in favour of single or multiple site operation are considered.

Objectives of operations design

The objectives of a business organization are usually expressed in terms of profitability and market share. These may be couched in terms of market leadership, customer satisfaction or even technological leadership, but generally they still lead ultimately to profit. Broadly, maximizing profit involves maximizing the appeal of the product/service to the customer while minimizing cost. While the philosophy behind just in time (JIT) (see Chapters 5 and 7) and total quality management (TQM) (Chapter 11) sees this as a perfectly reasonable ambition, it is more usual to recognize that there are trade-offs between customer satisfaction and cost.

In not-for-profit organizations, and this includes internal operations within commercial ventures, the issue is more complex. Profit is not an objective, so performance cannot easily be targeted or measured by simple equations such as (revenue-cost). Frequently there is no competition; a manufacturing manager seeking to recruit more labour must work through the human resource management (HRM) department of the firm; for most people seeking health care or education within the UK, there is little alternative but the state provision. Revenue is also frequently imposed in a manner that does not necessarily relate very clearly to expected or actual demand. Attempts have been made to introduce surrogates for competitive pressure into such organizations through customer charters and performance league tables, but with mixed results.

In education within the UK the performance of schools in a variety of parameters (examinations, attendance, inspection reports, etc.) is published. Coupled with this parents have, in theory, freedom of choice as to the schools they send their children to. This is intended to introduce competitive pressure into the 'market' for education and drive up standards. It has, however, been dogged by criticism of the performance measures and by capacity problems restricting parental choice.

In internal operations within commercial organizations the recent growth of outsourcing has introduced real competition. The HRM or information technology (IT) department can no longer assume that it is essential since both can be subcontracted.

The objectives of operations design can thus be expressed as optimizing the balance between effectiveness and efficiency whether in commercial or not-for-profit organizations. However, this must be seen in the long term. Both markets and technology are constantly developing and what is optimal at any one point in time will not remain so. An important subsidiary objective is therefore to retain an appropriate degree of flexibility both to cope with market changes and with the development of technology.

In the early days of the National Health Service in the UK, hospital care consisted mainly of looking after the sick until they were well enough to leave, or died. This demanded a large number of beds, adequate hotel services and fairly low technology nursing care. Technological development in the form of vaccination and drug therapy has greatly reduced the demand for simple nursing care, while surgical technique in particular has led to a much greater demand for high technology intervention. The result is that hospitals now are primarily concerned with providing high cost, high skill intervention and intensive high skill aftercare, but with much shorter recovery times – patients remain in hospital for days rather than weeks. Indeed many surgical procedures do not now involve any stay in hospital. Hospitals are now also expected to treat more serious trauma and disease which, even twenty years ago, would have led to the death of the patient.

Overall there has been a move from a low cost, high capacity service to a high cost, high technology service. Utilization has become much more important, with spare capacity being seen as a waste of expensive resource.

Unfortunately winter still sees substantial increases in cases of infectious disease (influenza, bronchitis, etc.) requiring hospital treatment.

Exercise

Identify the issues facing the hospital service in seeking to balance effectiveness and efficiency at present.

Effectiveness

Operations management is often seen as being more concerned with efficiency, but efficiency without effectiveness is at best a waste of resources and at worst positively damaging. Effectiveness can be defined simply as 'doing the right thing' and efficiency as 'doing things right'. Given this, operations management is about 'doing the right things right'.

Effectiveness is simply achieving the desired outcome. In the overall context of the organization this is usually expressed in terms of customer satisfaction. A product or service that meets customer needs will sell; one that does not meet those needs will not sell well (unless there is a monopoly). A product or service that meets customer needs better than the competition will capture market share.

In manufacturing, operations is usually dependent upon design and marketing to specify customer needs, so an effective manufacturing operation will be delivering the right quantity at the right time to the right specification. In services, where customers interact directly with the operation, the situation is much more fluid. The operation may be able to adjust to particular customer needs, but overall there are still constraints arising from the design of the service. In the public sector, the definition of a customer is often difficult, so effectiveness can sometimes be defined in terms of keeping the paymaster happy.

Operations can be effective in delivering to specification, but if the specification is inappropriate this will not lead to customer satisfaction. There is, however, little that operations itself can do to correct this. Satisfactory design of the product or service is a prerequisite for effective operations.

In not-for-profit organizations there is often far more difficulty in defining the customer. This is particularly true when the direct recipient of the service is not paying for it. Is a public health service there to satisfy the needs of the sick or the needs of society (possibly as represented by government)? It is widely recognized that the demand for public health services is almost unlimited, therefore, cost constraint is inevitable. This implies selection and rationing with the almost inevitable consequence of public dissatisfaction. It might be best to consider government (or society at large) as the customer at a strategic level, with the individual patient as the customer at an operational level. Meeting the patients' needs is a measure of effectiveness once the patient has been admitted to the system, but the decision on admission to treatment should be based upon overall social priorities. Unfortunately any government that publishes clear guidelines on what may or may not be treated will be subject to public opprobrium, so the issue is usually left vague and unspecified.

Exercise

The customers of charitable organizations are even more difficult to define. Do charities exist to satisfy the needs of the deprived that they ostensibly serve, the volunteers who work for them or the donors who give to them?

Efficiency

Efficiency is a much simpler concept than effectiveness. It is closely related to the concept of productivity (Chapter 5), but can be simply defined as achieving the required output at the lowest overall cost. Cost involves labour, materials, facilities, support services and time. The real danger with seeking to improve efficiency in isolation is that the real purpose is lost sight of. The result is suboptimal performance, or even, in the extreme case, dysfunctional performance.

Case Study

A computer systems designer is given the task of computerizing a manual creditor payments system. On investigation it is found that the existing system requires that every invoice received is not only checked against the order and goods received files, but also has to be authorized by the original requisitioning manager and by quality control. The process takes between eight and twelve weeks and must be completed before payment is authorized. It also takes a substantial amount of staff time and paperwork.

In the new computerized system, when an invoice is input, the system checks the order and delivery files automatically and, provided the invoice corresponds to a received order that has not been paid for, prints a cheque. Only if the invoice is for more than £5000 does payment require management authorization.

Exercise

Comment on the efficiency and the effectiveness of the new system.

An excessive stress on efficiency in control systems can also lead to suboptimal performance. In manufacturing, efficiency is often linked to utilization, and attempts are made to ensure that plant and labour are always fully occupied. However, it is a central tenet of optimized production technology (OPT) (see Chapter 8) that utilization only matters at bottlenecks in the process. Striving for high utilization at non-bottleneck processes is simply wasting resources.

Flexibility

There are four reasons for retaining flexibility in an operation.

Variation in the volume of demand

This is more fully dealt with under capacity planning (Chapter 6). It is sufficient to mention here that there are very few, if any, situations where demand is constant.

Development of the market

Markets change, sometimes gradually and sometimes dramatically. If the operation cannot respond to the change then the organization will certainly be less successful, and may fail altogether.

Case Study

The Ford model T car was an example of a perfect match between the production system and the product specification. The production line concept, perfected by Ford, meant that this highly standardized and very basic vehicle could be produced for a price that the competition simply could not match. Unfortunately for Ford, the increasingly sophisticated market began to demand much greater variety and much higher specification. The Ford production line was too inflexible to accommodate this change.

Development of technology

Technological development in the market is, perhaps the greatest challenge facing operations. In manufacturing there are very few areas which can be considered immune. In almost any area involving electronics the risk of obsolescence, or even the total failure of a technology, is very high.

Case Study

A selection of notable failures

- Quadraphonic sound – a technique for enhancing the sound quality of vinyl recordings by recording four channels instead of two, it struggled for a few years in the 1970s before vanishing.
- The 'squarial' – an alternative convention for satellite television transmission, it lasted about twelve months.
- Eight-track stereo – an alternative to the music casette.
- Betamax – an alternative video recording system, technically superior to VHS.

The jury is still out on high definition, wide screen, digital television – all developments where there is conflict over standards and technologies – and flat screen display – there are currently three or four competing technologies and are unlikely all to succeed.

Environmental changes

The political and social environment has an effect upon operations through improving standards of welfare, health and safety at work. For example, child labour and excessive working hours have been progressively discontinued in the developed world, and similar pressures are being felt in the developing economies. These are usually fairly long-term changes however. Changes in consumer or government sensitivities can be more dramatic. Concerns over the safety of products or processes can lead to rapid changes in consumer behaviour, and operations may well be unable to respond sufficiently quickly.

Technology

Any operations process is very susceptible to the effects of technology. In general the question of appropriate technology should always be addressed. This does not necessarily refer to advanced technology, but that technology which strikes the best balance between efficiency and effectiveness. This often depends upon external circumstances. An organization setting up a manufacturing facility in a developing country might be better advised to employ a well-established but robust technology rather than state-of-the-art methods. The latter may well seem more cost-effective, but is more likely to suffer failure.

Process organization

As operations management has developed, a number of ways of organizing the operations process have been discovered and progressively refined. These standard methods of organization and control have been developed through long experience (many of the approaches can be found as far back as in ancient Egypt) and are still appropriate today. Technology has certainly blurred some of the boundaries but, in general, the most important operations decision is still the process organization adopted.

Market influences

The appropriateness of method is usually related to the nature of the market for the product or service, and almost all market variables are relevant. The most important are:

1 *Variety* – the degree to which the product or service is customized to meet a particular customer need.
2 *Volume* – the total output of particular product/service lines.
3 *Availability* – the speed of response required by the market.
4 *Stability* – the life expectancy of individual products, and the variation in the volume of demand.

Variety and volume are obviously linked in that a high variety market will not require high volumes of individual products, but the relationship is not necessarily straightforward. Variation in product from the point of view of the market is not necessarily variation from the point of view of operations.

Cars are seen as mass market standardized products yet the standard Cadillac has 7.2 million configurations. This figure is arrived at by multiplying body variations by engine variations by trim variations, etc. The consumer is presented with almost limitless choice, yet from a manufacturing point of view there is very little variety.

Benetton, the clothing manufacturers and retailers, developed a process that allows colouring to be the final stage in garment manufacture. This greatly reduces the variety during the bulk of the manufacturing process, without diminishing the variety available in the market.

Other market factors that have some impact upon operations organization are:

1 *Price* – the more competitive a market is on price, the more pressure this will put on operations to reduce costs.
2 *Quality* – while the production of poor quality products or services can never be justified, different operations organizations do lend themselves to different levels of quality.

Low volume operations

The main characteristic of low volume operations is that economies of scale are not available. If a manufacturer produces a single item then all the setup costs must be recovered against that one item. Likewise a service provider designing a service to meet the precise needs of a particular customer incurs costs which can only be recovered from that customer.

Case Study

If seeking to invest money, a customer can use one of the many standard investment vehicles (bonds, individual saving accounts (ISAs), unit trusts, high interest building society or bank accounts) or engage the services of a financial adviser. The financial adviser may charge a fee, in which case the customer might hope that the expert advice is worth more than the fee in terms of investment performance. Alternatively the adviser may be paid commission, which will come out of the money invested by the customer. Again the expectation is that the performance of the investment will more than outweigh this additional cost.

Exercise

What are the additional activities that the customer is paying for when engaging a financial adviser?

Low volume operations are generally either customized to a high degree, or so rarely performed that there is little point in devoting effort towards achieving a high level of efficiency. In either case the effect is a situation with a fairly high level of uncertainty, which demands skill and flexibility from the operations system. The organization adopted in these cases is sometimes distinguished by the scale of the task, but the distinctions are relatively unimportant.

Job operations

These are usually small-scale low volume operations. The task of the jobbing builder is an example, or a garage carrying out maintenance and repair of motor vehicles. The builder carries out small-scale repairs, alterations and extensions on property and, while all contracts share a common repertoire of skills and context, each contract is different. The builder must possess, or have access to, all the skills and equipment necessary, although any one contract may use only a subset of these. Each contract is subject to detailed discussion with the client, usually leading to an estimate of time and cost. Since the actual contract may turn out rather differently from expectation, the actual cost and time may well be different.

Project operations

These differ from job operations only in scale and complexity. While, on the face of it there may be little similarity between building a conservatory on to an existing private house, building a new gas-fired power station, and developing a new passenger airliner, the differences are in scale and skills not essential organizational characteristics. All are characterized by a degree of uniqueness and the uncertainty that this generates. No two conservatory installations will be quite the same, and this variability is even more obvious with the power station and the airliner. All are characterized by the need to predict from past experience of variable relevance, and the need to develop and manage a complex and non-linear set of activities.

The characteristics of both job and project operations are:

- uncertainty about the precise breakdown and relationship of the activities required to carry out the task
- uncertainty about the resources (time, labour, facilities and materials) required for each activity
- the need to plan and co-ordinate activities and resources in an uncertain and complex environment
- job, and more especially project, operations usually involve a number of activities going on in parallel which must be brought together at some time during the operation.

This leads to the following requirements:

- high level of skill to deal with the uncertainty as it arises
- range of skills to deal with all possible requirements within the chosen field
- range of equipment and facilities to deal with all possible requirements within the chosen field
- skill at estimating time and resources and co-ordinating multiple activities,

all within the context of the type of service provided.

This inevitably leads to low utilization since not every skill and resource will be used on every project. In addition the project scheduling process must allow slack to compensate for unpredictability. One side effect of the flexibility that this gives job and project operations is the potential for very high quality. It is at least theoretically possible to spend as long on a particular task as is necessary to get it perfect, without causing massive disruption to other work.

Case Study

Rolls-Royce adopted a job approach for much of their car assembly until recently. Given that the Rolls-Royce is a standard car, if low volume, this might seem a rather reactionary approach. However, it did mean that a craftsperson could, for example, spend an extra hour or two perfecting the finish on a body panel to compensate for the natural variability of a previous process.

Project and job operations normally use a fixed position layout, since the facilities are usually taken to the object being worked on. In a motor repair workshop, tools will be sensibly stored and brought to the vehicle when needed. The precise location of the tools is not particularly important. In a building project, equipment and labour must obviously be brought to the building and the design of the building dictates their disposition.

High volume operations

With high volume operations, the fact that particular tasks, functions and activities are going to be carried out many times, under practically identical situations, justifies the expenditure of time and effort in achieving a high level of efficiency. There is very little point in trying to increase the efficiency of a task that is only carried out a few times a year, even if it takes several hours. On the other hand, the task of fitting the wheels to a new car may take only two minutes, but if this is carried out 200 000 times, then a 10 per cent improvement saves 300 hours or more.

Economies of scale are greatest when the task is carried out continuously. Not only is it worth investing substantial design effort to reduce non-productive resource usage, but there is no resource wastage in changeover from one task to another.

Case Study

A typist using a typewriter must stop at the end of each document, remove the paper and insert a new sheet. This must also be done at the end of each page of a multipage document. A word processor operator can type continuously without interruption, except to save each document on completion. In effect, each page represents a setup for the typist, and each document equally so for the word processor operator. The result is higher productivity with the word processor, but also less variety of work and greater risk of repetitive strain injury.

The extent to which such economies can be realized depends on the overall variety of products or services produced. If the output of a given product is such that resources can be devoted to that product full time, then a mass production or flowline process can be adopted. If demand is not that high, then a batch organization is more usual.

Batch operations

Batch operations are appropriate whenever:

● standard products/services are involved

- quantities of individual products/services required are significant
- quantities required at any one time are not great enough to justify the dedication of resources to the one product/service.

Normally the organization is providing a number of products/services with related process needs. Equipment and staff may be used on several different products.

In summary, batch operations are appropriate in medium variety, medium volume situations. Two examples illustrate the general principles.

A company makes electrical wiring for electrical equipment assemblers. This may be the wiring from the switch to the motor on a vacuum cleaner, or the various power leads found inside a personal computer. Whatever the application, the basic process is to cut the wires to length; trim them; bundle them together (if necessary); fit terminators; inspect and pack them. All products follow the same sequence using largely the same facilities, but each product requires different wires, sizes and terminators. A batch of personal computer power leads will be made and this may be followed by a batch of wiring looms for a hi-fi amplifier, and so on. Between batches materials have to be assembled and equipment adjusted – the setup.

A package holiday company is also a batch operation. A batch of holidaymakers is booked into a given resort at a given time. The process sequence is assemble holidaymakers at airport, fly them to their destination and distribute them to their hotels. A week later this process is reversed. In between holiday flights, planes are cleaned and refuelled, and hotel rooms cleaned – the set up.

In both the above cases, a group of products are processed as if they were a single unit. The sequence is fixed, and to a large extent so is the time available. There is little room for variation; the holi-daymaker who is late will miss the flight.

The key decision in batch operations is the batch size. This is frequently determined by economic constraints – a charter aircraft must be full if it is to show a profit – but may also be dictated by demand or even some combination of the two. Data from devices such as point of sale terminals is often sent to the central computer by telephone, at night, in a single burst. This allows records to be reasonably up to date without the cost of a continuous telephone connection. Issues of batch size and sequence will be considered in Chapters 6, 7 and 8.

Case Study

A manufacturer of toiletries produces a variety of products. Some are powder based (i.e. talcum powder), some are liquid and some are creams (i.e. moisturizer). Of the liquids, some are fluid (i.e. perfume/after shave) and some viscous (i.e. shampoo). Many of the products are packed in a variety of different sizes.

The basic process for all products is the same. Ingredients are mixed; containers are filled, capped, labelled and packed. Inspections are carried out at appropriate stages. The plant require-ments vary. The mixing of powders, liquids and creams requires quite different processes, and the filling technology also differs. However, the same equipment can be used for mixing hand lotion, body lotion, shampoo, conditioner, etc., provided it is cleaned between products. A batch organization may be used, so that a batch of say 5000 200 ml bottles of anti-dandruff shampoo is followed by a batch of 3000 50 ml bottles of moisturiser, etc. The layout might be as shown in Figure 3.1.

Flowline operations (mass production)

If the volume of output of a product or service is sufficient to justify dedicated facilities, then considerable scope for economies of scale arises. At this point it is worth devoting effort to making the oper-ation as efficient as possible since the frequent repetition gives large accumulated savings. In a flowline, the fixed sequence of operations

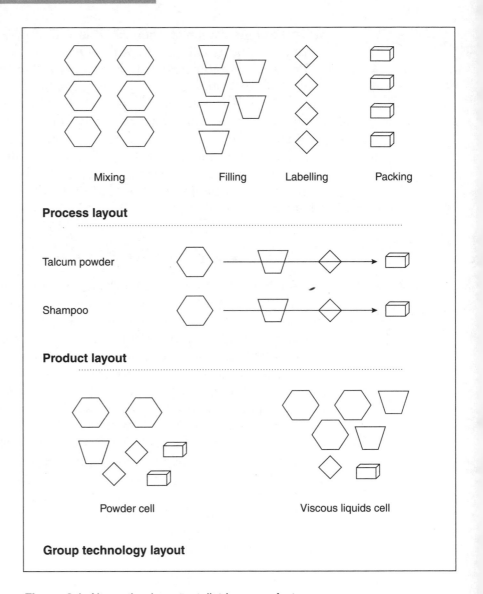

Figure 3.1 Alternative layouts, toiletries manufacturer

is embedded into the design of the line so that transport is minimized. Plant and facilities for consecutive stages in the process are physically adjacent. The processes themselves are designed to minimize non-productive effort.

Case Study

In a well-organized job shop, equipment is stored away when not in use, since a particular piece of equipment may be used only occasionally. As a result a great deal of the work carried out is actually retrieving and setting up equipment, then putting it away after use.

In a batch environment, the basic machinery is fixed in place, but it is used on different batches of different products. Setting-up equipment needs to be brought to the machine and the material to be worked on, for each batch needs to be collected and then removed afterwards. More of the actual effort is directly productive but much is still wasted in non-productive tasks.

In a flowline the work stage is designed so that everything is to hand. The material to be worked on arrives from the previous stage and is sent on to the next stage. Except for the occasional need to adjust, overhaul or clean the workstation, all effort is productive.

Figure 3.2 illustrates the relative productivity of the three methods.

A flowline need not be high technology or even powered. Operators sitting at adjacent tables can pass work from stage to stage.

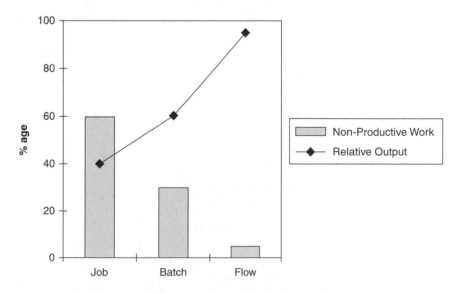

Figure 3.2 Relative efficiency of job, batch and flow

Individual efficiency of flowline stages is of little consequence compared with the overall efficiency of the line. A stage producing at 10 000 per hour is of little use if the following stage can only produce at 3000 per hour. A well-designed flowline must be balanced so that each stage is operating at the same rate of output. This is most easily achieved by reducing the units of work to their lowest common denominator, so that efficient flowlines are often characterized by very short operating cycles – a task is often completed in seconds. These short cycle flowlines are often criticized because the very repetitive nature of the work gives little opportunity for any sort of job satisfaction, and they have sometimes been associated with low productivity, absenteeism and poor industrial relations. Of course, many batch operations have equally short cycle times, but batch process operators do have more variety – batches come to an end and new batches are started.

Flowlines are intrinsically inflexible; they are designed to produce a particular product at a particular rate of output. If demand for the product rises or falls, there is little that can be done to respond. Capacity cannot be easily increased, and reducing output simply reduces utilization and may result in very little cost saving.

Case Study

If demand for individual products was great enough the toiletries manufacturer mentioned above might adopt a flow organization. This is shown in Figure 3.1. Again the sequence of operations is mix the ingredients, fill the container, label and pack. Each product has its own line with purpose designed plant, hence the term 'product layout'.

Group technology

Group technology can be seen as an attempt to obtain some of the cost benefits of flowlines in a batch environment. A company manufacturing 200 different products will often find that these products fall into families based upon their manufacturing characteristics, and a group of perhaps ten products could require very similar processing in terms of machinery, process sequence and operation times. While the demand for each product individually will not be great enough to justify dedicated plant and labour, the output for the whole group may be great enough to justify setting up dedicated facilities. The group technology organization rarely leads to fully fledged flowlines and is more likely to lead to small manufacturing cells containing the necessary plant and labour for that group of products. Setup and control are easier and transport is reduced compared with batch operations.

A frequently reported benefit of group technology is greater motivation and job satisfaction. Compared with a batch organization, workers gain a greater familiarity with the task, while still having a good variety. Compared with both batch and flow operations, workers can see the context of their work within the overall scheme since group technology cells are usually small enough so that all process stages are visible from every point.

Case Study

The toiletries manufacturer could consider a group technology organization based upon the four groups of products identified; powders; creams; viscous fluids; non-viscous fluids. This is also shown in Figure 3.1.

Continuous processes

Continuous processes are usually found in chemical processing industries, and generally are highly automated. Examples include petrochemical production, electricity generation and steel-making. They are usually of more concern to the engineer than to the operations manager.

Hybrid processes

Many systems overlap the boundaries defined above. Flowlines, and even continuous processes, may operate on a batch basis for minor variations. The changes are usually minor, at least in terms of the process requirements. The final colour of a product would simply involve cleaning and refilling the paint reservoir, whether it was a pencil manufacturer or a car manufacturer. A batch of red cars (or pencils) would be made and immediately followed by a batch of yellow with very little interruption.

The term 'mass customization' is sometimes used to describe a situation where an apparently inexhaustible range of choices is offered to the customer, but where the implications for operations are slight. The example of Cadillac cars with 7.2 million alternatives has already been mentioned. Increasingly technology is leading to greater variety in output from apparently standard processes. The flexibly manufacturing system described in Chapter 4 could be seen as a jobbing flowline.

Case Study

Avon manufactures cosmetics that are sold by agents from a catalogue. Much of the manufacture uses purpose-designed flowlines.

Because new catalogues must be issued regularly to stimulate sales, there are frequent changes to the product range. In order to accommodate this with a flow production system, Avon have developed flowlines which can be stripped down and rebuilt for another product in forty-eight hours or less.

Appropriate organization

There are no hard and fast rules about which type of organization to adopt, but different organizations lend themselves to different situations.

Key variables are variety, the number of different products/services produced, and volume, the total output of an individual product/service. These are, of course, related since high variety implies low volume and vice versa. Figure 3.3 illustrates the general relationship between these and process organization.

Other factors that are relevant include:

1 *Quality*. All systems allow good quality to be achieved, but batch and flow depend upon consistency for efficient operation. They are not tolerant of variation in the output required or in the input used. On a flowline in particular, additional time and resources devoted to one particular activity will have an adverse effect upon the whole output. A job/project organization allows the time and

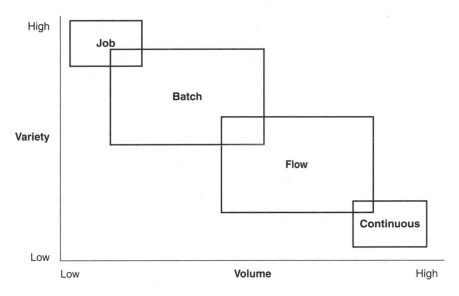

Figure 3.3 Relationship between volume, variety and process

resources required to achieve perfection to be devoted to a particular task without necessarily interfering with other activities as described in the case of Rolls-Royce above.

2 *Price*. Price competitive markets exert pressure on costs. The high utilization achieved in batch and, more especially, flow systems indicates that they are more appropriate where price competition is high.

Exercise

In your current course of study, different aspects of your interaction with the institution delivering the programme will adopt different processes. Identify those that are job/project, batch or flow, and comment upon the appropriateness of that organization.

Manufacturing and service operations

In many respects manufacturing and service operations are similar. Inputs are transformed into outputs. Resources are deployed to achieve this. The process organizations are similar, as are the general requirements for management and control.

An important difference is the presence of the customer. Although increasing customer involvement is found in manufacturing, through the development of partnerships customers are usually not present during the manufacturing process itself. By definition, the customer must be present during some, or all, of the service production process.

This leads to the following differences between service production and manufacturing:

1 *Simultaneity*. Production and consumption of the service are simultaneous. A haircut cannot be produced ready for the customer, but requires the customer's presence throughout.
2 *Volatility*. Service cannot be stocked. Unsold goods remain to be sold another day, but an unoccupied seat on a train, or table in a restaurant or bed in a hospital, is a wasted resource. It cannot be used twice tomorrow because it was not used at all today.
3 *Variability*. Demand for products tends to follow seasonal patterns. Demand for services not only follows seasonal patterns, but much shorter-term patterns as well, often with extreme variation. Demand for public transport, or restaurant meals, follows daily and weekly patterns, with swings of several hundred per cent over the space of an hour or less.
4 *Subjectivity*. Products are usually made to specification, which is often comprehensive and agreed with the customer. Services rarely have a comprehensive agreed specification. Indeed the precise nature of the service may not be agreed. (Do you choose your hairdresser for their skill or the quality of their conversation? What is the service offered by a public house?) Even if the nature of the service is clear, the customer's judgement of satisfaction is subjective, and the customer is the ultimate judge of quality. This is discussed further in Chapter 11.

Exercise

Identify a number of services and consider the relevance and impact of the above factors.

Approaches to service organization

In designing a service operation, the above factors must be taken into account. The variability and volatility mean that extreme problems of matching capacity and demand arise. This is sometimes dealt with merely by letting customers wait, through queues and appointment systems, or by holding sufficient spare capacity and charging appropriately. However a number of approaches have been developed to reduce the impact of these factors on the efficiency of the operation. The most important are standardization, self-service and the front office/back shop approach.

Standardization

The greater the degree of standardization of the service, the more predictable and reproducible its delivery. Customers who are presented with few choices will take less time to make a choice and will occupy the service facilities for less time as a result. In addition the presence of few options means that more preparation can be undertaken before the customer arrives, in the knowledge that that preparation will almost certainly be useful.

Case Study

Compare the expensive restaurant with the fast food outlet.

In the fast food outlet, the few choices can be prepared in advance because they will almost certainly be sold before they become stale. Customers spend only a few minutes choosing, are served almost immediately, and consume the meal within ten to fifteen minutes. Utilization is high, but queues build up at peak times.

In the restaurant, customers require time, and space, to sit and study the menu. Because the variety is high much of the food is cooked to order, and a meal may take one to two hours. At peak times demand is managed through a booking system. Utilization is low, so prices are high, and additional revenue is usually generated from the waiting customers by selling drinks.

Self-service

Using the customer as labour is one way of ensuring that some elements of capacity remain in step with demand. Given the intrinsic lack of skill and training of the customer, however, self-service operations generally need to be highly standardized. This is discussed further in Chapter 4.

Front office/back shop

One of the most widespread and successful approaches to improving service utilization, this involves identifying the minimum customer involvement necessary to provide the service. This is defined as the front office and in essence becomes the service operation. All other activities are seen as support activities, which do not require the presence of the customer and can take place in the back shop. Since the customer is not involved, they can be seen as manufacturing activities, subject to the economies and controls of any manufacturing operation. Back shop activities can be carried out using batch or flow systems as appropriate, they can be carried out at a time and rate to suit the operation rather than the customer, and they can be stocked.

The extent to which this separation is possible depends on the service requirement of the customer, the degree of standardization possible and sometimes the customer skill as the examples in Figures 3.4 and 3.5 indicate.

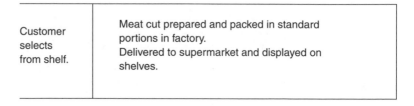

Front office	Back shop
Greet customer. Enquire needs. Possible discussion and preparation to order. Pack and take money	Receipt of bulk meat. Limited preparation of standard cuts.

Traditional butchers

Customer selects from shelf.	Meat cut prepared and packed in standard portions in factory. Delivered to supermarket and displayed on shelves.

Meat display in self-service supermarket

Figure 3.4 Front office/back shop in meat

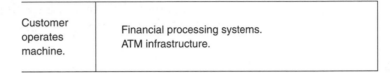

Teller service in Bank

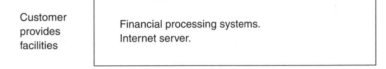

ATM in high street

Customer provides facilities	Financial processing systems. Internet server.

Home Internet banking

Figure 3.5 Front office/back shop in retail banking

The example of meat retailing (Figure 3.4) shows the diminution of choice, i.e. the standardization implicit in this approach, and supermarkets are increasingly introducing counter service for those customers who prefer it. The example of retail banking (Figure 3.5) shows an extreme where the front office has become the property and premises of the customer. It also indicates the extent to which the willingness and skill of the customer determines participation.

Exercise

To what extent can the front office/back shop principle be applied to a college offering qualification courses? What advantages and disadvantages would arise from maximizing the back shop content?

Location

The actual location of operations, whether manufacturing or service, is often a matter of historical accident, and involvement in a location or relocation decision is a rare event for an operations manager. However, the pressure of global competition, and the relative ease of transport and communications, is increasing the importance and frequency of location decisions. Multinationals seem always willing to move production facilities to the latest low labour cost economy, and as one economy develops as a result of this investment, pushing up labour costs, then another appears to undercut it.

Case Study

At the time of writing BMW and the UK government are seeking to determine the fate of the Longbridge car assembly plant, not only for its present output but also as a location for future car models.

Location factors

Ideally the following factors all need to be taken into account in arriving at a location decision.

Market

Location near the market is seen as advantageous in many cases. This was true in manufacturing when transport was difficult and expensive since it reduced costs and increased responsiveness. Although it is still seen as relevant today in some industries, effective transport has made it irrelevant in most cases.

Case Study

In construction products manufacture, bricks, cement and glass are not generally seen as exportable products because of their high bulk, high transport costs and relatively low cost.

In contrast copper tubes and fittings and woodwork, with a lower bulk and higher value, are seen as exportable.

Location near the market has always been much more relevant in the service sector, but again technology and mobility have changed this. Retail outlets that used to need to be within walking distance of the customer (the corner shop), or within a town centre served by public transport, have increasingly been replaced by out-of-town shopping centres to which customers drive. The customer without a car is a low spending, low priority customer.

With over 90 per cent of households having a telephone, many services that do not require face-to-face contact can be carried out remotely. There is no need to visit a bank to open a savings account or negotiate a loan, and there is no need to visit an insurance office to take out property or car insurance. The development of Internet shopping will accelerate this trend. In effect the location of the service outlet has been brought into every home, but without investment by the service provider. Only in personal services is location near the market likely to remain a dominant factor.

Materials

Location near a source of raw materials is obviously a prerequisite for extraction processes; coal can only be mined where it is found. The first stage processing of raw materials is sometimes located near the source of those materials, and this makes economic sense if processing results in a substantial reduction in bulk.

Case Study

Sugar beet is grown in the UK primarily in East Anglia. Sugar beet is a bulky low value crop whose only function is to be converted into sugar, and most of the sugar mills are also located in East Anglia.

It is perhaps surprising how rarely this seems to be an important issue. Crude oil is frequently shipped halfway round the world for refining, and metal ores are rarely refined at source.

Labour

A ready source of skilled labour is essential to any operation, and the lower the labour cost the more efficient the operation.

Manufacturers of sportswear and equipment frequently locate in Far Eastern countries such as Indonesia, Myanmar or China because of the ready supply of labour at very low relative costs.

A US insurance company transferred its data entry operation to the Republic of Ireland because labour was both cheaper and more reliable.

The cost of shipping goods in the first case and documentation in the second is more than offset by the savings.

Location near labour is not always possible. The location of motorway service areas and offshore oil platforms is determined by other factors, and labour must be bussed in or be resident.

Transport

An effective transport system is almost always a prerequisite for any location option. This is frequently a given for any developed world decision, but transport infrastructure development is sometimes offered as an inducement if a major investment is at stake. For example a government might promise road and rail access to attract a new car assembly plant.

Identifying an optimal location based on minimizing transport costs is a well-established operational research technique, but transport costs are rarely significant enough in themselves to dominate the decision.

Infrastructure

Apart from transport, most operations require reliable communications, power and water supply, and waste disposal. They may also require social facilities for staff and labour, and possibly access to technical support and advice. High technology companies tend to cluster around centres of technical excellence, frequently universities.

The issue of infrastructure is more likely to be important when considering location in a developing country. Are power, communications and water supplies reliable enough? What facilities and support are available for expatriate management?

Political issues

Manufacturing in the target market may be necessary to overcome import barriers, both tariff – additional duties charged on imported goods compared with home produced goods – and non-tariff – bureaucratic delays and complexities with paperwork – or the need to satisfy local 'standards' which may not be so stringently required of local products. As world trade becomes freer these needs may reduce but they will probably never be eliminated.

Political incentives can also dominate location decisions. The location of a new car assembly plant may ultimately be decided by the grants and tax breaks made available to the company.

Centralization or decentralization

There are obvious advantages to having a single central location for an operation. These include the following.

Economies of scale

Support services such as personnel, purchasing, goods inwards and outwards, etc. need only be provided on the one site.

Smoother demand and supply

The smaller the operation the greater the effect of variation in demand, and the greater the impact of such issues as staff absenteeism, holidays or machine breakdown. This is particularly marked in services where small branches can be easily overwhelmed by demand at peak times, particularly if a member of staff is absent.

A bank branch normally employs three tellers. Demand can vary during the day from two customers per fifteen minutes to twelve customers per fifteen minutes. Off-peak, staff may have other work to do, but the overall utilization is not high. At peak times queues build up. If one member of staff is sick, then capacity is reduced by 33 per cent, and service becomes intolerably slow at peak times. Such a small unit cannot carry surplus capacity to allow for such shortages and planned absences would normally be covered by staff from a central reserve, but unanticipated absences cause serious problems.

A telephone banking service such as First Direct has a single centre accepting calls from all over the country. While variation is still large, it is proportionally less because of the very large number of customers. There may be a staff of several hundred at any one time, so that absenteeism and sickness will probably never exceed 5 per cent. Provided the capacity has been well planned, the centralized system should always give a service that is acceptable or better while still maintaining a high utilization.

Easier communications

With everything and everyone on the same site, the transport of both goods and information becomes simpler.

Better facilities

A wider range of skills and equipment can be carried at a centralized site because the demand will be great enough to justify it. The small bank branch will probably have to refer mortgage or insurance enquiries on because the demand will not justify their maintaining that expertise on site. This introduces delays and increases the risk of misunderstanding.

There are, however, advantages to decentralization as well. Among these are the following.

Easier to manage

It is generally found that managing a small facility is easier. The span of control is smaller. The knowledge of staff about the position of their task within the overall scheme is greater and this generally leads to greater satisfaction. Problems, when they arise, are likely to become more visible more quickly and can thus be dealt with before they become major issues.

More flexible

It is much easier to reduce capacity by closing one or more small branches than seeking to lay off labour at one central site. In addition closing a branch saves the overhead as well as the direct costs, while reducing labour at a single site rarely has a proportional effect upon overheads. Small branches can also be used to try new products, processes or working methods with less disruption, particularly if they prove unsuccessful.

More responsive

Location of facilities near their markets can lead to a greater degree of sensitivity to local needs. It is easier to establish a close rapport with the market, which makes it more difficult for competitors.

More secure

Any location is always at risk from industrial or political unrest or natural disaster. If an organization is centralized then there is always a possibility that such an event will completely prevent it operating, and could even destroy the organization. A decentralized organization may suffer the same events, but probably not at all branches, so it is much more likely to continue operations.

The balance of advantage varies with the circumstances. In much of the service sector decentralization is essential since the service must be located in the market. However some degree of centralization may still be appropriate as the following examples show.

Benetton retail franchise holders are linked to a central stock control and dispatch system through point of sale terminals. Decisions about demand and supply are centralized with the result that the demand forecasting system has a great deal of good quality data to work on, and manufacturing can be closely integrated with this. The disadvantage is possibly that the franchise holder has little discretion.

Many retail banks centralize insurance, loan and mortgage services. Customers deal with the bank branch, but this is really just a vehicle for transferring the request. The advantage is an efficient and skilled service available to everyone. The disadvantage is delay and communication failure.

Many companies decentralize to the extent of having representatives call at the customers home, i.e. Avon cosmetics, Betterware household cleaning, Prudential financial services, but all other activities are centralized.

Functional or total decentralization

If an organization is decentralized, this can be done on a functional basis, i.e. a particular location carries out only one of the functions of the whole organization. Many car manufacturers have separate plants for engine manufacture, body panel manufacture etc., with the parts being shipped to final assembly plants.

Case Study

The European Airbus is assembled throughout Europe. This is partly the result of a political decision, to ensure that all partners get a share of the revenue and the work. To have each partner setting up plant to make whole aircraft would have resulted in substantial diseconomies of scale, with each plant achieving very low output. Instead each country manufactures a component of the aircraft, The UK manufactures the wings, and these are shipped to one site for final assembly.

The advantages of functional decentralization include:

● location near a source of skilled labour, raw material, etc.
● easier to manage since a simpler subset of the total operation
● specialization leads to greater skill in both labour and management
● retains many economies of scale.

The alternative to functional decentralization is total decentralization, where each location carries out the full range of activities. Full total decentralization is rare in manufacturing now, but a high degree is often found in the service sector.

Case Study

CenterParcs operate a number of holiday villages based around an all-weather water-based leisure facility. Each village is completely self-sufficient, and provides the full range of activities.

The main advantages of full decentralization are:

- allows location near the market
- reduces transport and communication problems
- easier to co-ordinate activities.

However, the loss of economies of scale can be a major disadvantage.

Objectives

The objective of any operation is to achieve an appropriate balance between effectiveness – the ability to produce the outputs required by the market – efficiency – producing those outputs at minimum cost and flexibility – the ability to respond to changes in the market, and in the technological and economic environment.

Process organization

The organization of the operations process is a key factor in determining its ability to meet the objectives. Five broad process types are used:

1. *Job/project*. Suitable for operations with a high degree of variety and customization, essentially one-offs.
2. *Batch*. Medium variety medium volume products/services are produced in batches, groups of the same product/service that progress through the process as a single unit.
3. *Flow/mass*. With low variety, high volume products/services, dedicated plant becomes economically feasible. The process for each product/service is independently designed and optimized.
4. *Group technology*. An attempt to obtain the economies of flow production in a batch environment. Products/services are grouped according to their operations characteristics.
5. *Continuous*. Used in chemical processing and other industries where dedicated, usually automated, plant continuously produces a single product.

Many operations use processes which mix the characteristics of the above process types. The process organization particularly relates to the volume/variety dimension of the market.

Manufacturing and service operations

There is a great deal of common ground between manufacturing and service operations but the nature of services imposes constraints and demands upon the operation which are unique. The most important of these are caused by the presence of the customer during the operation. This gives rise to simultaneity, volatility, variability and subjectivity.

In order to overcome these problems a number of approaches to service operations design have been adopted, including standardization, self-service and the front office/back shop division.

Location

The location of the premises is often an important, and difficult to change, decision. The main factors to be considered include market, materials, labour, transport and infrastructure, and political issues. Manufacturing in the target market may be necessary to overcome import barriers. Political incentives can also dominate location decisions.

Centralization or decentralization

The advantages of a single central location include economies of scale, smoother demand and supply, easier communications and better facilities.

The advantages of decentralization include easier to manage, more flexible, more responsive and more secure. The balance of advantage varies with the circumstances. If decentralization is to be adopted it can be functional or total. In functional decentralization a location carries out only one of the functions of the whole organization. With total decentralization each location carries out the full range of activities.

Self Assessment

1 The objectives of operations design are:
   (a) maximizing throughput
   (b) minimizing cost
   (c) maximizing utilization
   (d) maximizing customer satisfaction?
2 Effectiveness means:
   (a) meeting market requirements
   (b) producing to specification
   (c) producing as cheaply as possible?
3 Efficiency means:
   (a) keeping the operation going at all costs
   (b) maximizing utilisation
   (c) satisfying customers immediately
   (d) minimizing cost?

4 List four reasons why efficiency and effectiveness are important in not-for-profit organizations.

5 List four reasons why flexibility is required in operations design.

6 List four market factors which need to be taken into account in designing a process organization.

7 A job organization would be used when:
(a) variety is high
(b) volume is high
(c) the task is very complex
(d) the task is small scale?

8 A project organization would be used when:
(a) variety is high
(b) volume is high
(c) the task is very complex
(d) the task is small scale?

9 Which would be used when both volume and variety are medium:
(a) job
(b) batch
(c) flow
(d) group technology?

10 Which would be used when both volume is high and variety low:
(a) job
(b) batch
(c) flow
(d) group technology?

11 A product layout is used for:
(a) job
(b) batch
(c) flow
(d) group technology?

12 A process layout is used for:
(a) job
(b) batch
(c) flow
(d) group technology?

13 Which of these gives the lowest non-productive work content:
(a) job
(b) batch
(c) flow
(d) group technology?

14 List four differences between manufacturing and service operations.

15 Standardization is useful in service design because:

(a) customers are easily confused
(b) it reduces variability
(c) it allows more advance preparation
(d) service staff are not skilled enough?

16 Self-service is useful because:
(a) the customer has more choice
(b) it gives better quality
(c) it allows capacity to vary with demand?

17 The front office is:
(a) where senior management work
(b) where the customer is served
(c) where most of the staff work?

18 List four reasons for splitting the front office from the back shop.

19 List three disadvantages of maximizing the back shop content of a service.

20 List four factors that have an important bearing on location decisions.

21 List four advantages of a centralized location.

22 Decentralization:
(a) reduces vulnerability
(b) increases vulnerability
(c) is better for manufacture that service operations
(d) is more efficient?

23 List four advantages of functional decentralization.

Further reading

Francis, R. L. and White, J. A. (1987). *Facility Layout and Location.* Prentice-Hall.

Heskett, J. L., Sasser, W. E. and Hart, C. W. L. (1990). *Service Breakthroughs: Changing the Rules of the Game.* The Free Press.

Schmenner, R. W. (1982). *Making Business Location Decisions.* Prentice-Hall.

Slack, N., Chambers, S., Harland, C., Harrison, A. and Johnston, R. (1998). *Operations Management.* Pitman.

Wu, B. (1994). *Manufacturing System Design and Analysis.* Chapman and Hall.

Chapter 4

Design and measurement of work

In Chapter 3 the overall role and organization of operations was considered, together with the major classifications of operations, and the major differences between manufacturing and service. The importance of getting the overall operation right was identified. In practice, however, it is equally important to get the detail right, and much of operations management is more concerned with detail than with the 'big picture'. It is one thing to establish the role of operations within the organization, the nature of the transformation, the type of process organization and the balance of front office and back shop, etc. These are all important, but of little value unless the people charged with carrying out the activities can actually do so. The detailed tasks must be relevant, co-ordinated and feasible, otherwise the effort will be wasted.

This chapter considers the various approaches to the design of the task, with particular emphasis on method study:

Learning Objectives

1 *Objectives.* What are we seeking to achieve in the design of the task? What are the constraints and trade-offs involved? Issues of effectiveness, efficiency and flexibility are considered, along with competence and skill.

2 *Approaches to work design.* A number of alternative ways of addressing the issue of the design of work have arisen. These are described and their suitability considered.

3 *Layout.* The layout of the premises is important for effective and efficient operation. It also frequently has important implications for safety. The main issues, constraints and methods are discussed.

4 *Role of automation.* No discussion of the design of work would be complete without consideration of whether the task should be carried out by a person or a machine. The general capabilities of automation are considered, together with the issues of suitability.

5 *Work measurement.* The measurement of work is not strictly an aspect of work design, but it is an essential prerequisite for any realistic capacity planning and scheduling. Since it is closely associated with method study, it is discussed here. The main techniques are described along with the circumstances in which their use is appropriate.

Objectives of work design

The objective of balancing effectiveness and efficiency is just as important in the design of the task as in the design of the operation as a whole (see Chapter 3), although the consequences of a wrong decision are likely to be less damaging and more easily rectified. The task must above all achieve the required output; thereafter it should be carried out at minimum cost.

Flexibility is a less certain requirement, and the basic approach of much of scientific management has always been that the worker needed to be trained and constrained to be predictable, not flexible. This is probably still the case for large-scale, largely manual, tasks where unpredictability and 'initiative' on the part of the workforce will always be disruptive, however well intentioned.

As automation has reduced the labour force in many organizations, there has been a growth in the realization that the labour force has knowledge and insight to contribute as well as basic mechanical skills. The increasing rate of change due to technological development and globalization have also increased the pressure to utilize all the resources of the organization fully, and labour flexibility can be seen as an important element of such developments as Kaizen (see Chapter 5).

Flexibility is not the same as anarchy, however, and tasks still need to be well designed and specified. What is, perhaps, different in more modern and empowered organizations is the extent to which task design specifically recognizes discretion and the extent to which the operator is allowed or encouraged to contribute to the design of the task.

The task must, of course, be within the competence of the operator, the equipment and the materials used, so the task design process, at its broadest, involves product/service design, engineering, recruitment and training. In the case of service operations, where the customer is expected to contribute to the process, it may also involve customer selection through market segmentation and customer training.

There is also a need for the measurement of work, usually in the form of the time taken for a task. Planning and scheduling are impossible without some measure of resource inputs required for a given output, and unit costing cannot be carried out accurately unless the precise resource inputs for a given output are known. Since labour is usually paid according to time worked, and machinery is certainly used in time, time is the usual unit for measuring work.

Approaches to work design

It is often believed that formal specification of working methods was a result of the scientific management school, which developed, in the late eighteenth and throughout the nineteenth centuries. Certainly such authorities as Adam Smith, Eli Whitney, James Watt, James Mill and Charles Babbage all advocate the division of labour, and the careful observation and analysis of tasks prior to rational design. The driving force behind this was the advent of industrialization and with it mass production. Prior to this most output was fairly small scale; labourers laboured and no one thought it worth paying much attention to how; craftsmen passed on their craft through apprenticeships, and the craft was frequently deliberately complicated and confused to prevent copying, so maintaining a monopoly.

Whenever the need for mass production has arisen throughout history, however, similar techniques have been developed. For example, however the pyramids and temples of ancient Egypt were actually built, the fabrication involved a large, specialized labour force working to predefined standards; the materials and components used were also standardized.

Large-scale output is only possible through the application of the two principles of division of labour and standardized parts.

Division of labour

A craftsman will carry out a large number of operations in producing an object. Producing a wooden table would involve, among other things, rough-cutting then turning the legs, sawing, shaping and smoothing the top, drilling holes for the legs then fitting and gluing them. This demands many and varied skills and also demands a great deal of setting up and general non-productive work. If many tables are to be made, then it is far more efficient if one person specializes in rough-cutting the legs (a task of relatively low skill), another in turning them (higher skill), etc. Non-productive effort is reduced, since frequent setups and changeovers are avoided. The overall skill level required is also reduced since each person needs only to learn their own designated task. A larger, competent, work-force is available so output can be increased, while costs are substantially reduced. In division of labour, the task is divided into discrete elements, and a different person specializes in each of the elements.

Standardized parts

The craftsman can shape the legs to fit the tabletop, or vice versa, since each table is individually made from start to finish. Division of labour demands standardization. Each table leg must be the same since they are produced quite independently of the tabletop. All legs must fit all tabletops, and all legs must look the same so that any four, when assembled, will look like a set. Division of labour demands standardization of parts. Standardization of parts allows the use of inventory and the flexibility that this brings (see Chapter 7).

Case Study

The Venice arsenal (fifteenth century) was to large extent responsible for the position of Venice as a major world power at the time. It used standardized parts, limited and well-defined tasks, careful inventory management and flowline principles. It could turn out a fully assembled war galley in twenty-four hours. The techniques of operations management were a state secret, and unauthorized knowledge an act of treason.

Whatever its origin, the scientific management approach led to the set of methodologies and techniques known as 'work study'. Initially applied in manufacturing these were applied to administrative (office) work once offices became large enough and the work repetitive enough to justify the investment. Work study in the office is frequently known as organization and methods, but the methods are much the same.

Work study divides into two disciplines: method study, which is concerned with the design of the task; and work measurement, which is concerned with the measurement of work, exactly as its name implies. These will be considered separately.

Method study

Except when a completely new task is being designed, method study is firmly based upon the principle that improvement should always stem from existing practice. No changes should be made without a thorough understanding of current practice, and the context in which it operates. While this approach tends to lead to gradual and incremental improvement rather than major breakthroughs, it does have the advantage that the proposed working methods will usually at least be feasible.

To ensure that changes are feasible a well-developed and tested six-stage methodology is used. It is frequently represented by the mnemonic SREDIM:

● *Select.* The area or activity to be studied is selected. The criteria for selection vary. A problem may have arisen in the task, indicated by poorer quality, lower output, machine breakdowns or simply operator complaints. Product or service redesign might force a change of working methods. The simple passage of time might indicate a need to reassess a task, since new technologies and methods become available, and established methods do tend to drift over time. The selection process will take into account the cost-effectiveness of the study. A task that is rarely carried out, or is going to be discontinued in the near future, will probably not be worth investigating even if it is performing poorly. On the other hand, quite minor improvements in a task carried out many thousands of times a week will lead to significant savings.

● *Record.* The activity is recorded in detail. The aim is to obtain a representative sample of task performance so observations will be taken over several days and several operators. Direct observation by the method study engineer is the most common approach, although video might also be used.

● *Examine.* The record is carefully analysed, usually through some form of chart. The objective is to seek out areas where improvement is possible. This is discussed in more detail later.

● *Develop.* Improved procedures are developed out of the analysis. These are then tested, in the abstract, by 'walking through' the charts of the procedures and comparing them with existing practice. Again this is considered in more detail below.

● *Install.* The revised procedures are installed. Procedure manuals are written, staff training is given. If necessary new plant is obtained and installed and existing workplace layout revised. In a major project, installation may even involve the lay-off, redeployment or recruitment of staff.

● *Maintain.* Problems frequently arise when procedures are changed. It is a rare method study engineer who manages to anticipate and allow for every eventuality. A presence is required to ensure that problems are dealt with promptly during the early days of a new or revised procedure.

Exercise

List the activities you carry out in a normal working week. Which one would you nominate for a method study investigation and why?

Successful method study depends upon the co-operation of both local management and the workforce. The objective of the recording phase is to record the process as it is actually carried out in practice, and without co-operation this is not possible. A workforce that is hostile or distrustful is likely to distort working practice while being observed, perhaps by 'working to rule'. Even when there is no hostility there is often a tendency to try and 'do the job properly' while being observed. While it is sometimes suggested that covert observation can overcome these problems, this is rarely acceptable in practice, and will usually be discovered, leading to even poorer co-operation between labour and management.

Method study should be seen as a means of improving operations for everyone, and full consultation with labour before starting will help to ensure reliable and valid results. It will also improve co-operation when the revised methods are introduced. If sufficient observations are carried out then the presence of the observer eventually ceases to have any effect on working practices.

Charting methods

A variety of charting methods has been developed to facilitate recording and analysis in method study. The most important are the various forms of process chart. At its simplest the process chart shows the sequence of actions undertaken. For example, on entering a lecture room for a class a student might first look around to see that it is the correct class, find a seat, sit down, take out paper and pen, etc. A very simple representation in chart format is shown in Figure 4.1

The example in Figure 4.1 is little better than a list. Method study process charts use different symbols for different types of activity, which enables the chart to show a first-level analysis of the structure of the process.

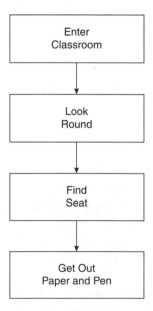

Figure 4.1 Basic process chart

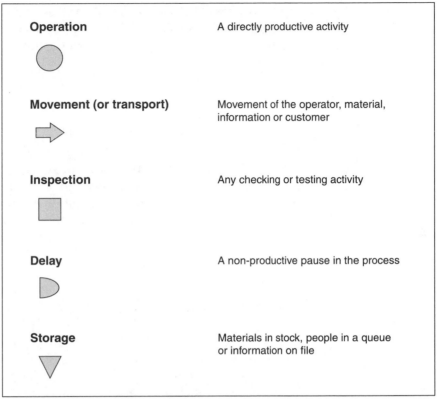

Operation   A directly productive activity

Movement (or transport)   Movement of the operator, material,
                                       information or customer

Inspection   Any checking or testing activity

Delay   A non-productive pause in the process

Storage   Materials in stock, people in a queue
                                       or information on file

Figure 4.2 Process chart symbols

Figure 4.2 shows the activity types and the symbols associated with them.

These different types of activity can be broadly classified according to their desirability – the extent to which they are likely to be adding value – in the following sequence:

1 *Operation* – a core part of the process, making a direct contribution to the finished product/service.
2 *Inspection* – a part of the process concerned with ensuring appropriate quality.
3 *Storage* – possibly contributing to efficiency or service in some way, but not directly productive.
4 *Transport* – generally non-productive and to be minimized.
5 *Delay* – invariably non-productive and to be eliminated.

Of course, operations and inspections can be badly designed and sometimes completely unnecessary, so the above sequence should be used only as a general guide.

The process chart takes several forms, according to the needs of the study. These include the material flow chart, the operator chart, the two-handed chart and the customer flow chart.

The operator chart

Taking the example shown in Figure 4.1, arriving for a class, and applying the flow chart symbols, gives the result shown in Figure 4.3.

Charts are sometimes produced in the free form manner shown in Figure 4.3, but it is more usual to use a pro forma of the type shown in Figure 4.4, where each symbol is represented by a column. Additional columns are included for the description of the activity and, where relevant, time taken and distance travelled.

Exercise

In investigating a warehouse operation, a method study engineer discovers the following procedure:

Twice a day a warehouse operative collects a small watering can and a notebook from the office. He fills the watering can then walks round the warehouse checking six wet and dry bulb thermometers (wet and dry bulb thermometers record temperature, but one bulb is kept damp by a wick resting in a reservoir of water – this enables humidity to be calculated). At each thermometer

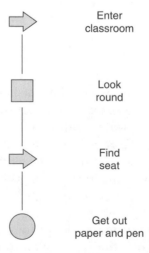

Figure 4.3 Arriving for a class

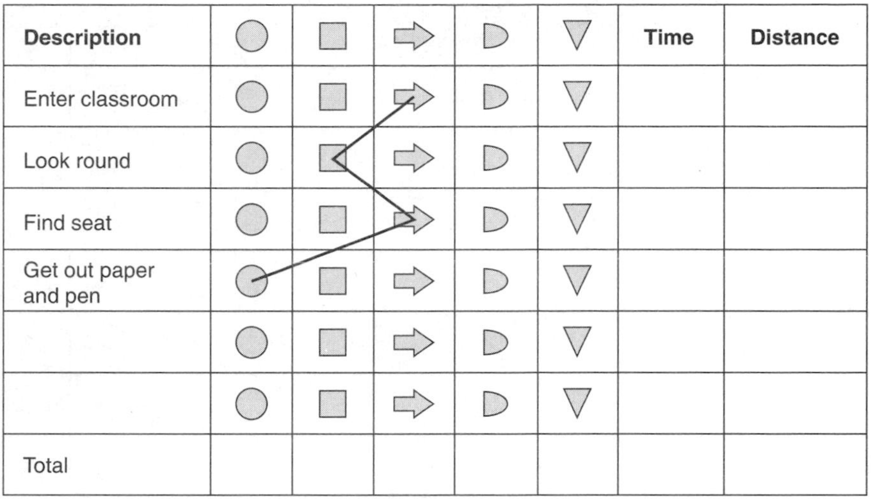

Description	○	□	⇨	D	▽	Time	Distance
Enter classroom	○	□	⇨	D	▽		
Look round	○	◁	⇨	D	▽		
Find seat	○	□	⇨	D	▽		
Get out paper and pen	○	□	⇨	D	▽		
	○	□	⇨	D	▽		
	○	□	⇨	D	▽		
Total							

Figure 4.4 Chart pro forma

the operative writes the two temperature readings in the note-book and checks and tops up the water reservoir from the water-ing can. On completion he returns to the office and telephones the laboratory to read out the temperatures. A laboratory assistant records them in a record book in the laboratory.

Produce a process chart for the procedure.

The two-handed chart

When investigating manual activities in detail, the two-handed chart is sometimes used as a way of showing the activities of each of the operators' hands. Two charts of the form shown in Figure 4.4 are presented side by side as mirror images. This type of chart is really only of use to method study engineers and is not illustrated. It is mentioned to show that the level of detail presented in a flow chart will vary depending on the nature of the study.

The material flow chart

The operator chart is useful for considering how well a particular activity is being carried out, but has the disadvantage that it does

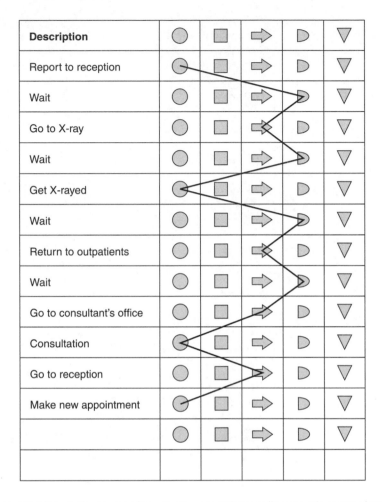

Description	○	□	⇨	▷	▽
Report to reception					
Wait					
Go to X-ray					
Wait					
Get X-rayed					
Wait					
Return to outpatients					
Wait					
Go to consultant's office					
Consultation					
Go to reception					
Make new appointment					

Figure 4.5 Material/customer flow chart – an orthopaedic outpatient appointment

not show the links between process stages. The material flow chart overcomes this problem by considering the process from the point of view of the material being worked upon. An example, based upon attending an outpatient clinic at a hospital, is shown in Figure 4.5. Here the customer is seen as the material being processed.

The customer chart

This can be seen as a variation of the material flow chart for use in services, or as an alternative form of the operator chart where the customer is the operator. Figure 4.6 shows a customer chart for obtaining cash from an automatic teller machine.

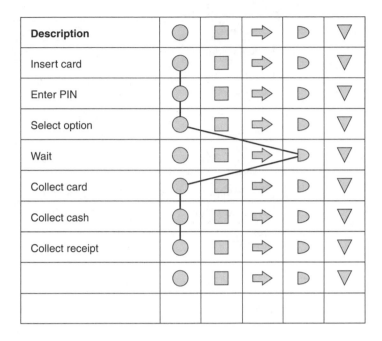

Description	○	■	⇨	D	▽
Insert card	○	■	⇨	D	▽
Enter PIN	○	■	⇨	D	▽
Select option	○	■	⇨	D	▽
Wait	○	■	⇨	D	▽
Collect card	○	■	⇨	D	▽
Collect cash	○	■	⇨	D	▽
Collect receipt	○	■	⇨	D	▽
	○	■	⇨	D	▽

Figure 4.6 Customer chart: drawing cash from an automatic teller machine

Figure 4.6 illustrates an obviously efficient procedure, with little in the way of delay and transport. Compared with this the procedure in Figure 4.5 is incredibly inefficient, with four delays, four transports and only three substantive operations (in fact the delays and transports are understated).

The customer chart can often be combined with the operator chart to very good effect when looking at the interaction between customer and service personnel. It frequently shows up inefficiencies on both sides, for example, when a customer is waiting while some peripheral service task is performed or where the server is waiting for some action or decision from the customer.

Waiting in services is often seen as undesirable by the customer and can be an important quality issue. Equally, idle staff are wasteful and increase costs. Perhaps the most useful aspect of the customer/operator chart is to show the process from the customer's perspective, to ensure that the service designer/provider considers the customer's viewpoint.

A customer/operator chart for the X-ray activity in Figure 4.5 is shown in Figure 4.7. This serves to illustrate that, while the customer is doing little or nothing, the service staff are fully occupied. The service is designed around the principle that the service staff are much more valuable/expensive than the customer. High utilization

Description	Operator					Customer				
Check paperwork	○	☐	⇨	▷	▽	○	☐	⇨	▷	▽
Call patient	○	☐	⇨	▷	▽	○	☐	⇨	▷	▽
X-ray patient	○	☐	⇨	▷	▽	○	☐	⇨	▷	▽
Send patient to waiting room	○	☐	⇨	▷	▽	○	☐	⇨	▷	▽
Develop X-ray	○	☐	⇨	▷	▽	○	☐	⇨	▷	▽
Inspect X-ray	○	☐	⇨	▷	▽	○	☐	⇨	▷	▽
Complete paperwork	○	☐	⇨	▷	▽	○	☐	⇨	▷	▽
Take paperwork to patient	○	☐	⇨	▷	▽	○	☐	⇨	▷	▽
Start new patient	○	☐	⇨	▷	▽	○	☐	⇨	▷	▽
Total	6	1	1			2		3	4	

Figure 4.7 Operator/customer chart for X-ray example

of service staff requires both the waiting and the movement of the customer. Given that public sector health care is invariably overloaded and under-resourced, this is probably a reasonable presumption.

Exercise

Consider a service with which you are familiar: for example, applying to extend your overdraft at your bank; having a meal in a restaurant; visiting the doctor; enrolling on a college course. Produce a customer/operator chart for the service encounter and consider where inefficiencies occur from the point of view of both the customer and the operator.

Examine and develop

The examination stage of method study is concerned with establishing potential for improvement and should lead directly to the development of the improved process.

The self evidently non-productive elements, delay and transport, are obviously prime candidates for improvement, however the impact upon adjacent elements must always be considered. The normal procedure is therefore to address each stage in the process through the following questions:

- *Purpose*: What is being done? Why? What alternatives are there? What should be done?
- *Place*: Where is it being done? Why? Where else is possible? Where would be best?
- *Sequence*: When is it done? Why? When else is possible? When would be best?
- *Person*: Who does it? Why? Who else could do it? Who would be best?
- *Means*: How is it done? Why? How else could it be done? How best should it be done?

By asking these questions of the apparently productive elements, operation, inspection and storage, it is often possible to eliminate or combine them. This automatically reduces transport and delay. The revised process is further developed by charting it, and carefully 'walking through' it. This walk through is carried out not only by the method study engineer, but also with shopfloor supervision and sometimes, particularly in team-based organizations, with the operators. In services it is obviously desirable to test out the proposals on customers, though this is often not done.

Exercise

Carry out a detailed analysis of the warehouse procedure previously charted.

- How might it be improved?
- Should it be improved?

While method study is the most common approach to task design, it does not stand alone and is often supplemented by two other approaches.

Ergonomics

Ergonomics treats the human operator both as a mechanical and a sensory device, and applies scientific principles to the investigation of capabilities and the optimization of the working environment and equipment. In operations the main contribution is to the detailed design of the work area with the aim of minimizing unnecessary movement and to maximizing the comfort of the operator. A casual examination of many work areas in both manufacturing and service shows that ergonomics is often not used.

Exercise

What do you think are the main ergonomic factors reflected in the design of a car seat? How does this differ from a class/lecture room seat?

The human resources school

Method study tends to treat the human operator as simply another component in the process, to be commanded and controlled. Partly in response to Japanese approaches, the human operator is now increasingly seen as a valuable resource with a contribution to make to the operation beyond merely following instructions. In any case, treating the human operator as an unthinking component has never worked well, since it is simply not true.

The human resources approach is based upon the idea that the well-motivated worker will work harder, faster and better. This will in its turn lead to higher productivity, higher quality, lower absenteeism and better industrial relations. While this is certainly true, identifying the motivating factors is not straightforward. Job enrichment, for example, identifies job satisfaction as an important motivator and so aims to make jobs interesting, challenging and complete. The operator will then feel a sense of achievement and participation in carrying out the task. However, the operator often sees this as an unnecessary complication of the task, and it can result in even lower motivation.

More recent developments in this area, based around such concepts as Kaizen, are discussed in Chapter 5.

Method study, ergonomics and the human resources approaches are not mutually exclusive, and the best approach to the design of the task is to use all three in concert. Method study is best at designing and improving the overall flow and organization of the task, while ergonomics is applied to the detailed design of the work area. The human resources approach suggests that the best outcome will be achieved by consultation and involvement of the workforce throughout the design and implementation process.

Layout

The basic layout of an operation is usually determined by the choice of process organization, as discussed in Chapter 3. Job and project operations usually adopt a fixed product layout, since it is the nature of the object being worked upon which dictates the disposition of the labour and plant.

Case Study

In a civil engineering project, for instance the building of a bridge, water treatment works or even the Millennium Dome, the bulk of the work must take place on site, and at the precise location determined by the design.

Even in a car maintenance workshop, although the car is usually brought to the workshop, the necessary tools and equipment are then brought to the car.

In a batch organization, layout is based upon process type, with processes requiring similar equipment and skills being grouped together. In flow or mass production, each product (or product type – allowing for minor variations) has its own dedicated production resources. These are all discussed in more detail in Chapter 3.

The detailed design of the layout presumes that the basic layout type has been decided. In arriving at a detailed layout, the following objectives are relevant:

● Maximize utilization of space. Space is an expensive resource and no more should be used than is necessary.
● Minimize unnecessary movement.
● Conform to relevant safety legislation.
● Ensure free access for process and maintenance operatives.
● Maintain appropriate flexibility.

In addition, constraints are often imposed by the space available. It is only when the process is designed in conjunction with the building that is to house it that such constraints can be disregarded. More usually a process is being arranged, or rearranged, within an existing building, and the space is unlikely to be of an ideal shape.

The overall interaction of the various objectives and constraints is very complex and the usual approach to designing the layout of an operation is based upon simplification. Safety, access and available space are taken as necessary constraints, and the layout is designed to achieve an acceptable balance between utilization of space and minimization of unnecessary movement. It is more usual to aim for a satisfactory solution in a reasonable time rather than strive for an optimal layout.

The most commonly used design tools are charts. These may be simple paper devices, more complex three-dimensional models or computer simulations. All use the same principle of trial and error to seek a satisfactory layout. The only real advantage of computer simulation over simpler methods is the ability of the computer package to review far more options, and therefore arrive somewhat nearer an optimal solution than might a work study engineer with paper and pencil.

Two of the most common charting methods will be described.

From/to or movement chart

An efficient layout is one that minimizes the total distance travelled by materials, customers or staff. It must therefore take into account not only the distance travelled but also the frequency of the journey.

The movement chart is a simple device for recording the frequency with which each journey occurs. Its use is best illustrated with a simple example.

Example

An office building has five departments of approximately equal size. The present layout is shown in Figure 4.8. The number of journeys between departments is recorded over a period of one week.

A matrix is constructed showing each location as a potential source and a potential destination, as shown in Figure 4.9. The number of times specific journeys arise is then entered in the matrix.

In this case the direction of the journey is not relevant, so the totals of from journeys and of to journeys can be combined. A ranking by total number of journeys, shown in Figure 4.9, gives a priority list for the layout of the work area.

In this case A and C would be located as close together as possible, followed by D and E and so on down the list.

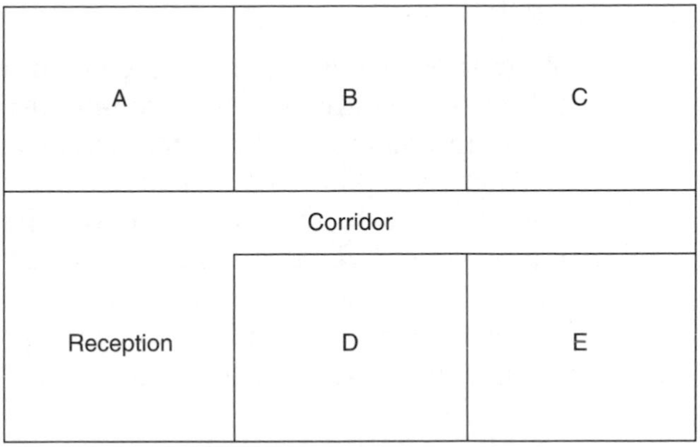

Figure 4.8 Office layout

Department	A	B	C	D	E
A			150		60
B	110		20	20	35
C	64	30		90	
D		15			40
E		50		100	

Journey	**Number**
A to B	110
A to C	214
A to D	0
A to E	60
B to C	50
B to D	35
B to E	85
C to D	90
C to E	0
D to E	140

Prioritized

Journey	**Number**
A to C	214
D to E	140
A to B	110
C to D	90
B to E	85
A to E	60
B to C	50
B to D	35
A to D	0
C to E	0

Figure 4.9 Movement chart and journey ranking

Redesign of layout would, of course, only take place as part of a full method study of the tasks, and effort should always be put into trying to combine tasks which involve a high level of transport.

Strictly speaking, the objective is to reduce the total cost of transport. This can be measured by determining the cost of each journey, multiplying this by the number of journeys and producing a weighted total. The same procedure carried out for each alternative layout evaluated identifies the best layout. Frequently cost per metre is considered to be fixed and only the distance is considered.

Layout charts

Layout charts are simply scale diagrams of the work area, as in Figure 4.8. At their simplest they are produced on squared paper, with pieces of cardboard representing the plant and equipment in question. Plastic models can be used to give a three-dimensional image, but contribute little to the overall design process.

Decisions on relative location are based upon the movement chart output, and total distance or transport cost, as described above, is calculated for each feasible solution as a basis for selecting the best.

Figure 4.10 shows an improved layout chart for the office example above. Assuming an equal distance between offices, this reduces the total distance travelled by about 15 per cent. In this particular case, since the departments are of equal size, any department can occupy any of the five locations. As a result there are 5 factorial (120) possible layouts. While it is feasible to calculate all 120 solutions and select the best, more realistic problems can rarely be analysed completely.

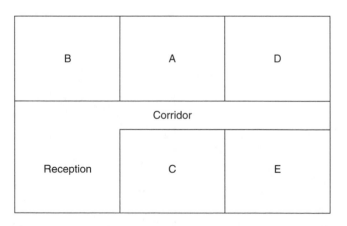

Figure 4.10 Improved office layout

Usually a number of the more obvious solutions are considered and the vast majority rejected without investigation.

The main merit of computer simulations in this is that far more alternatives can be considered and evaluated but, in simple layout decisions, this does not necessarily justify the extra effort required to set up the simulation.

Total distance is, of course, not the only criterion. There may be very strong safety reasons for separating two processes. It would, for example, be inappropriate to place a process involving naked flame next to one involving flammable solvents. At the other extreme, the delay between two processes could be critical, so even if this transport were rare, it would be essential to have the two processes in close proximity. This is not easily quantified, but a relationship chart can be constructed to guide the decisions arising out of the movement chart. The usual classification of relationships, together with an example of a relationship chart is shown in Figure 4.11.

Code	Closeness
A	Absolutely necessary
E	Especially important
I	Important
O	Ordinary closeness
U	Unimportant
X	Undesirable

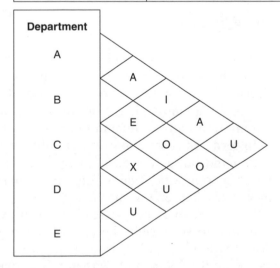

Figure 4.11 A relationship chart

A company manufactures four products using a six-stage process, however not all products go through all processes, and not all follow the same process sequence. Table 4.1 shows the number of batches of each product made in a typical month and the process route for each product.

Table 4.1 Product batches and process routes

Product	Route	Batches
1	A, B, C, D, E, F	15
2	A, B, C, E	20
3	A, B, C, E, D, F	10
4	A, C, D, F	5
5	A, B, F, D	20
6	A, C, D, F	30

Each process (A, B, C, D, E and F) needs to occupy the same sized rectangular space, each batch incurs the same transport cost, and there are no other restrictions.

Construct a movement chart for the situation, and use this to produce a layout.

Role of automation

A key decision in the design of work is the extent to which the work should be performed by human operators or machines. The decision is ultimately based upon cost, but there are a number of less easily quantifiable factors to be considered. Table 4.2 contrasts automation and the human operator.

In terms of cost, labour is a variable cost and cost can be reduced if demand falls, by reducing overtime, short-time working or even laying people off. Against this, machinery is a capital cost that is incurred whether the machinery is used or not. The cost balance between the two alternatives is constantly changing as labour costs continue to rise, while the cost of technology continues to fall.

Automation is generally best at simple repetitive tasks, which will be carried out reliably and consistently provided that the input is reliable and consistent. Where high levels of variability are required then

Table 4.2 Characteristics of human and machine operation

Factor	Human	Machine
Cost	Variable, increasing	Fixed, reducing
Reliability	Lower	High
Flexibility	High	Low
Consistency	Lower	High
Robustness	High	Low
Failure	Gradual	Sudden
Judgement	Possible	None

the human operator is generally to be preferred. Failure in automation is usually total and sudden. While such a failure can occur with human operators (for example, the coach driver who has a heart attack while driving) people generally realize that there is something wrong with their performance before that stage is reached.

The trend is certainly towards automation as it is becoming increasingly cost-effective with advances in technical development. Automation is also becoming increasingly flexible, and established technologies are generally robust and not prone to failure.

Automation in manufacturing

Although the earliest examples of numerical control (NC) occurred in fabric processing (the Jacquard Loom, operated by punched cards, was developed early in the nineteenth century), most development has taken place in the handling of rigid materials, specifically metal. Numerically controlled machine tools (lathes, drills, etc.) were the first major development. They work by recording the actions of skilled operators in carrying out a particular task on punched paper tape. These tapes can then be used independently to drive the machine. Operators are still required to fit the material to be worked on into the machine, supervise the operation, change tooling, etc. but less skill is required. Simple NC machines have largely been superseded by computer numerical control (CNC). A computer controls one or more machines from a repertoire of programs. Often these programs have been produced directly by computer-aided design (CAD) packages.

The flexible manufacturing cell takes this development a stage further by including its own tool store so that it can locate and load the correct tools for the job without human intervention. The work-piece is usually loaded on to a pallet with a machine-readable barcode so that no human intervention is required.

The flexible manufacturing system (FMS) links CNC machines, flexible manufacturing cells, automatic inspection devices and a flexible transfer line into one integrated computer-controlled manufacturing facility. Human intervention is restricted to loading work on to pallets, removing completed work and replenishing the tool stores as required. Such sophistication is, of course, expensive and can only be justified if fully utilized. An FMS will usually operate continuously, while personnel will operate on a three-shift system. The first shift will be fully manned and will load and unload pallets and replenish tool stores. The second shift will be a reduced crew maintaining the supply of loaded pallets. The third shift will usually be unmanned.

Automation is not a universal panacea, and such is the cost of the more sophisticated forms that careful matching to demand is essential. Figure 4.12 shows a broad match between technology and product volume/variety.

Other areas where automation is well established include the forming and welding of metal panels (i.e. car assembly) and painting. Automation is also widely used in the assembly of electronic circuit boards and in a great deal of food processing and packaging.

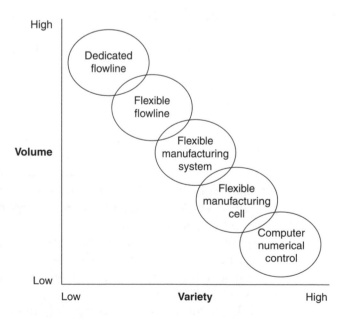

Figure 4.12 Appropriate manufacturing technology

It is less well established in industries dealing with fabric or timber, largely because these materials are less rigid and predictable than metal, however developments in automatic cutting and handling of fabrics are accelerating. It may well be that garment production will become as automated as car production in the foreseeable future.

Automation in services

The computer has, of course, had a dramatic effect upon back office service activities. The substantial and continuing reduction in employment in banking is an example of this. The impact of automation on the customer interface has taken place in three distinct but linked areas.

1 *Automated services*. The customer interacts directly with service providing machinery. The best example of this is the automated teller machine (ATM). This provides a cost-effective twenty-four hour service, but with a limited range of options compared with personal contact. Banks are striving to develop greater flexibility and offer a wider range of services through ATMs, but a limiting factor is the actual skill of the customer. Developments in retail distribution are also tending to eliminate personal contact, for example, credit-card accepting petrol pumps, customer-only checking out in supermarkets and Internet shopping in general. The aim in most of these is cost reduction, or widening accessibility without cost increase (banks could stay open twenty-four hours a day, but bank charges would rise substantially).

2 *Computer assisted services*. The service personnel depend upon automated support in providing the service. Examples include the travel agent with on-line access to availability databases, the service engineer with an expert system to aid diagnosis on a laptop computer, the financial services adviser with a database of services and built in checklists on a laptop computer. The aim here is to improve the service to the customer by giving wider choice and faster response.

3 *Back office automation*. The impact here is indirect, and may be largely cost reduction as in retail banking, but generally there is at least the potential for improved service. The use of point of sale terminals linked to a central storage and distribution system has enabled supermarkets to reduce costs substantially in all areas. In particular, clerical activities have been almost eliminated, and

storage and logistics costs greatly reduced; however, the customer is also seeing better stocked shops with a greater variety of products as a direct result of the improved material control and flow.

It is quite certain that service automation will continue to develop, but much of this will depend upon public acceptance. Not everyone has the skill, inclination or resources to use the Internet for banking, shopping or whatever. Many people still prefer to deal with other people face to face rather than via the phone or dealing with computers. The development of expert systems in computing has consistently failed to live up to the predictions of the pundits. What seems to be in question, however, is not whether services will continue to become automated, but simply the speed with which it will happen.

Work measurement

Method study is usually grouped with work measurement in the overall discipline known as work study, although the purpose of work measurement is quite different.

Operations management is concerned with the efficient and effective use of resources in the conversion of inputs (raw materials and/or customers) into outputs (finished products and/or satisfied customers). While the inputs and outputs are counted as units – number of refrigerators shipped, number of customers served, etc. – resources can only be effectively measured in terms of time available – 100 operators working an eight-hour shift gives 800 hours of available labour. Work measurement is concerned with the relationship between units of output and resource time. It provides the factor that converts units to time and vice versa.

Work measurement has the following main uses:

- *Capacity planning and scheduling.* Discussed in more detail in Chapters 6, 8 and 9, the efficient planning of operations depends upon accurate information on how demand relates to capacity. Capacity can only be effectively planned if the known and forecast demand can be converted into accurate capacity measurements, i.e. time requirements.
- *Payment systems.* Many payment systems reward employees on the basis of output, either completely, as in piecework systems where the employee is paid a fixed amount for each item completed, or partially where a bonus is paid for output above

a certain level. For any output-related payment system to work properly, fair time standards must be established for the tasks in question.

● *Productivity monitoring.* While overall productivity can be measured using quite crude indicators such as total output to total labour hours, detailed investigation of change and of scope for improvement requires measurement of the actual tasks.

Of these, the first is without question the most important.

Like method study, work measurement uses a well-established procedure:

● *Select.* The area or activity to be studied is selected. The criteria for selection vary. A problem may have arisen in the task, indicated by lower output or operator complaints. The process may have changed, requiring new time standards. Changes to payment systems will generally require a revision of time standards. Simply the passage of time might indicate a need to reassess a task.

● *Record.* The activity is recorded in detail. The aim is to obtain a representative sample of task performance so observations will be taken over several days and of several operators. Direct observation by the work measurement engineer is the most common approach, although video might also be used. The record is charted in the same way as in method study.

● *Measure.* Using the detailed record of the stages of the task, the time taken for each element is determined. This is the most difficult area of work measurement, since the rate at which people work varies. In administrative or clerical activities it can be almost impossible. Is the person sitting staring out of the office window thinking constructively about the task in hand, thinking about their holiday or simply not thinking at all? The various methods of measurement are discussed later.

● *Publish.* The results are collated and published in a form suitable for use.

● *Maintain.* Problems frequently arise when procedures are changed and drift occurs in any situation, so regular monitoring is usually considered necessary.

There are two basic approaches to the actual measurement phase: time study and activity sampling.

Time study

Perhaps the most obvious, but also the most difficult method, time study simply uses a stopwatch to measure the time taken for the task. In order to overcome the natural variability of any process, a suitably large number of timings must be taken, covering several points during a working shift and a working week to ensure representative sampling. Several operators should also be timed if it is a task carried out by different people.

The real difficulty with time study is determining how hard the operator is working during the observation. There is a natural reaction among some people to work harder when being observed, but there is also the possibility that people will deliberately work more slowly in order to get an easier time standard. The objective of work measurement is usually to establish a realistic time standard for planning purposes, so neither of these reactions is helpful. Nor is it acceptable to use covert observation (via closed circuit television say) to avoid the observer effect. Trade unions are usually fairly sensitive to issues concerned with work measurement and covert observation would certainly be unacceptable to the workforce.

Time study overcomes this problem by the use of rating. The engineer not only times the task with a stopwatch, but estimates how hard the operator is working. A common rating scale uses a rate of 100 to describe a skilled and motivated operator working at a rate that they could reasonably keep up through a normal working shift. A rate of 100 is equivalent to walking at four miles per hour and is sometimes described as 'brisk'. Rating is, of course, subjective, but frequent retraining with videos of workers performing at different rates ensures that a competent time study engineer will produce consistent ratings.

Rate is not the only variable that affects actual output, and the following procedure is used to convert the observed time, recorded by the stopwatch into the standard time, used for planning and control purposes.

Standard time is the time that a skilled and motivated operator would take, on average, during a normal working shift, to complete the task. Standard time is determined in the following sequence:

● Observed time – recorded by the stopwatch; for example, 2.5 seconds.
● Rate – recorded by the engineer at the same time as the time is recorded; for example, 110 (i.e. 10 per cent harder than the standard rate of 100).

- Basic time – the time that would have been taken at a rate of 100; using the above examples, observed time $\times$ rate $\div$ 100 gives; $2.5 \times 110 \div 100 = 2.75$ seconds

Allowances are now added.

- Relaxation allowance – no operator can be expected to work continuously so this is added to allow for toilet breaks, tea breaks, etc. It varies according to the difficulty of the working conditions. It is usually negotiated within the company or across the industry sector; 12.5 per cent is common in light assembly tasks.
- Contingency allowance – to cover for example extra work due to faulty tooling or materials.
- Unoccupied time allowance – for delays caused by breakdowns, work not available, or any other event which prevents work being carried out. These are arrived at from observation during the time study. Assume 20 per cent in total in this example.
- Standard time – the average time taken at a rate of 100 during a normal shift; continuing the above example, basic time + allowances gives; $2.75 \times 120 \div 100 = 3.3$ seconds.

This illustration shows only one observation of one small element of a task. The standard time for the whole task would be generated by summing the individual elements, but would also be based upon a statistically representative sample of observations. Time study is a skilled, time-consuming, and expensive task.

Exercise

An operation during the assembly of a computer consists of a number of activities. These are identified in Table 4.3, together with the observed times and rates from a time study exercise.

Table 4.3 Computer assembly activities

	Time	Rate
Place circuit board in case	3.2	95
Place four bolts in bolt holes	4.1	110
Tighten four bolts	4.7	92
Connect power lead	1.3	115

All times are in seconds. The time for the placing and tightening the bolts is the total for all four.

If a relaxation allowance of 10 per cent is given, what is the standard time for the whole operation?

Activity sampling

Time study provides accurate and detailed information on the time taken to carry out defined tasks, but it is an expensive process requiring a high level of skill. In many cases such detail is not required but, rather, an overall impression of how long a task takes or even of how time is broadly shared between different tasks. Time study also suffers from the disadvantage that it requires the task to be consistent and capable of fairly detailed analysis. It is not appropriate for many administrative or service tasks, which are neither predictable nor amenable to detailed analysis.

Exercise

Consider the problem of carrying out a time study on patients' consultations with their general practitioner.

Activity sampling overcomes many of the problems of time study by giving a broad overview of how time is spent. It requires relatively little skill and does not involve detailed observation, stopwatches or rating. It is widely used in measuring administrative work and service activities for this reason.

Activity sampling uses the principle of making spot observations over a period of time. Activities are classified into a relatively small number of important categories, and the particular activity that is taking place at the time of the observation is noted. When enough observations have been taken it is possible to determine what proportion of the available time is spent on each activity, and to establish from this approximately how long each activity takes. Since rating is not involved, no great skill or training is required to carry out an activity sample, and since continuous observation is not involved, the observer effect upon worker behaviour is minimized. The first step is to determine the categories of activity that are to be measured. These should be well enough defined to enable unambiguous classification, few enough to allow ease of recording (and to minimize cost since the more categories there are the greater the sample size must be), but detailed enough to give useful information.

The required accuracy must then be decided, and from this the sample size determined. The sample size (number of observations) is given by:

$$N = \frac{4P(100 - P)}{L^2} \qquad\qquad (4.1)$$

where P is the estimated percentage of time spent on the major activity and L is the maximum permitted percentage error in this. If P cannot reasonably be estimated then a value of fifty should be used.

A schedule of N observations is then drawn up over a period of time that represents a typical cross-section of activity, a week or even a month rather than a half-day.

At the appointed times, a tick is placed against the activity actually happening at the time of observation. The total number of ticks against each activity divided by N gives the proportion of time spent on the activity.

Case Study

An activity sample is carried out on the sales assistants in a retail clothes shop. For the sake of simplicity only one assistant will be considered. The relevant activities are:

- Talking to a customer.
- Waiting for a customer in the changing room.
- Operating the till.
- Arranging clothes.
- Talking to other sales staff
- Other.

It is estimated that the major activity will take 30 per cent of the time and an estimate is required with a 5 per cent accuracy.

The number of observations required is $4 \times 30 \times 70 \div 5^2 = 336$.

Given a 37 hour week this means one observation every 6.6 minutes for one week. For the sake of simplicity this may be changed to one observation every half-hour for four weeks.

The results are shown in Table 4.4.

Table 4.4 Activity sample: results

	Number	percentage
Talking to a customer	80	27
Waiting for a customer	36	12
Operating the till	41	14
Arranging clothes	65	22
Talking to staff	41	14
Other	33	11

The advantages of activity sampling are its simplicity and low cost. Its main disadvantage is a lack of accuracy and precision. Any attempt to calculate individual task times would give a very approximate estimate. High levels of accuracy are almost impossible to achieve with low frequency tasks. Very low frequency tasks can be missed altogether, no matter how important.

Exercise

1 What sample size is necessary to give an accuracy of 5 per cent on an activity which is estimated to take 30 per cent of the available time?
2 Accuracy is usually quoted as percentage of the total time for all tasks, i.e. an accuracy of 5 per cent on a task taking 10 per cent of the available time means that it takes between 5 and 15 per cent of the time. What sample size would be required if it was necessary to know the percentage of time taken by a task, estimated to take 10 per cent of the available time, to within +/− 5 per cent of that proportion?

Summary

Objectives
Work design seeks the same balance between effectiveness, efficiency and flexibility as operations design as a whole, but being on a smaller scale is more focused upon efficient conduct of established activities.

Approaches to work design

Method study, concerned with an engineering approach to work design and arising out of scientific management, is the main approach used in manufacturing. Its use in administration is less obvious, but still well established.

Method study uses the well-established methodology of select, record, examine, develop, install and maintain. It is based upon the idea of progressive improvement. Record and examine usually using flow charts.

Complementary approaches include ergonomics, which considers physical and sensory capabilities of the human operator, and human resources which considers issues of human relations and motivation.

Layout

Basic layout is determined by the process organization adopted, i.e. job/project, batch or flow. Detailed layout is concerned with maximizing utilization of space while minimizing unnecessary movement. Safety and access are necessary constraints on this.

Minimization of movement is achieved through the use of travel or from/to charts, which identify the frequency of various transports in an operation. These may use actual costs of journeys, but more usually assume cost is proportional to distance, and therefore only consider the distance travelled. Other factors are taken into account using a relationship chart, which identifies less easily quantifiable factors.

The detailed design of the layout is developed using layout charts or computer simulations, but is essentially a matter of trial and error.

Role of automation

The criteria for use of automation or labour are discussed, together with the continuing advance of automation in both manufacture and service. Automation tends to be more successful with predictable and consistent tasks, but these constraints are increasingly eroded. The main criterion for selecting is, increasingly, simply relative costs. Service automation in the back shop is driven almost exclusively by cost-effectiveness. In the front office an important constraint is the customer whose attitude determines acceptability and whose skill determines capability.

Work measurement

An essential input into planning and control of operations, work measurement provides time standards for tasks. The procedure is very similar to that of method study. The commonest and most accurate approach is that of time study, which measures the precise time, taken for a task. Problems of variable effort are overcome by rating. The output is the standard time representing a realistic average for a working shift.

Activity sampling is a simpler substitute requiring less skill and detailed analysis. It gives a broad overview of the proportion of time spent on major tasks. It is more useful in administrative and service operations.

Self Assessment

1 Division of labour means:
   (a) separating members of the workforce
   (b) having different departments in different places
   (c) workers specialize in small elements of the task?
2 List the stages of a method study.
3 Which of the following might give rise to a method study:
   (a) a fall in quality
   (b) a fall in output
   (c) operator complaints
   (d) customer complaints
   (e) all the above?
4 Method study is best carried out by experts without considering labour or management opinion. True or false?
5 Name the five types of activity symbolized in process charts.
6 Name four types of process chart.
7 Name the five areas considered in analysing a flow chart.
8 Ergonomics is primarily concerned with:
   (a) ensuring the operator is comfortable
   (b) ensuring the task is within the operator's capabilities?
9 The human resources approach is primarily concerned with:
   (a) ensuring the operator is happy
   (b) maximizing utilization of the operators
   (c) maximizing motivation
   (d) maximizing contribution
   (e) (c) and d)?
10 Which of the following are major objectives of layout design:
   (a) that the layout should be attractive
   (b) that it should be comfortable
   (c) that space should be used efficiently.
   (d) that transport should be minimized
   (e) that safety should be maximized?
11 A from/to chart is intended to show:
   (a) the direction of a journey between locations

(b) the total number of journeys between locations
(c) the distance travelled
(d) the relationship between locations?

12 Computer packages can optimize layout. True or false?

13 A relationship chart is intended to show:
(a) the direction of a journey between locations
(b) the total number of journeys between locations
(c) the distance travelled
(d) the need for proximity between locations?

14 Compared with labour, automation:
(a) increases costs
(b) reduces costs
(c) increases fixed costs?

15 In which of the following is automation usually better than labour:
(a) reliability
(b) flexibility
(c) consistency
(d) robustness?

16 Which of the following is most suited to high volume manufacture:
(a) dedicated flowline
(b) flexible flowline
(c) flexible manufacturing system
(d) flexible manufacturing cell
(e) computer numerical control machine tool?

17 Which of the following is most suited to low volume manufacture:
(a) dedicated flowline
(b) flexible flowline
(c) flexible manufacturing system
(d) flexible manufacturing cell
(e) computer numerical control machine tool?

18 A flexible manufacturing system is best for:
(a) high variety output
(b) low variety output
(c) medium variety output?

19 Name three uses for work measurement.

20 Name the five stages of a work measurement project.

21 Standard time is:
(a) the time a job should take
(b) the time management wants the job to take
(c) the time a job will take under normal circumstances?

22 Name the four stages in obtaining a standard time.

23 Name three allowances that may be used to obtain a standard time.

24 Activity sampling is concerned with:
(a) finding out what activities are going on
(b) finding out which is the most common activity
(c) finding out how time is shared between activities?
25 Activity sampling is:
(a) more accurate than time study
(b) less expensive than time study
(c) requires more skill than time study?

Further reading

Bailey, J. (1983) *Job Design and Work Organization.* Prentice-Hall.
Bessant, J. (1991) *Managing Advanced Manufacturing Technology: The Challenge of the Fifth Wave.* Blackwell.
Collier, D. A. (1985) *Service Management: The Automation of Services.* Reston.
Francis, R. L. and White, J. A. (1987) *Facility Layout and Location.* Prentice-Hall.
Slack, N., Chambers, S., Harland, C., Harrison, A. and Johnston, R. (1998). *Operations Management.* Pitman.
Wu, B. (1994). *Manufacturing System Design and Analysis.* Chapman and Hall.

Chapter 5

Managing productivity at work

This chapter is concerned with productivity – its relevance and definition, its measurement, control and improvement. Among the topics considered are:

1 *Relevance.* Productivity is seen as one of the most important measures of performance in operations management. In order to make any improvement in the utilization of input resources and to the performance of the transformation process, there must be methods for measuring their current efficiencies. Productivity is also vitally important in terms of profits, customer satisfaction and competition in all types of organization.

2 *Definition.* Productivity is not easy to define. But in any situation it is largely dependent on factors such as people performance, level of technology used, and the quality of the operational managers involved.

3 *Measurement.* Productivity of a resource and performance of a process will not be improved without first being measured. Various ways of measuring productivity will be examined. These will include both the traditional elements and the new criteria such as costs, quality, delivery and flexibility.

4 *Control and improvement.* Performance of organizations in all sectors, both at home and overseas, depends on their ability to develop sound strategies and effective control policies that will enable them to make full use of their available resources by continuously developing these resources and improving their products and processes using world-class techniques and measurements. Some of the Western and Japanese management approaches used to improve productivity will be outlined.
5 *World-class performance.* Emphasis on global market and international competition has led many companies to aim for world-class status. Steps that can be taken by organizations to become world-class performers are discussed.

Definition and types of productivity

Efficiency of an operation is usually measured in terms of its output or productivity. However, these two terms are not the same. Output of an operation is the outcome achieved when operation resources such as people, materials, equipment, etc. are put into work. Whereas, productivity is expressed as a ratio of output produced against the input used to achieve it. This can be shown as follow:

$$\text{Productivity} = \frac{\text{Output produced}}{\text{Input consumed}} \qquad (5.1)$$

Productivity measures of individual resources can then be related to the amount of output produced against the amount of input used. For instance:

$$\text{Staff productivity} = \frac{\text{Output produced}}{\text{No. of staff used}} \qquad (5.2)$$

Example

Six hundred patients have visited a dental clinic in one week. There are four dental surgeons employed by the clinic. Assuming equal distribution of work, what is the productivity of individual dentist per week?

We can use the above ratio to determine productivity for each dentist:

$$\text{Productivity per dentist} = \frac{600}{4} = 150 \text{ patients per week}$$

$$(5.3)$$

Traditionally, productivity has been measured at national, industry and organizational levels. These are usually assessed as follows:

1 *National productivity*. This is where the productivity of different nations are measured and compared. This is usually expressed in terms of percentage of exports by each country per annum.
2 *Industry productivity*. This is where the productivity of different industrial sectors is measured. Statistical comparisons are then made of their relative performance. This information, which is often expressed in terms of output per employee per hour, is a useful way for individual companies in a particular sector to compare their performance with the industry average.
3 *Organizational productivity*. This is where productivity of a particular organization is measured. It is usually measured in monetary terms and expressed as the ratio of the output sold to the costs of inputs (e.g., labour, materials, equipment) used to produce that output. The total factor productivity ratio is obtained by dividing total output by the total of labour, materials, and capital inputs. Therefore we have, for total factor productivity:

Total factor productivity

$$= \frac{\text{Output (£ value)}}{\text{labour + materials + capital (all in cost terms)}} \qquad (5.4)$$

There are also partial productivity ratios, e.g.:

$$\text{Labour productivity} = \frac{\text{Output (£ value)}}{\text{Labour hours (or costs)}} \qquad (5.5)$$

Example

The gross national product (GNP) of a country as well as the value of labour, material, and capital inputs in the past three years are shown in Table 5.1. Calculate the improvement in the total factor productivity.

Table 5.1 Example of factors in a country's productivity (£ billions)

Years	1	2	3
GNP	1400	1480	1520
Labour+Materials	800	980	820
Capital	400	240	360

Total factor productivity can be determined using the following ratio for each year:

$$TFP = \frac{Output (£ \ value)}{Labour + Materials + Capital \ (all \ in \ £ \ cost)}$$

$$TFP \ in \ year \ 1 = \frac{1400}{1200} = 1.16 \qquad (5.6)$$

$$TFP \ in \ year \ 2 = \frac{1480}{1220} = 1.21$$

$$TFP \ in \ year \ 3 = \frac{1520}{1180} = 1.28$$

The results indicate improvements in year 2 and 3.

Improving resource productivity

There are various ways that the productivity of a resource or operation can be improved. These are:

● Increasing the working speed by improving the output from the operation whilst utilizing the same amount of input.
● Improving the working methods by obtaining the same output from the operation using less input.

● Reducing cost and wastage by increasing output from the operation whilst reducing the input to the operation.

Vauxhall has been operating a productivity plan where payment is triggered by achieving a productivity ratio calculated broadly by the number of vehicles passed to sales, divided by the total number of hours taken to produce the vehicles. The fewer the hours taken, the better the reward. The payment from this incentive plan reflects well on the efforts being put in by the employees.

Explain from national, management, and labour perspective why it is desirable to improve productivity.

Operations managers are responsible for improving productivity and reducing operating costs. They should look regularly in a systematic and critical way at the resources under their control in order to find where they can be used more efficiently. Some of the key resources to review are:

1 *People.* The efficiency, utilization, and effectiveness of the workforce within an operation can be improved with sound planning, motivation, innovating new work methods, and by raising people awareness through effective training and empowerment.

Body Shop International Plc is a value-driven, high quality skin and hair care producer and retailer operating in forty-seven countries. It has developed a global strategy that focuses on organizational behaviour, leadership and communication, skills development, and measurement. The company has been transformed into an international centre of excellence on human resource practices, including the full implementation of employee consultation systems for preserving well-being, justice and honesty in the workforce.

Case Study

Newlife Cleaning Systems is the second largest private sector employer in South Shields. The company is organized in three divisions: cleaning support services, daily cleaning services and industrial cleaning services. It has offices in Manchester, Leeds and Falkirk. Amongst its corporate clients are Barclays Bank, Nestlé Rowntree, Rolls-Royce and Sanyo. The company believes that 'people' are the business. So, careful recruitment and selection can introduce an active ingredient into the change process.

The company has experienced that personal qualifications encourage commitment to quality practice and that the National Vocational Qualification (NVQ) system has produced greater understanding at operative level than the International Standards Organization's (ISO's) ISO 9000 procedures. The company has shown its commitment by becoming the first NVQs assessment centre in UK for the cleaning industry. This has sent out the motivating message to staff that they work for a progressive organization. The company policy is to back its staff even when they are wrong. It is the company view that giving operatives the chance to make on-the-spot decisions is important to the quality/productivity improvement process – but so, too, is creating the confidence to be open about their mistakes in order to learn from them.

2 *Equipment.* The utilization, efficiency and availability of equipment and machines can be improved through effective capacity planning and control, simplifying operations and efficient management of maintenance activities.

3 *Materials.* The availability and utilization of materials can be improved through efficient planning and control of materials and effective sourcing and management of the supply chain.

4 *Space.* Efficient use of available space can be made through better layout design and organization of productive resources.

5 *Money.* The amount of working capital allocated to an operation in the form of stock, consumable and services can be optimized through sound budgetary planning and control, structural and improvement decisions.

6 *Time.* People being late for work or absenteeism can be reduced through listening to employees concerns, better communication, motivation, development of their skills and recognition and appropriate reward for their efforts and outstanding contribution.

Exercise

Give examples of specific approaches or techniques that can be used by operations managers in both service and manufacturing organizations to improve productivity of the following resources:

- people
- space
- equipment.

Value-added and non-value-added activities

Productivity in manufacturing and service operations can be influenced by two types of activities: those which add value to the end product or the end service, and those which waste resources and fail to add value to the end product. Of course, value here refers to all those features or specifications in a product or a service that a customer is paying for, or all those service characteristics which will satisfy specific needs of the consumer in the public sector organizations.

As seen in Chapter 2, all types of operations take in various inputs and use some processes to add value to those inputs, in order to produce the desired output that is passed on to the next link in the total value-chain. This is shown in Figure 5.1. As the product or the service travels along this chain, value should be added at each point based on the customer requirements.

Porter (1990) has divided up the value chain activities in any type of organization into two categories of primary and support activities. This is shown in Table 5.2.

A company can improve its performance, profits and competitive superiority by analysing its value-chain activities and identifying and focusing on increasing productivity of those primary and support

Table 5.2 Value-chain activities

Primary activities	Support activities
Inbound logistics	Human resource development
Operations	Procurement
Outbound logistics	Technological development
Marketing and sales	Firm's infrastructure
After-sales services	

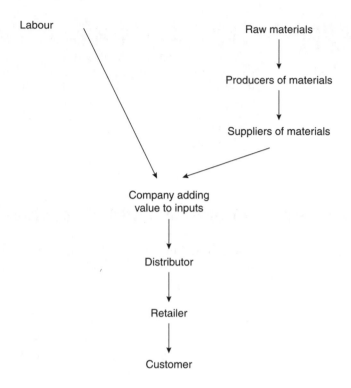

Figure 5.1 Total value chain

activities which are most important to the firm's competitive position. This can be achieved either by reducing the operating costs or optimizing quality and performance of the products or services offered to the consumer.

The Safeway supermarket chain kept its costs competitive by concentrating on and decentralizing the primary activities of inbound logistics (such as receiving, sorting, handling and distributing of goods in), and the support activities of procurement (such as administrative task of ordering goods).

Productivity in manufacturing organizations

Despite some slight improvements, the manufacturing productivity in the UK, USA and even in Japan has suffered significantly in recent years. Several factors can be considered as primary causes of poor performance of manufacturing industries.

International competition

Over the years manufacturing organizations in some European and Scandinavian countries, Canada and Australia have suffered greatly from their lack of investment and innovation in all aspects of their business. They have been rather slow in taking advantages of 'best practices' such as CAD, computer-aided manufacturing (CAM), manufacturing resources planning (MRP), business process re-engineering (BPR), just in time (JIT), etc. (see Chapters 4 and 8). A closer examination of their commitment to competitiveness demonstrates alarming evidence of their disappointing positions in the league table of industrialized nations. This is shown in Table 5.3

Lack of graduate engineers

Traditionally, in some developed countries such as the UK, engineers have not been given the status and the remuneration they deserve.

Table 5.3 Competitive league of industrialized nations

Country	Ranking	Country	Ranking
USA	1	Taiwan	11
Singapore	2	Canada	12
Hong Kong	3	Australia	13
Japan	4	Austria	14
Switzerland	5	Sweden	15
Germany	6	Finland	16
Holland	7	France	17
New Zealand	8	UK	18
Denmark	9	Belgium	19
Norway	10	Chile	20

Source : *Daily Telegraph*, 12 February 1998.

Table 5.4 University output of engineers per annum

Country	Output of engineers per annum
Japan	70 000
USA	65 000
France	30 000
UK	8 000

Source: Coopers and Lybrand

This has led to engineering degrees as a qualification not being popular amongst university applicants. It can be said that, unlike Germany, the USA and Japan, engineering as a profession does not attract good quality graduates in some countries. This is shown in Table 5.4

Further statistics indicate that out of the above numbers 15–20 per cent of engineers each year prefer to choose a career in a non-engineering field such as sales or marketing where financial rewards are usually much better. Therefore, it seems clear that unless governments in these countries change their policies to genuinely review and improve the status and salaries of engineers, manufacturing productivity will be negatively affected. After all, engineers everywhere make a significant contribution to the productivity of manufacturing companies.

Fluctuation in interest rate

High interest rates always lead to having a stronger currency abroad, which in turn makes it difficult for local companies to export their manufactured goods. It also makes it hard for companies to raise finances to fund any investment to improve their performance. In the past decade, variation in interest rates worldwide have both improved and reduced the productivity of manufacturing organizations.

Strikes

Disputes over pay and working conditions have often interrupted output on factory floors and resulted in loss of productivity. However, due to recession in the 1990s, unlike the 1970s and 1980s, this factor has not played a significant role in reducing manufacturing productivity.

It is equally important to understand that, with the exception of graduate engineers, each of the above factors can have serious implication on productivity of service organizations worldwide.

Productivity in service industries

In the past three decades there has been a gradual reduction in the number of people employed in manufacturing organizations, with increasing numbers of people joining the service sectors particularly in the European countries. For instance, it has been estimated that by the year 2000, only 19 per cent of UK employment will be in manufacturing, with 81 per cent of the working population being employed in the service industries. Therefore, improving productivity in the service organizations is as important as in manufacturing industries.

Like in manufacturing, service productivity can be expressed as a ratio of output produced to input consumed. In service industries people are usually the key resources. Other inputs are money, materials, equipment and information.

Output in service sectors can be such things as healthy patients, educated students and satisfied passengers. Hence service productivity depends on how efficiently management can utilize resources at its disposal and how effectively service personnel can achieve their operational goals. This in turn means that results achieved by a service organization can be significantly affected by:

● efficiency of resources – the method by which resources are used
● utilisation of resources – the actual use of resources to their potential use
● effectiveness of resources – the extent to which resources achieve the corporate goals of the organization in what they do.

Armistead et al. (1988) have identified that service managers can control the three main influences on productivity, namely the input costs, the transformation of these resources into output and the utilization of these resources or capacity management. They stress that managing capacity is not just an issue of maximizing the utilization of the total operating system, but also the utilization of the operating subsystems. For example, it is possible for a hospital to be operating at 100 per cent but for part of the operation to be underutilized.

Exercise

Outline tactics that can be applied by the following operations in order to optimize the utilization of the total operating system and its subsystems:

- an air line
- a hotel.

Strategic determinants of productivity

In service industries the following elements are considered to be the strategic determinants of productivity:

- volume of demand
- variety of services offered
- variation in the volume and nature of demand over time

The management of service productivity will be affected by each of the above elements.

Volume effects

Traditionally, volume of demand has always had a major influence on service productivity. The input costs are usually reduced by the 'economies of scale', especially in those service organizations with low customer contact. High volume allows efficient transformation of resources and development of specialization and learning effects. Furthermore, high volume can facilitate balanced capacity especially if combined with low variety, resulting in all the subsystems operating at optimum levels. Examples include a library or an airport service.

Variety effects

Generally, high variety can be considered as the main cause of low productivity. According to Armistead et al. (1988), high variety reduces volume per service line and demands a wide range of skills, both of which increase input costs. Therefore, effective management of variety requires time. It may need specialized units, equipment and employees to accommodate different services, all of which reduces efficiency of resources. Full system utilization examples include hospital services or lawyers' practices.

Variation effects

The impact of variation over time in the demand and the nature of services provided requires that service operations adopt a flexible approach to systems utilization. Two broad alternative strategies can be considered:

1 The chase demand planning is used in situations where resource provision is flexible enough to reflect the fluctuation in demand. For example, in the fast food industry, staff are mainly hired on a part time basis; they are semi-skilled and the shift patterns are varied.
2 The alternative is the level capacity strategy which is used in service operations with relatively low customer contacts. For example, in a bank operation, staff are normally employed on a full time basis. During the period of high demand (usually lunchtime), staff tend to undertake customer contact activities, but in slack times they switch to the 'back room' activities such as document handling and information processing.

Exercise   Discuss the volume, variety, and variation effects on the service productivity of a theme park.

Critical issues in productivity improvement

Organizations in all sectors wishing to improve their productivity should give special attention to the following critical success factors:

Change management

Change should be considered a way of life and everyone in the organization should expect change. It must be initiated, clearly communicated, co-ordinated and continuously supported by the company's top management.

Case Study

British Airways has moved from being a government-subsidized company that flew planes, to a leader in customer service. This was achieved through the senior management commitment to a culture of change. The company had to make radical changes to its corporate, business and operations strategies. For this to succeed British Airways used innovative open learning opportunities together with traditional class-based training.

Empowerment

Senior managers should be able to release the full potential of their employees through involvement, training, recognition and effective communication. Highly productive firms treat their workforce as a source of ideas and not as costs. It is important that people's contributions are constantly recognized and rewarded through a combination of informal, instant and sincere appreciation from colleagues and formal recognition schemes. Examples are the 'Magic Moment ' award used by the former Birmingham Midshires Building Society for great, unprompted acts of service, and the 'Professional of the season' award used by the TNT Delivery Express for staff who have exceeded normal performance expectations. The latter includes a certificate, a bottle of champagne and a £250 cash prize.

Customer orientation

Organizations should make every effort to know their immediate markets and clearly understand their customers requirements. These can be better achieved by companies through partnership with their customers and suppliers, and by listening to their views through regular meetings.

Innovation

Companies should welcome the pressure put upon them by demanding customers in terms of price reduction, flexibility, delivery, and design and quality improvements. This can be achieved by constantly developing new products and services. They should continuously benchmark every aspect of their operations against the 'best' in the world in order to lower their operating costs, increase their product variety and globally improve their manufacturing/service responsiveness, productivity and competitiveness.

Customer delight

Customers should always be regarded as the 'focal point' whenever companies are considering any change or innovation in their products, services and processes. By delighting its customers a company can improve its market standing, and increase its productivity and overall profits.

Case Study

Lawson Mardon Plastics (LMP) is part of LM Packaging, which became a wholly owned subsidiary of the Alusuisse Lanza Group in 1994. Alusuisse Lanza is one of the largest packaging groups in the world. Lawson Mardon Plastics operates from a single site in Nottingham, and employs over 165 people. Its core business is the production of high volume plastic packaging for leading food, cosmetics and pharmaceuticals companies. Consistently high and improving customer satisfaction is a target set in LMP's mission statement.

The company has established a thirty-five point survey covering issues such as sales support, delivery performance and pricing and gained maximum benefit by targeting actions on those areas where performance improvement has the greatest effect on customers perceptions. These have been identified through 'gap analysis' – comparing LMP's results to customer expectations and the company's competition. Over the past few years, the gap has closed substantially to a point where LMP does better than its customers expect. The company encourages customer complaints, however small, to drive improvement. Lawson Mardon Plastics has won a range of industry awards for design innovation, including a Goldstar Award from the UK's institute for packaging (won jointly with Whitbread for a draught beer insert for bottles).

Exercise

Outline some questions that a firm may ask itself as part of its company-wide productivity improvement programme.

Japanese management techniques

In Chapter 10 some of the Japanese management practices to improve product and service quality are outlined. This section deals with other approaches widely used and developed by Japanese firms in order to increase their productivity.

Continuous improvement (kaizen)

This approach requires that organizations in all sectors consider their operations as an integrated process with a view to continuously review, redesign and constantly improve every process in the light of changes that take place in the needs of the customer and in the actions of their competitors.

For kaizen to work in an organization it must be applied at all levels. It is vital that management at top, middle and supervisory levels and the workers, participate in the control, maintenance and the continuous improvement of business processes. It is important to remember that kaizen is not a system, but an environment for total quality to succeed. It is a never-ending journey based on the principle that methods and performances can always be improved. Amongst the key success factors are:

● quality leadership
● employees involvement in decision-making
● partnership with customers and suppliers
● teamworking.

Through a culture of continuous improvement organizations can achieve continuous competitiveness. For this to work successfully operational managers need to be 'process'-orientated. They need to value time management, skills development, participation, employees morale and effective communication whilst continuously evaluating and improving their people and process performance.

Case Study

National Westminster Life Assurance Ltd was founded in January 1993 with an initial capital of £150 million, making it the largest life assurance start-up in Europe. It markets life assurance, pensions and longer-term investment products in the UK. The company established the culture of constant improvement and development from day one. It is one of the very few European organizations that demonstrates its understanding and belief in continuous improvement in the way it works. One consequence of the continuous improvement culture is the creation of a central register which empowered people to log the improvement opportunities. Furthermore, all initiative teams are aware that the key objective throughout the organization is to create a lifetime relationship with the customer. The company has an understanding of what customers want and how many purchases they are likely to make throughout a lifetime. It gives customers the opportunity and very good reasons to want to come back to them.

Teamworking

Japanese firms are well known for encouraging and developing team-work. Group-based activities such as quality control circles have been used increasingly in Japan since 1962 as a strategy to aid problem-solving and to improve productivity and employee morale (see Chapter 10).

Team characteristics

Traditionally Japanese work teams:

- are customer focused
- understand the mission and their work objectives
- are well motivated
- co-ordinate their activity in order to achieve team objectives
- have the necessary skills and problem-solving abilities within the team to achieve their goals
- are well balanced; members respect their team leader and each other roles

- learn quickly from their mistakes
- set measurable milestones
- communicate regularly in order to review their performance.

Team culture

Japanese companies have worked very hard to promote and create a team culture within their business operations. This is successfully achieved by:

- organizing teams around the key processes rather than the key functions. Such a policy helps in reducing conflict and power struggles between departments, which in turn results in meeting customer needs rather than detracting from them
- building teams using cross-functional departments
- early recognition of the team's existence and achievements
- adopting team performance ratings through rewarding the whole team rather than an individual member in the team
- integrating people and connecting their abilities to objectives that should be achieved by the team
- encouraging individual and team commitment through provision of non-financial rewards such as team uniforms, social events, team of the month awards, etc.

Dutton Engineering is a subcontract sheet-metalworking company based in Sandy, Bedfordshire. It employs twenty-seven people and supplies stainless steel housings for the electronics industry. Trust and training are the key words in an approach to continuous improvement that has made Dutton Engineering a Mecca for those looking to see how quality techniques can pay dividends in the small business sector.

Teamworking has proved the most important element of the new business structure. The shopfloor has been divided into three teams, named by their members 'red', 'blue' and 'green'. At first individual employees found it difficult to overcome ingrained habits and work as part of a defined group. The company overcome the problem when it introduced a system of annualized hours, contracting employees to work a set number of hours per year rather than per week. Once the tasks for the week are finished, teams can go home. Such flexibility allowed Dutton to retain sales during the last recession. Teamworking is effective at Dutton because the shopfloor teams have power in all aspects of the business – not just production. They have direct contact with customers and suppliers in areas such as design, ordering and costing.

Case Study

Westfield Health private scheme provides health care services to over 280 000 people. The company actively promotes teamworking as an effective way of enhancing performance, while recognizing the value of each individual. Self-managed teams are responsible for key operational processes such as claims reimbursement, registration, subscriptions and customers enquiries, allocating and monitoring their own performance against objectives.

Advantages of teamworking

Amongst its many benefits, teamworking can bring about:

- better co-ordination between individuals
- greater job satisfaction
- lower absenteeism and employee turnover
- improved productivity
- increased profit
- higher social satisfaction.

Exercise

Given the benefits associated with teamworking, explain why it is it that some teams fail to achieve their objectives.

The 5S system

The 5S system is a Japanese 'housekeeping' approach that has been around for a long time. It is applied by companies as an early step in implementing the total quality management concept. Table 5.5 shows what the five Ss stands for.

Table 5.5 Definition of the 5S system

Japanese	English	Meaning
Seiri	Organize	Discard the unnecessary. This means, distinguish those items needed from those not needed and throw away those unneeded.
Seiton	Neatness	Put things in order. This means, keep things tidy and ready for use.
Seisou	Sweep	Clean up/find defects. This means, to find minor defects while sweeping clean.
Seiketsu	Cleanliness	Personal cleanliness. This means, to improve the environment around the facilities to minimize deterioration.
Shitsuk	Discipline	This means, obey what has been decided.

The reason why the 5S system is needed at work is because there are many things people do at the workplace without thinking which can affect the organizational productivity. The 5S are like a mirror reflecting our attitudes and behavioural patterns. Its effective implementation can lead to:

● prevention of waste
● better safety
● improved efficiency
● prevention of facilities breakdown
● improved quality
● standardization.

Case Study

Excel (Electronic) Assemblies have a culture of challenging everything that they do. They have created a process of ongoing improvement where effectiveness is measured at the point of use, with extraordinary results in quality. The production lead time has been slashed by focusing on adding value for the customer through elimination of wasteful and inappropriate processes, using techniques such as pull systems (kanban), the 5S system and visible management.

Lean production

The term 'lean production' was first advocated in 1990 by the publication of the American book *The Machine that Changed the World*. However, the concept had long been developed in Japan in particular at the Toyota plant.

Lean production is seen as a successor to mass production. Through the application of methodologies such as JIT, TQM and total productive maintenance (TPM), lean production usually requires half of the input resources as compared to mass production system. For example:

● less materials/parts
● less human effort
● less space
● less investment in tools.

The Japanese have been enjoying the results of this integrated approach because of their dedicated practice of the kaizen techniques such as teamworking, the 5S system, quality circles, etc. They also succeeded in transforming supplier relationship in order to reduce waste, increase flexibility and improve quality and delivery service by involving suppliers in the design of the products and processes.

The 'five why' system

As part of the lean production Japanese developed the 'five why' system. This is an investigative approach in which workers are trained to trace every fault back to its ultimate cause by asking 'why' as each level of the problem is uncovered, and then think of a solution so that it would not happen again.

Total integrated management

In recent years top management of the Japanese companies has realized that the productivity programmes, total quality control systems and other operational measures are no longer sufficient to improve business performance. They have been focusing more on innovating frameworks that can enhance the quality of management practice as a way of maximizing organizational performance. Total integrated management (TIM) is an integrated Japanese approach developed to examine and evaluate the quality of management factors affecting the performance of a company.

The TIM framework has a checklist of twelve primary factors. These factors are shown in Table 5.6.

From the twelve management factors, six are thought to be particularly important to the success and productivity of an effective organization. These are shown in Table 5.7.

Figure 5.2 illustrates the interrelationship between the above six factors. It shows that the quality of management cycle affects the four factors of management structure, resources, design and culture. In turn the quality of these four factors affects the management performance that can further influence organizational productivity and business results.

Japanese experience shows that if the quality level of the management cycle is low, then the six factors generate a 'passive feedback loop', in which management waits until poor results within management performance force reactionary feedback into the management flow. On the other hand, if the quality level of the management cycle is high, then the six factors generate an 'excellent feed-forward loop' in which management perceives the plans and strategies

Table 5.6 Twelve factors of management quality

Management factors	Management factors
1 Corporate history	7 Management targets
2 Corporate climate	8 Business structure
3 Strategic alliances	9 Management resources
4 Channels	10 Management design
5 Management cycle	11 Management functions
6 Environment	12 Management performance

Source : Yahaqi (1992).

Table 5.7 TIM critical success factors

Management factors	Description
Management cycle	Company vision, strategy, planning, control, and operations
Business structure	Various fields in which the company operates, its business mixture, and standing in the marketplace
Management resources	Money, materials, information, and people available to the company
Management design	Management system, organization, authority and responsibility
Corporate culture	The values and beliefs of management and employees within the company
Management performance	The growth, stability, and market share of the company

needed for the success of each management factor, and then productively formulates and implements them.

Following scenario illustrates how the TIM concept has been applied in the Scandinavian Air System (SAS).

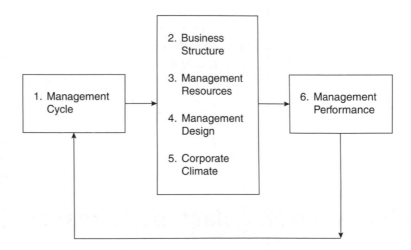

Figure 5.2 Interrelationship between key management factors affecting management quality

1 *Management cycle*. Like many other successful airlines, SAS has the vision of providing extraordinary customer satisfaction. This is supported by sound strategic planning, effective control and efficient operations.

2 *Business structure*. In the airline business one seat on an airplane is much like any other. It is passenger service quality that makes the big difference in the treatment by the front-line personnel. This includes situations on board, at the ticket counter, and at the baggage area. The international airline's challenge is complex: what has to be done to ensure the traveller's complete satisfaction with long hours' experience of flying 10 000m above the sea level at 800 kilometres per hour?

3 *Management resources.* John Carzon, President of SAS, said that SAS is not the aeroplane or the airport gate, or the overhaul station. It is the contact between the employee and the passenger. The 'moment of truth' occurs when the customer, consciously or unconsciously, has a need and turns to an employee or the physical facilities for a solution.

4 *Management design*. In SAS, each time an employee interacts with a customer it is noted as a 'moment of truth'. Carzon estimated that some 50 000 moments of truth occur daily as SAS personnel interact face to face with customers.

5 *Corporate culture*. The moment of truth is successful because the design of the physical facilities anticipated those needs, and the service plan provides anticipatory human intervention. Above all the corporate culture takes into account the values, beliefs, customs and behaviour of passengers and employees.

6 *Management performance*. The growth rate, scale, stability, profit and market share of the company have been increased dramatically after the transition.

Achieving world-class performance

Today, manufacturing and service organizations are operating in a global market; therefore their success depends on having the right products/services and providing customers with what they want at the right time and at the right price continuously and competitively.

Various awards are used to measure the world-class status of potential companies. For example, Deming Award in Japan, Malcom Baldrige Award in the USA and the UK/EFQM Award in Europe (see Chapter10).

In order for companies of all types to enhance their productivity and to become world-class performers they need to develop policies and apply strategies which will continuously:

- satisfy the quality expectation of their customers
- lower their costs whilst sustaining or even improving the standards of their products and services
- deliver their products and services at the right time.

World-class companies regard continuous improvement (kaizen) as a means of achieving the above three minimum requirements, and make every effort to move beyond these 'order entry criteria' to increase their market share and achieve higher productivity, profitability and customer delight. The key to continuous improvement is generating an enthusiasm for ongoing changes based on teamworking, innovation and benchmarking, together with individual and team motivation.

Companies wishing to achieve world-class performance can benefit from the following.

Planning competitively

As discussed in Chapter 2, it is the responsibility of senior management in any organization to set out a vision and a strategic direction for the company. They should know where the company ought to be going. Having competitively developed long-, medium- and short-term plans is the first important step for a firm seeking to achieve world-class performance in every aspects of its business.

1 *Long-term planning.* This should decide company mission and its long-term objective over a three to five years' period. Management at all levels should be involved in formulating the long-rang goals of the organization.
2 *Medium-term planning.* This should identify the functional strategies that are going to be implemented over the next eighteen months to two years.
3 *Short-term planning.* This should set out the day to day operational tactics and specify the people and resources involved.

Table 5.8 Relationship between personal and company objectives

Staff/function	Objectives
Research and development	Reducing time to introduce new products and services
Marketing	Reduce logistics cycle time
Quality	Reducing quality costs
Cost accounting	Reducing invoice time
Order entry	Reducing order handling time
Production	Reducing manufacturing lead time

In a world-class company productivity is improved by everyone in the organization taking part and making daily contribution to meeting the goals and objectives of the company. This means that everyone's personal objective should be doing something every day to assist the company to achieve its goals in areas such as improving quality of products and services, reducing lead times, increasing flexibility and reducing costs. This is shown in Table 5.8.

Exercise

In relation to the goals of a world class company what should be the personal objectives of a:

● hospital chief executive
● IT software designer.

Selecting world-class measurements

In quality companies business, personal objectives and strategies cannot be implemented successfully unless they are monitored continuously and measured against the world-class targets and achievements. This means that meeting, for instance, the business goal of satisfying customers in terms of quality, cost, delivery, flexibility, etc., necessitates performance of people and technology and the quality of policies and strategies used within an organization to be evaluated continuously and compared with those of world-class performers. A company should assess:

- the extent to which people within the firm are capable, involved and effective in what they do, as compared to the 'best ' in the world
- the level of technology and the nature of processes used in the company in terms of the simplicity of operations, stability and quality of operational processes
- the quality of policies and strategies used by the firm in terms of the degree of their impact on company's productivity, sales and competitiveness in the global market.

Case Study   Coca-Cola and Schweppes Beverages is a world-class soft drink manufacture. Through its best operating practice initiative the company strives continually to improve a climate of flexibility and adaptability, enabling its team to achieve at the highest level.

Meeting the goals

Any manufacturing or service organization wishing to become the best in its field and to achieve world-class performance needs to :

- have visible commitment from the top
- instigate total communication at all levels
- initiate and encourage formal employee involvement on strategic issues and decision-making
- promote effective delegation and management accountability
- make investment on time, employees training and participation
- integrate strategies with day-to-day operations
- incorporate strategy measures in management processes.

Case Study   Hospitals worldwide are struggling to achieve higher quality, shorter waiting lists and lower medical costs and public expenditure on health. They now have a corporate focus and their biggest challenge is to produce better care with similar resources through better management. The new structures mean that doctors, nurses, midwifes, managers and directors have the opportunity for a wider participation in strategic decision-making and in the running of hospitals. However, a process of understanding and effective communication at all levels is essential. Many positive results have been achieved through teamworking, self-analysis and self-development.

Summary

Relevance

1 *Effectiveness*. Management of productivity in all types of organization depends on how effectively companies manage their productive resources and how rapidly they innovate and develop their products, services and their transformation processes. It can also be affected by the volume of demand, the variety of products and services offered, and the variation in demand over time.
2 *Value*. There is a direct link between productivity and profits. The performance of a firm can be affected by two types of activities: those that add value to the end product or the end service, and those that fail to add value. Value here means all those features in a product or a service that the customer is paying for.
3 *Competition*. During the past decade the industrial productivity of Western nations has suffered more than that of the Japanese and some other countries in the Far East such as Singapore and Hong Kong. This is mainly due to the inability of the West to compete effectively in terms of innovation and investment, and a lack of well-qualified and well-motivated engineers.

Definition

Productivity is the most common measure of performance. With current trends in organizations and external environment, some other criteria are also used. These include quality of products and services, cost of conversion processes, delivery to customer and process flexibility.

Measurement

Productivity is expressed as the ratio of output achieved to input consumed. There are three levels of productivity:

1 *National* – where international comparison can be made between the productivity of a group of nations.
2 *Industrial* – where productivity of different sectors within the economy is measured. This is often expressed as output per employee per hour. Comparison can then be made by individual companies against industry average.

3 *Organizational* – where productivity of any firm is measured in monetary term. This is expressed as the ratio of output sold to cost of input used to produce the output.

Control and improvement

Production and operations managers are responsible for improving productivity and reducing operating costs. Regular evaluation and efficient, and effective utilization of available resources such as people, equipment, materials, space, time and money, can help managers to enhance productivity and cost-effectiveness of their operations.

Productivity of a resource can be improved by increasing the working speed, or improving the work method, or reducing cost and wastage.

Companies in all sectors can improve their productivity through welcoming change, empowering their workforce, knowing their markets, producing new products and services regularly, and understanding and delighting their customer.

The efficiency, utilization and effectiveness of resources used can improve productivity, particularly in service organizations. Service managers are able to control the cost of the input resources, the conversion processes of these resources into the desired output and the capacity or utilization of these resources.

World-class performance

Awards such as Deming, Malcom Baldridge, and UK/EFQM European model for business excellence are used to measure the world-class standards of progressive companies.

Continuous improvement of products, services, and internal and external processes should be considered by all types of organization as a means of satisfying the changing needs of their customers, reducing costs, and meeting their consumers' delivery times. This can be facilitated through teamworking and other Japanese management techniques such as; the 5S system, lean production, the five whys system, and the total integrated management approach.

Companies in all sectors can achieve world-class performance through competitively developing long-, medium- and short-term plans, assessing their business objectives and business results using world-class targets and measurements. This can be achieved through quality leadership and management practices that promote, learning, employee involvement, empowerment, reward, recognition and effective communication at all levels.

1 State three levels of productivity.
2 Differentiate between industry and organizational productivity.
3 Outline three way by which productivity of a resource can be improved.
4 List three types of 'resources' important in to the operation of a service organization.
5 List five types of 'resources' used in a manufacturing organization.
6 The following will result in improving operations productivity, except:
(a) increasing working speed
(b) improving working methods
(c) reducing cost
(d) reducing wastage
(e) reducing participation?
7 Productivity can be expressed by the following ratios, except:
(a) results achieved to resources consumed
(b) output produced to number of hours used
(c) output achieved to number of people employed
(d) input used divided by output produced
(e) output produced to number of machine used?
8 Employee productivity can be improved by which of the following:
(a) structure of the organization
(b) goals of the organization
(c) unionization of the company
(d) none of the above
(e) all of the above?
9 Which of the following factors have lesser affect on productivity of an organization:
(a) government regulations
(b) process automation
(c) diversification
(d) process layout
(e) inventory management?
10 The following are the primary activities in an organization, except:
(a) operations
(b) marketing and sales
(c) human resource development
(d) inbound logistics
(e) after sales services?
11 Which of the following can have the most impact on a company's productivity:

(a) innovation
(b) industrial dispute
(c) investment
(d) interest rate
(e) inflation rate?

12 Organizational productivity can be improved by the following, except:
(a) employees involvement and empowerment
(b) customer orientation
(c) effective leadership and change management
(d) continuous development of products and services
(e) economic contraction?

13 Service productivity can be influenced by the following, except:
(a) efficiency of the resources
(b) utilization of the resources
(c) number of service outlets
(d) cost of input resources
(e) effectiveness of the resources?

14 Which of the following is not a strategic determinant of service productivity:
(a) economies of scale
(b) number of suppliers
(c) variation over time in demand
(d) variety of services offered
(e) variability of demand for the range of services offered?

15 Which of the following may not be an order-winning criteria:
(a) meeting customer quality expectation
(b) lowering costs
(c) on-time delivery
(d) all of the above
(e) only (a)?

16 Continuous improvement is a system to improve total quality. True or false?

17 The kaizen approach requires operational managers to be process orientated. True or false?

18 A process-orientated manager should put high value on:
(a) skills development
(b) employee morale
(c) communication
(d) all of the above
(e) only (a)?

19 The 5S system include the following elements:
(a) tidiness

(b) order

(c) discipline

(d) cleanliness

(e) all of the above?

20 The 5S system is an initial stage of TQM implementation. True or false?

21 Japanese companies are not famous for group-based activities. True or false?

22 List three Japanese teamwork characteristics.

23 Group-based activity achieves the following, except:

(a) improved productivity

(b) increased profits

(c) financial rewards for group leader

(d) improved morale

(e) none of the above?

24 To create a team culture, organizations should do the following, except:

(a) organize teams around functions

(b) use cross-functional teams

(c) integrate people's abilities with the team objectives

(d) encourage commitment through non-financial rewards

(e) recognize team effort early?

25 Teamworking can lead to the following, except:

(a) co-operation between individuals

(b) higher staff turnover

(c) greater job satisfaction

(d) higher social satisfaction

(e) lower absenteeism?

26 Lean production is 'lean' because it results in less of the following, except:

(a) human effort

(b) manufacturing space

(c) investment

(d) inventory to keep

(e) defects?

27 Briefly explain the 'five whys' investigative system.

28 Total integrated management is a Japanese approach aimed at improving product quality. True or false?

29 List six management factors of the Japanese TIM framework which can significantly influence management and organizational productivity.

30 The TIM 'management cycle' include the following elements, except:

    (a) vision
    (b) strategy
    (c) planning
    (d) control
    (e) processes?

31 Key elements of a continuous improvement programme include:
    (a) benchmarking
    (b) teamworking
    (c) process redesign
    (d) all of the above
    (e) none of the above?

32 Companies aiming to achieve world-class status will benefit from the following, except:
    (a) only top management involvement in strategic decision-making
    (b) competitive planning
    (c) visible commitment from the top
    (d) delegation and management accountability
    (e) total communication at all levels?

References and further reading

Armistead, C., Johnston, R. and Slack, N. (1988). The strategic determinants of service productivity. In Johnston, R. (ed) *The Management of Service Operations*. IFS Publications.

Coulson, T. C. (1997). *Future of Organization*. Kogan Page.

Hannaghan, T. (1995). *Management:Concepts and Practice*. Pitman.

Johnston, R. (1988). *Management of Service Operations*. IFS.

Norton, C. (1993). *Becoming World Class*. Macmillan Business.

Porter, M. (1990). Competitive Advantage of Nations. Macmillan.

Slack, N., Chambers, S., Harland, C., Harrison, A. and Johnston, R. (1998). *Operations Management*. Pitman.

Stacey, R. (1993). *Strategic Management and Organizational Dynamics*. Pitman.

Womack, J., Jones, D. and Roos, D. (1990). *The Machine That Changed the World*. Rawson Association.

Yahaqi, S. (1992). After product quality in Japan: management quality. *National Productivity Review*, Autumn, 501–15.

Chapter 6

Planning and control of work: the management of capacity

This chapter deals with the management of capacity, which is the ability of an organization to process the amount of work demanded of it. In considering this area of operations management several topics are covered:

1 *Planning and control.* The basic task of capacity management is to provide the right number of staff, with the right facilities and technology in the right place at the right time. This task cannot be achieved without there first being a plan showing how these resources are to be allocated. Once framed, the implementation of the plan needs to be monitored. Feedback is required from the operation to show if the plan is being achieved. The planning process is thus a dynamic one and plans seldom stay unchanged as the operation attempts to adjust to the demands placed upon it.

2 *Forecasting.* One of the basic difficulties in planning for the

future allocation of capacity is to know what the future demand for work is likely to be. In part, the prediction of future demands will rest upon what the managers of the organization know about the behaviours of their customers and users. This knowledge is qualitative and is obviously a potentially very useful source of ideas about what the pattern of demand is likely to be. However, it is unwise to rely solely upon such 'instincts' and quantitative data showing the history of actual demand patterns is vital to help the managers of the operation make as accurate an estimate as possible. Some of the simpler quantitative forecasting techniques are illustrated in the supplement to this chapter.

3 *Differing planning time horizons.* Some of the lead times involved in allocating capacity can be very long. The building of a brand new operation, for instance, will require a long process of research, planning and execution. It is quite likely that this process will be measured in terms of years. Such capacity decisions as these, therefore, have to be made with a long-term perspective. Other decisions are made in a much shorter time frame. Changing working patterns to accommodate sudden staff illness is an example of such a decision. The long- and short-term aspects of managing capacity are both vital to the primary objective of meeting the workload required.

4 *Scheduling.* The act of allocating people to tasks in the short term is called scheduling. Scheduling is a complex activity, with most situations involving an array of different possible schedules. Some of the basic principles are outlined.

How does the operation work?

The capacity of an organization may be defined as its ability to undertake the work demanded by its users. For example, a university might define its overall capacity in terms of the numbers of students it can teach, an airline by the number of passengers it can carry and an amusement park by the number of visitors it can accommodate. These numbers in turn will reflect the individual abilities of the various components that make up the working organization. Broadly, these individual components are the staff, the technology and the facilities. This ability to undertake the work demanded clearly cannot exist without the managers of the organization providing it.

It is this task, the task of providing the ability to undertake work, which is the focus of this chapter. More specifically, the chapter looks at how managers can plan and control the operation so that it meets the volume and variety demands of its users. Some of the decisions involved are long term, for example, the planning, building and execution of a new facility such as a new hospital will take many years. However, some decisions are of a much shorter duration, so deciding on the allocation of tasks amongst the nursing staff to meet the running of the maternity unit for the next eight hours is much less complicated. The chapter therefore deals with both the macro and the micro aspects of providing the capacity of the operation. At the macro level, the topics are the importance of forecasting, the relationship between capacity and anticipated demand, design of the operations network, the scope of the tasks to be undertaken and the balance of capacities.

At the micro level the areas covered are some of the techniques for making a forecast, techniques to manage capacity in the short term and the basic principles of scheduling. At the end of the chapter, therefore, the reader will have developed an understanding of some of the approaches available in this field and the issues involved.

The meaning of planning and control

In the first part of this chapter it was said that the chapter looks at how managers can plan and control the operation so that it meets the volume and variety demands of its users. Before embarking upon the various techniques and issues involved, it is important to understand what the term 'plan and control' actually means in this context.

Planning and control defined

In general terms, a plan is a worked out set of actions and decisions that we will undertake in the future. In our social lives we might organize a party, a trip to the zoo or a holiday. In the area of capacity management, a plan is similarly a worked out set of actions and decisions, but in this case it tells the people of the operation how they will meet the volume and variety demands of the users. At the same time, like all operational plans, it must also help

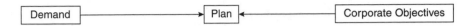

Figure 6.1 Operational plan relationships

to implement the overall objectives of the organization. This relationship is illustrated in Figure 6.1.

As a result of the planning exercise there will be a document (manual or computerized) specifying how the resources of the operation will be allocated in order to meet both the demand and the wider operation's objectives. Once the plan is agreed, the people in the operation will then begin to put it into action. The people responsible for making sure that the plan is achieved will need to know how the actions are proceeding and how far the plan is being realized. Obtaining information on the implementation of the plan and comparing progress against its detail is the control aspect of managing capacity. If there are any variances between what is actually being achieved and what the plan expects to be achieved then the performance of the process has to be altered. If the process cannot be altered to meet the plan then the plan has to be modified to accommodate this. The diagram in Figure 6.1 can be developed slightly to show this (see Figure 6.2).

Planning and control is easiest to perform where both the process and the demand are predictable. In the service sector, this task is complicated by the fact that service usually cannot be stored ahead of demand and that the customer usually has a direct role in the provision of the service (see Chapter 3 for further discussion of these points).

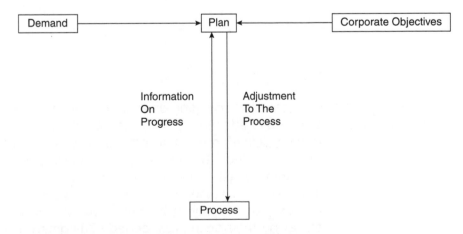

Figure 6.2 Developed operational plan relationships

The planning hierarchy

In order to plan and control its capacity effectively the organization needs to review all time horizons, i.e., it needs to think in the long term, the medium term and the short term. The more short-term aspects of capacity decisions are usually referred to as scheduling. Thus scheduling is introduced as a heading in the final section of this chapter.

How does the management of capacity affect the key operations objectives of quality, cost, speed, dependability and flexibility?

Capacity planning and control

The role of forecasting demand

The basic task of capacity planning is to provide the resources necessary to cope with the volume and variety of demands placed by the users of the operation. It follows that some assessment of the future patterns of this demand is crucial to the planning task. If the resources are deployed to cope with an estimate of the demand that is inaccurate, then the potential consequences range from a process which is unable to meet the demand to a process which is idle. Some estimate of the future usage is therefore essential, and the more accurate the estimate can be then the more precise the allocation of the resources can be.

Egg, the direct banking operation, was launched by the Prudential. Eight days after the launch the company was warning customers of long delays in opening accounts. In the first five days of operation they took 65 000 telephone calls, more than double the amount forecast. The company had badly underestimated demand. The problem was so great that customers were told that they might have to wait twenty-eight days from submitting their applications to having their accounts opened. Customers were also urged not to send in cheques, as the processing of these would take a long time and also add to the work with customers phoning to find out if their cheques had been cleared.

Dependent and independent demand

In some cases the demand is known for certain because, for instance, firm orders are in place or the process actually supplies another process and the requirements of the latter operation have been stipulated. This type of situation is referred to as one of dependent demand, i.e., the actual demand for work from the system depends upon some higher level of demand and this quantity is known. In such a situation the planning of capacity can be carried out with a greater degree of certainty than if the demand can only be estimated. Where the requirement can only be estimated it is known as independent demand. One way of viewing this is to think of the demand as independent of the control of the operation. In these circumstances the planning task is trying to cope with a higher level of uncertainty and the risks of the plan being wrong are therefore larger. Independent demand has to be predicted by a forecast.

Case Study

Hospitals are only too aware of the difference between dependent and independent demand. The former is represented by elective surgery, where medical operations are booked in advance. In these cases the hospital can plan to provide the necessary capacity knowing what type and number of operations will be required. Primary care capacity, in the form of operating theatres, clinical and nursing staff, medical supplies and beds can be allocated with a high degree of certainty. Supporting services, such as catering and laundry, can also be planned. The position with emergency surgery, i.e., independent demand, is far more difficult to plan for. If the number of emergency surgery operations exceeds the capacity of the hospital then usually booked appointments are cancelled. This releases the necessary resources to cope, but risks causing high levels of dissatisfaction amongst those patients whose operations are cancelled at very short notice.

The components of demand

Demand patterns usually show a trend and often some element of seasonality. The trend is the general direction of the demand pattern, which might be for the demand to rise or fall over a given period. This upward or downward trajectory may not be reflected, however, in every individual demand figure. The trend is the broad drift of the demand data. Seasonality means that the demand will fluctuate, thus giving rise to peaks and troughs. These fluctuations may occur on a daily, weekly, monthly or a longer-term basis. Swimming pool sales peak in the spring, heavy clothing sales in the autumn and winter, and holidays in the summer. A simple diagram can illustrate these two components of demand. Suppose that the scattergraph of the demand shows the pattern as in Figure 6.3.

It can be seen that the broad drift of the plotted values is upwards. This broad direction is the trend. Drawing a freehand line, as shown in Figure 6.4, can indicate it very roughly.

The movement around the trend line indicates the seasonal component of the demand. In this case there are two peaks and two troughs (Figure 6.5).

Seasonal demand patterns are common in many sectors. For example, the tourist industry will show most holidays being booked for the summer, with lower peaks at Easter and Christmas and troughs in the intervening periods. In the UK car industry in the past, most cars were sold at the time of the new registration period,

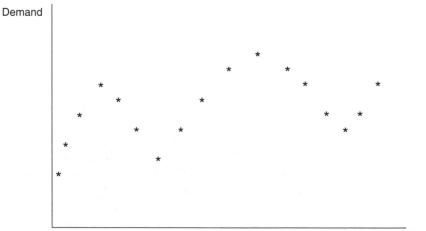

Figure 6.3 Scattergraph of demand

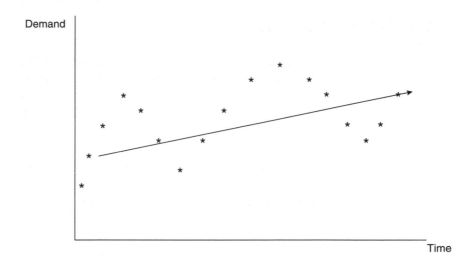

Figure 6.4 The trend line

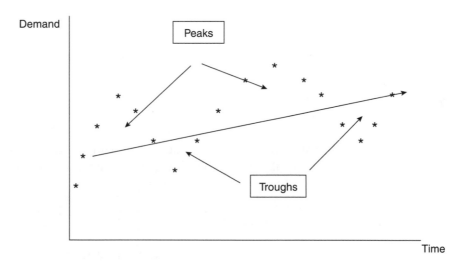

Figure 6.5 Seasonal demand

a peak in demand that caused the manufacturers serious capacity management problems.

The variations which are not accounted for by the trend and the seasonality factors are known as unassignable variations. These are movements in the data for which the cause is unknown.

The accuracy of forecasts

One common measure of the accuracy of forecasts is the mean absolute deviation. This measure is the measure of the average deviation of the forecast from the actual demand, ignoring whether the deviation is negative or positive. This can be illustrated from Table 6.1.

Table 6.1 Data for mean absolute deviation calculation

Week	Demand	Forecast	Error
1	120	123	3
2	101	101	0
3	115	116	1
4	114	109	5
5	98	109	11

The mean absolute deviation is:

$$\frac{20}{5} = 4 \tag{6.1}$$

Using this measure, the forecasting method producing the lowest mean absolute deviation is considered to be the best.

What makes a good forecast?

To be useful to the operation a good forecast should be:

● clear about the units of capacity needed
● as accurate as possible
● issued in sufficient time.

It should be noted that where a service involves the random arrival of customers, queuing theory might also be used to help predict the pattern of demand. This topic is dealt with in the literature on operations research. The formulae can be complicated and for most practical applications computers are used.

Long-term capacity planning

Case Study

- After purchasing the Rolls-Royce car manufacturing plant, Volkswagen undertook a £500 million investment programme to lift the annual output of Bentley motor cars from around 1400 to 9000 in a five-year period.
- Philips, Europe's largest consumer electronics company, plans to close about a third of its factories over a four-year period. The president of the company said that they had built up too big a production capacity.
- Overcapacity in the D-Ram industry was one important factor in the decision by Siemens to close down its manufacturing plant in the North-East of England.
- Kingfisher, the retail conglomerate that includes B&Q and Castorama, plans to invest £750 million and create 20 000 jobs over a period of five years. This expansion is based on opening 125 out-of-town superstores.

The long-term issues concern major decisions that affect the total size of the operation. For example, the building or closing down of major facilities is an issue which has great implications for the operation overall. If the long term is to be dealt with in a properly planned manner, then the thinking underpinning the decision should be based upon the ability of the operation to cope with the expected demand several years hence.

The key questions

When looking to the long-term future of the capacity of the operation the following are the key questions to be resolved:

1 What relationship should there be between the capacity and anticipated demand? Should the capacity to be put in place exceed anticipated demand, be less than the demand or aim to match the volume and variety exactly?
2 What should be the design of the operations network? Should there be one facility serving the total demand or should there be

several facilities? Should the organization do all of the work itself or should some of the tasks be undertaken by third parties?

3 If there is to be more than one facility what capacity should the individual operations making up the total network of the organization have?

Each of these questions is now dealt with in turn. In reality, the decisions made by operations are likely to be a mix of the options raised.

What relationship should there be between the capacity and anticipated demand?

If the operation is designed to exceed the expected demand then certain consequences will follow. On the plus side, the operation will always be able to meet the volume and variety demands placed upon it. This will lead to users satisfied in terms of the time that the process takes. On the debit side, the costs of providing the excess capacity will have to be absorbed. In addition, services that are underutilized may be perceived as lacking in valued experiences such as excitement levels.

Excitement levels are a particular concern of services in the entertainment sector. The following operations may deliver service to their usual standards, but if there are few users then the perceived excitement, and therefore value, will usually fall:

- zoos
- pop concerts
- restaurants
- theatres
- football matches.

Clearly there are financial implications too. The staff costs and other fixed costs will largely remain the same if the operation is busy or quiet, but in the latter case revenues will be substantially lower.

Placing capacity at below demand ensures the opposite. In this case there will be users dissatisfied with the waiting time, but the operation will make full use of the costs of its resources. In the commercial service sector much attention has been paid to 'yield management' as organizations attempt to decide which demand to meet and which to turn away. The yield of a unit of capacity is the amount of revenue that it generates. Airlines, hotels and car rental firms commonly use yield management. The goal is to maximize this yield so that profitability is improved. In a hotel, for instance, the yield of its bedroom capacity might be calculated by the ratio of total revenues received to the theoretical revenue which could have been received had the capacity been sold for the highest price.

The policy of matching capacity to demand attempts to gain the benefits of both courses without their attendant demerits. It can, however, be difficult and costly to achieve, requiring different amounts of capacity in different periods. Moreover, matching demand exactly may not be adequate enough to provide the correct level of quality. In service organizations in particular, operating at full capacity may be associated by customers with negative perceptions of service, such as that it is 'too busy,' 'overcrowded' or 'lacking the personal touch'.

What should be the design of the operations network?

This aspect of the long-term capacity decision area is dealt with in Chapter 3 under the heading of 'Location', to which the reader is referred.

Should the organization do all of the work itself or should some of the tasks be undertaken by third parties?

An integral part of the Philips four-year restructuring plan was to draw more upon outside suppliers for products and services. The complex issues raised by such decisions may lead to different solutions even in very similar operations. All the water authorities in England and Wales, for instance, except for Severn Trent Water Limited, contract out their engineering services.

In many cases the operation does not necessarily have to do the whole range of tasks associated with delivering the basic product or service. In manufacturing, this is usually referred to as the make or buy decision. In the commercial service sector, the issue is sometimes referred to as focusing upon what is the core business of the organization. In the public sector it has become more common to put some aspects of the operation out to competitive tendering. Which way an organization should decide this question will depend upon a complex mix of factors. Some of the relevant items to be considered might be:

- the degree to which involving third parties might compromise confidentiality
- the confidence that third parties can cope not only with the volume and variety, but also with the other performance objectives such as quality and cost
- the availability of competent suppliers
- the effects upon the skill and knowledge base of the people of the operation
- the size of any start-up investment which might be required.

What capacity should the individual operations making up the total network of the organization have?

Once the shape of the network is decided it is necessary to determine the capacities of the individual units. One important factor to be considered here is the degree of connection between the units. If they effectively amount to a chain of internal suppliers and customers, then the real capacity of the network will be governed by the process with least capacity. Such a process is called a bottleneck. The principles developed under optimized production technology might be relevant in this case and these are dealt with in Chapter 8.

Short-term capacity planning

All the above decisions will effectively set the opportunities and constraints within which the operation will have to provide the capacity to meet demand on a shorter timescale. In providing this capacity, other issues arise and there are different approaches available to enable the operation to deal with this task effectively.

Techniques to manage capacity in the short term

1 *Increase the human resources available.* There are various ways in which operations managers can provide extra human resources.

Encouraging overtime work and employing subcontractors will add to the total number of labour hours to be used. Some other means of adding to the labour pool would be to recruit an extra shift and employ part-time workers, either as permanent staff or on temporary contracts.

In dealing with its undercapacity problem in support of its launch, Egg took on several hundred more staff to handle telephone calls.

The cost implications of all of these options will have to be borne in mind and weighed against the benefits of improved performance on the primary objective of meeting the volume and variety demand.

Pizza Hut employs many staff on short-term contracts. Amongst other problems, this has led to very high staff turnover (160 per cent three years ago) and low employee morale. In order to combat these problems the company has transformed its personnel policies. Initiatives have included personal development reviews, new pay and career structures, common induction schemes and one-to-one coaching for new recruits. As a result, the turnover of staff in general has reduced to 100 per cent. Pizza Hut wants to reduce this still further, so that by the year 2000 it is seen as the UK's favourite restaurant employer.

2 *Improve the usage of resources.* Staff can be encouraged to become available at the same time as the peaks in demand occur. Changing shift patterns, part-time work and training staff to have multi-skills will all help in this respect.

The London Borough of Bromley Environmental Health and Trading Standards Service has experienced rising demand and budget reductions. It has still managed to improve its service and one way that this has been achieved is by the introduction of flexible working hours. The Environmental Health Complaints Team has been able to schedule its working hours so that the service is now provided out of office hours until midnight, to the benefit of both users and employees. The Trading Standards Complaint Team introduced home-working and this has increased productivity.

First Direct offers a full banking service via the telephone twenty-four hours a day, seven days a week. All the people who answer telephone calls are trained to handle over eighty per cent of calls without having to transfer callers to some other department within First Direct.

Multiskilling also enables staff to be transferred from one part of the operation to another according to changes in demand. In the service sector especially, the use of part-time employees is a common occurrence.

Where a service involves direct contact with the customer the scheduling of appointments will help to smooth the arrival of the demand and make it more predictable. This will have the effect of improving the utilization of the operation's resources by allocating the demand to times when the operation is available. One problem for the operation is people who reserve a place and do not turn up. Failure to turn up leads to idle capacity. Equally problematic are people who turn up late. This adds to the potential idle capacity problem by introducing an excess of demand when the person does eventually arrive. Some hotels, knowing the average failure to turn up rate from their own experience, in fact reserve over 100 per cent of their capacity. In the event of all the reservations being kept they then pass customers on to other hotels. Hospital appointment systems usually book over

100 per cent to accommodate DNAs (do not attends). In the Magistrates' Courts work is listed knowing that some defendants will change their plea on the day from not guilty to guilty. In order to manage this some courts have introduced systems to enquire into cases before they come to the court to ensure that time is not set aside for trials which will never take place.

In manufacturing, inventory can also be used to similarly smooth the effects of peaks in demand. Where materials are involved, these may be produced ahead of the demand and stored until they are required. (This point was made in Chapter 3 under the heading of 'Manufacturing and service operations'.) In this way, the capacity needed to process the materials (i.e., the material components, people and technology) may be applied when it is available. This gives an operation the ability to produce ahead of peaks in demand, so that it can run with a level capacity that does not vary and yet still meets peaks of demand which exceed this level of capacity. Figure 6.6 makes this point clearer.

By producing to full capacity in the first seven periods, the materials can be stored and used to meet the excessive demand in the following five periods.

These techniques attempt to maintain the capacity at a standard level and this approach is usually described as level capacity planning. If it can be achieved, a level plan will deliver the benefits of high utilization such as high productivity (productivity is discussed in more detail in Chapter 5). On the other hand, such

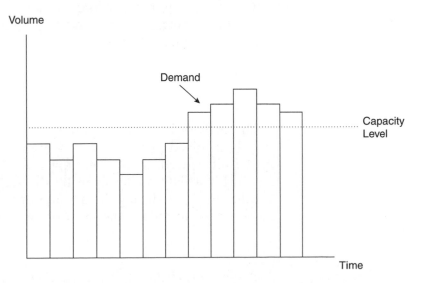

Figure 6.6 Capacity level in relation to peaks and troughs of demand

an approach might have cost implications in areas such as training, inventory and possibly remuneration.

What are the risks associated with an inventory policy aimed at smoothing demand?

3 *Modify the output.* By changing the output the operations manager can reduce the amount of processing required. One way of doing this is to reduce the amount of customization of the output. This has the effect of standardizing the task and making the process more efficient.

Case Study

An example of such an approach can be seen in many supermarket butchery departments. By prepacking cuts of meat the supermarket can greatly increase its output compared with the traditional butcher. The operation is standardized, so that efficiency gains in terms of the usage of people, materials and equipment are secured. This leads to lower operational costs. In contrast, a traditional butcher will offer an individual service. Each customer will have highly differentiated requirements, which means that the times of the transactions are much greater than in the corresponding supermarket operation.

Where there is the opportunity for the customer to become actively involved in the process a greater degree of self-service can be introduced, thereby getting the customer to do some of the work currently undertaken by the staff of the organization. Another way of reducing the amount of time spent on delivering the service is to reduce the level of personal service involved.

Exercise

Think about your involvement in the following processes as a user or customer and identify what aspects of the work of the operation you undertake:

● a supermarket
● a general practitioners' surgery.

4 *Modify the demand.* Marketing tools may be employed to try to influence the pattern of demand. Changing the pricing structure to encourage off-peak usage is a common example. Organizations such as railway operators offer off-peak travel discounts and public houses offer 'happy hours.' Promotion may also be used to achieve the same effect.

5 *Share capacity.* There may be opportunities to share the capacity of other operations at times of peak demand. This is often used in the emergency services, where, say, one police force will transfer some of its officers and detectives to a neighbouring force which is experiencing an exceptional strain upon its resources. Tourist operations like hotels sometimes also share capacity when one hotel is full.

6 *Introduce new products and services for the low demand periods.* Low utilization means high resource costs and some operations are therefore attracted to the idea of offering new products and services in times of low demand. A hotel, for instance, might develop special interest short breaks outside the peak summer season.

7 *Customer queues.* One option is to make the customers of the process wait for their product or service. In manufacturing, Morgan cars are a classic example of this. The average Morgan car owner has to wait several years for delivery. In the service sector, queues are a common phenomenon. This approach ensures that the process is fully occupied but it runs the risk of losing customers who are not prepared to wait. For this reason the service sector has to pay keen attention to the management of queues. Waiting in a queue is a psychological experience and operations managers can take steps to make the experience a positive one rather than a negative one. The following have been suggested as factors that make the queuing experience seem longer and which operations managers can address:

(a) unoccupied time
(b) waiting for the process to begin feels longer than waiting in the process
(c) anxiety
(d) uncertainty about the duration of the wait
(e) unexplained queuing
(f) perceived unfairness of the queue
(g) solo waiting.

Case Study

Queues are a common occurrence in theme parks, and many of the factors identified above are addressed in the design of the parks. At Legoland, Windsor, the time spent queuing for the more popular attractions is occupied by a variety of techniques, including:

● letting the people in the queue see the attraction from where they are standing, so that they observe it as spectators
● installing video players which actually instruct people in the queue about how the attraction works and how they should behave once inside it
● installing video screens to show the attraction as people are currently enjoying it
● employing small distraction games along the length of the longer queues.

Uncertainty about how long the wait will be is reduced by signs indicating the approximate waiting times from various points in the queue.

The fairness of the queues is built into the design of the entry and exit points and also the barriers, so that queue jumping is a blatant act likely to be controlled by adverse reactions from the rest of the people in the queue.

At no point in the park is there a queue that accommodates individuals only. All queues are designed to include groups.

Interestingly, the more valuable the service is to people the more they seem to be prepared to wait for its delivery.

Think of a variety of queues in which you have taken part. How well was your experience of these queues managed by the organizations concerned and why do you think this?

Operations scheduling

The task of allocating people to processes in order to get the work done is known as operations scheduling. In order to accomplish this task operations managers need reliable information on the various elements of capacity at their disposal. Information on some or all of the following may be relevant:

● what the existing and currently projected workload actually is
● the efficiencies of the people and processes concerned
● known holidays
● what tasks have to be completed by the staff and the processes
● how much time each task is likely to take
● expected sick leave.

What information, excluding demand patterns for this exercise, would you need to know in order to schedule the films for a given week at your local multiscreen cinema?

The objectives of scheduling

The main objectives of scheduling are to arrange the jobs to be done so that:

● the product or service is delivered on time
● the operation performs smoothly, giving optimum efficiencies
● the cash flow involved in the operation is balanced.

Forward versus backward scheduling

In planning when to start tasks there are basically two approaches. First, you can decide to begin working at the first possible opportunity. This is called forward scheduling. Second, you can plan to begin working at the latest possible time. This approach is known as backward scheduling.

Forward scheduling brings with it certain advantages. By always planning to start jobs at the first opportunity the utilization of the processes will be high. This approach also means that the future schedule has spare capacity in it, because work is not put off until a later date. As soon as tasks are scheduled for later dates then the capacity required to fulfil them is obviously unavailable for other work that might occur.

Backward scheduling also possesses certain advantages. By delaying the start of the work until the latest possible time the schedule is also putting off committing the cash of the organization until absolutely necessary. The operation is also giving the customers time to solidify their ideas, and any resulting changes will probably be easier to accommodate than under the forward scheduling regime. There is also the, perhaps less obvious, merit that the schedule focuses the operation on customer due dates.

As an example of the way that the two approaches can lead to differing patterns of work consider this situation.

Example

A student has three assignments issued this week. The details are shown in Table 6.2.

Table 6.2

Topic	Date issued	Date due
Managing operations	Week 1	Week 9
Marketing	Week 2	Week 7
Finance	Week 3	Week 6.

The student estimates that the work involved in each is as in Table 6.3.

Table 6.3

	Gathering information	Reading and analysing	Writing answer
Managing operations	1 week	3 weeks	3 days
Marketing	2 weeks	1 week	2 days
Finance	1 week	1 week	1 day

The student also calculates that she can only undertake reading and analysing or writing for one assignment at any one time. For example, she cannot perform reading and analysing for Operations in parallel with reading and analysing or writing for either Marketing or Finance. In addition, she can only work on the assignments for five days per week.

Adopting forward scheduling principles leads to the following schedule. All the activities for Operations are scheduled first, then the activities for Marketing and finally the activities for Finance:

Table 6.4

	Week1	Week2	Week3	Week4	Week5	Week6	Week7	Week8	Week9
Gather information	Ops	M	MF						
Read and analyse		Ops	Ops	Ops	M	M	F		
Write					Ops	M			F

Note: Ops = Managing Operations; M = Marketing; F = Finance

The Operations assignment is ready three-and-a-half weeks before the due week, Marketing one week before and Finance is late.

Under backward scheduling the activities are now scheduled in the order of due date first, which means that time is allocated first to Finance, then to Marketing and finally to Operations. The pattern of the schedule changes to that in Table 6.5. In this case all of the assignments are now delivered on time.

Table 6.5

	Week1	Week2	Week3	Week4	Week5	Week6	Week7	Week8	Week9
Gather information	M, Ops	M	F	F					
Read and analyse	Ops	M	F	F	Ops	Ops	Ops		
Write		F	M	Ops					

Exercise

Using first forward scheduling and then backward scheduling, plan using the grids in Figure 6.7 the following two jobs on two facilities:

● Job 1 (due at hour 10): three hours on facility A, two hours on facility B, one hour on A and two hours on B.
● Job 2 (due at hour 12): one hour on A, one hour on B, two hours on A, three hours on B.

Note that the sequence A, B, A, B must be followed.
    Then see if Job 3 can also be accommodated. It is due at hour 15 and requires two hours on A, two on B, one on A and one on B.
    Note that the sequence A, B, A, B must still be followed.

The complexity of scheduling

Study of the above exercise reveals that these two schedules are not the only ones possible for the student concerned. You might, for instance, feel that the backward schedule is preferable but want to change it so that the student begins reading and analysing Operations in parallel with gathering the information in week 1. In other words, you might want to change the schedule slightly by forward scheduling this particular activity. The ability to find more than two options in this situation should not be surprising, as scheduling often

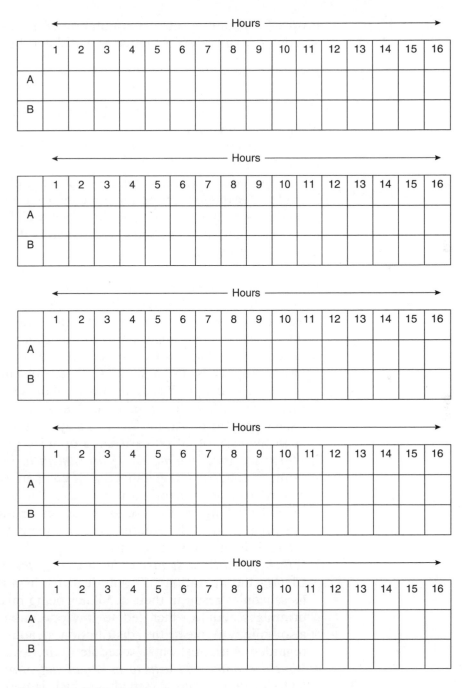

Figure 6.7 Grids for exercise

involves a complex set of permutations. The possible number of schedules in any given situation is calculated by

$$(n!)^m \qquad\qquad (6.2)$$

where n = the number of jobs to be scheduled and m = the number of processes involved.

In the example of the assignments there are thus $(3!)^3$ options, i.e., 216 permutations.

Any proposed schedule will, therefore, not be the only one possible. Deciding which option appears to be the best will depend upon the particular situation and there may well be a range of factors to be taken into account. Some of the factors that might be relevant include the following.

1 *Which schedule actually leads to the lowest cost for the operation?* Generally, a schedule requiring few changes to the process will lead to lower costs than one that needs the process to change often. The changes might be to the skills, equipment or facilities needed. Such changes usually require downtime, i.e., the process has to stop whilst the new skills etc. are put in place. Downtime is a waste of the productive resources of the operation and should, therefore, be kept to a minimum. This is an especially important issue where the downtime involves major capital investments, such as in the case of oil refineries and brewing plants.

2 *Which schedule minimizes the investment in inventory?* This is a primary concern for manufacturing companies, where materials can represent a major part of the costs of the operation. A schedule calling for the use of expensive or bulky items later in the programme will require less investment than one that calls for such items to be used earlier.

3 *Which schedule best meets the needs of the customer or user?* Clearly the operation will only lead to dissatisfied customers if its schedules result in their deadlines being missed. A newspaper printing schedule which led to low operations costs but which also failed to meet the distribution deadlines would not be regarded as a satisfactory schedule by its readers.

4 *Which schedule will help to maintain staff morale and individual levels of motivation?* A schedule which is perceived by the staff who have to make it work as unfair or unreasonable will risk damaging the levels of both morale and motivation within the operation.

Exercise

Imagine that you are to draw up a schedule for your examination revision. What factors would you use to determine which was the best schedule?

In order to help schedulers through the complex set of options that might be available certain guidelines have been formulated. These cannot be followed slavishly, but they can help to indicate what priority rule might be most appropriate in a given situation. Amongst these guidelines are the following:

● Meet the delivery requirements of the important customers first.
● Begin work on the earliest due date job first.
● Begin work on the job that arrived first in time.
● Begin work on the job that arrived last in time.
● Undertake the longest job first.
● Start the quickest job first.

The relevance of each of these guidelines will vary according to the circumstances faced by the scheduler.

Gantt charts

The Gantt chart is a useful tool for both devising and communicating schedules. The basic format of the chart is to list all the required activities down the left axis of the chart and display the relevant planning time horizon across the top axis running from left to right. It is then a matter of depicting the start and end dates of each activity against the time horizon by blotting out the relevant time periods with a bar. The basic format of the chart is as shown in Figure 6.8.

For the backward schedule for the student's assignments exercise earlier in this section, a Gantt chart might look like the one shown in Figure 6.9.

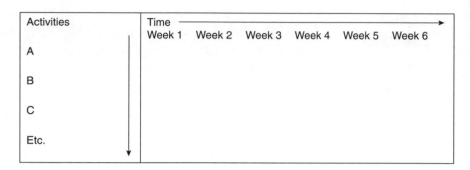

Figure 6.8 Basic format of a Gantt chart

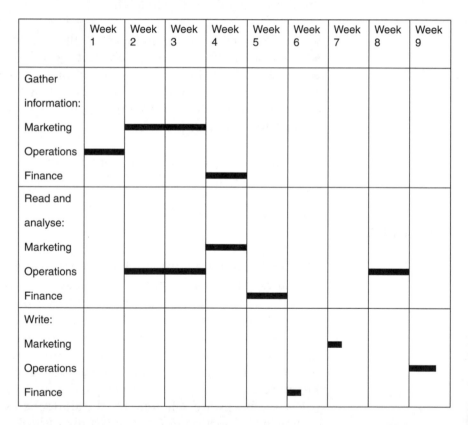

Figure 6.9 A backward scheduling Gantt chart for the previous example

Bob is in charge of two production lines at a crisp factory. The schedule of work allocated to these two lines for next week is as follows:

Line A for private label
Plain: Monday a.m.
Salt and vinegar: Monday p.m., Tuesday a.m.
Beef: Tuesday p.m.
Prawn: Wednesday a.m.
Cheese and onion: Wednesday p.m., all Thursday
Chicken: Friday all day
Line B for own label
Plain: Monday all day
Salt and vinegar: Tuesday am
Beef: Tuesday p.m.
Prawn: all Wednesday
Cheese and onion: all Thursday, Friday a.m.
Chicken: Friday p.m.

Draw a Gantt chart to communicate this schedule.

Planning and control
In any operation the allocation of capacity will be more orderly and effective if it is well planned. The test for deciding if a plan is good is to ask how far it supports the overall objectives of the organization and meets the volume and variety demands of the users and customers.

Forecasting
Fundamental to the success of the capacity plan is the accuracy of the estimate of demand underpinning it. Where the demand is from an internal customer the demand is said to be dependent, and this requirement can be estimated with a high degree of certainty. If the demand is from an external customer, then it is described as independent and forecasting such demand is a riskier business. Analysis of past data is very important, especially in the case of independent demand. An essential pattern to look for in the data is its trend.

A number of techniques have been described (see 'Appendix: a summary of forecasting techniques' at the end of this chapter for details):

- time series methods – moving average, seasonal indexing and exponential smoothing
- regression analysis.

The factors influencing the usefulness of a forecast are its clarity over the units of capacity, the degree of its accuracy and the timeliness with which its information is delivered. One measure of accuracy is the mean absolute deviation. The lower this figure, the more accurate the forecast.

Differing planning time horizons

This topic has been dealt with under two broad headings, namely, the long term and the short term.

Long-term capacity planning has to resolve some difficult problems. Those highlighted in the chapter are:

- Should capacity be provided in excess of demand, below demand or to match demand as exactly as possible?
- Where should the facilities making up the operation be located?
- How much of the total task should the organization do itself and how much should it employ others to do on its behalf?
- How should the capacities of each individual operational unit be balanced?

Short-term capacity planning involves a number of techniques to adjust the ability of the operation to meet the volume and variety demands placed upon it. A number of these techniques are described:

- *Increasing the human resources available*, by offering overtime work and employing extra labour.
- *Improving the usage of resources*, by adjusting working patterns, multiskilling, scheduling appointments and building inventory stocks.
- *Modifying the output*, by reducing the amount of customization, introducing self-service and making the service less personal.
- *Modifying the demand*, through the marketing tools of price and promotion.
- *Sharing capacity* with other operations of a similar nature.
- *Introducing new products and services* to stimulate demand for the quieter periods.
- *Queuing customers*, thereby making people wait for their product or service.

Scheduling

The aim of scheduling is to allocate people to jobs in the short term so that the operation runs smoothly, giving both timely delivery and an acceptable cash flow. Most scheduling situations involve a wide range of choices and some of the more important principles involved have been covered. By taking a forward scheduling approach jobs will be allocated to begin as soon as possible. In contrast, a backward scheduling approach begins jobs at the latest possible moment. Over time several rules of thumb to guide scheduling decisions have been developed and six of these have been mentioned. A useful tool for both devising and communicating plans is the Gantt chart. This presents the tasks to be completed down the left side of the chart and indicates their start and duration times against the planning horizon, which is shown at the top of the chart.

Appendix: a summary of forecasting techniques

Time series forecasting methods

Time series techniques are useful in the short term, for instance where the demand for a service is hard to predict intuitively and the operation does not have the spare capacity in place to cope with the peaks. Time series analysis uses the past records of demand to predict what the future volume and variety is likely to be.

One method of time series forecasting is *moving average forecasting*. The simple moving average combines data over a past period and how far back the data goes is determined by the forecaster. The formula for calculating the simple moving average is

$$\frac{\Sigma n \, demands}{n} \tag{6.3}$$

where n = the number of past periods to be used.

Example

Demand for the past six months has been: January, 200; February, 300; March, 200; April, 400; May, 300; June, 500.
   Using a six-month moving average, the forecast for July is given by:

$$\frac{200 + 300 + 200 + 400 + 300 + 500}{6} = \frac{1900}{6} = 317 \ (6.4)$$

Given that this is substantially lower than the June experience it would be wise to check whether those close to the source of the demand expect a reduction in July.

Demand for the last six months is: January 9; February 12; March 11; April 6; May 13; June 10.

What is the forecast for July using a six month moving average?

The simple moving average can also be used to identify the trend in past data.

Example

Suppose that the simple moving average is to be calculated on a four-week basis and that we have the data in Table 6.6.

Table 6.6

Week	Demand
1	110
2	100
3	112
4	114
5	98
6	120
7	101
8	115
9	118
10	102

The four-week moving average gives the trend in Table 6.7.

Table 6.7

Week	Demand	Trend
1	110	
2	100	
3	112	
4	114	109
5	98	106
6	120	111
7	101	108
8	115	109
9	118	114
10	102	109

The trend can be used as the basis for analysing the seasonality of the data. One approach is by calculating the seasonal index for the data. This is a development of the moving average method and the data used in the computation of the trend can be used to illustrate the approach. The data is reproduced again in Table 6.8.

Table 6.8

1	110
2	100
3	112
4	114
5	98
6	120
7	101
8	115
9	118
10	102

Exercise

The presence of a seasonal pattern in the data can be detected by a straight-line graph. Draw such a graph of the data for the ten weeks.

The seasonal pattern runs across a five-week cycle, with the pattern of week one being higher than week 2, week 2 being lower than week 3, week 3 being lower than week 4 and week 5 dips significantly. Table 6.9 below shows this more clearly.

Table 6.9

Seasonal period	Demand for season 1	Demand for season 2
1	110	120
2	100	101
3	112	115
4	114	118
5	98	102

In order to identify the relevant trend the moving average should, therefore, be calculated on a five-week basis. Before proceeding with the calculation of the moving average, the seasonal index approach requires that the trend be 'centred'. This is slightly different from the way in which the trend was positioned in the previous section. A centred trend is one where each moving average figure is located in the centre of the data from which it is drawn. For example, the first moving average figure is given by:

$$\frac{110 + 100 + 112 + 114 + 98}{5} = 106.8 \tag{6.5}$$

This figure is now located in the middle of its data set, i.e., 106.8 is the trend figure for period 3. Progressing in this manner through the data gives the results as in Table 6.10.

Table 6.10

Week	Demand	Centred trend
1	110	
2	100	
3	112	106.8
4	114	108.8
5	98	109
6	120	109.6
7	101	110.4
8	115	111.2
9	118	
10	102	

By dividing each actual demand figure by its corresponding centred trend figure the seasonal effect (and the unassignable factors) in the data can be identified. Thus, week 3 shows $112 \div 106.8$ as the seasonal effect, i.e. 1.049. The full seasonal-unassignable effect is shown in Table 6.11.

Table 6.11

Week	Demand	Centred trend	Seasonal-unassignable component
1	110		
2	100		
3	112	106.8	1.049
4	114	108.8	1.048
5	98	109	0.899
6	120	109.6	1.095
7	101	110.4	0.915
8	115	111.2	1.034
9	118		
10	102		

The variations in the seasonal-unassignable component for any one period in the season across time are due to the unassignable factors. These effects can be smoothed out by calculating the mean seasonal-unassignable figure for each period. The resulting figure is called the seasonal index. For example, weeks 3 and 8 share the same point in the seasonal pattern, so that the mean of their seasonal-unassignable components can be taken as the more accurate guide to the seasonal effect in the middle period of the season. The mean in this case is 1.049 + 1.034 ÷ 2 = 1.042, so that the seasonal index for the middle period of the whole season is 1.042 (Table 6.12).

Table 6.12

Week	Demand	Centred trend	Seasonal unassignable component	Seasonal index
1	110			
2	100			
3	112	106.8	1.049	1.042
4	114	108.8	1.048	
5	98	109	0.899	
6	120	109.6	1.095	
7	101	110.4	0.915	
8	115	111.2	1.034	1.042
9	118			
10	102			

This means that for the middle period of the season, demand will be 4.2 per cent higher than the trend. The forecast for the middle period of the next season is thus:

$$111.2 \times 1.042 = 115.87 \tag{6.6}$$

Given that the last two demands have been 112 and 115, this might be thought to be too pessimistic. An alternative forecast would be the last demand experienced multiplied by the seasonal index:

$$115 \times 1.042 = 119.83 \tag{6.7}$$

One final adjustment to the seasonal index is sometimes necessary. The mean of the index figures should equal 1. If this is not the case, then each seasonal index figure must be multiplied by:

$$\frac{\textit{the number of periods in the season}}{\textit{the sum of the unadjusted seasonal index figures}} \tag{6.8}$$

Incorporate the additional demand data in Table 6.13 into the format of the demand table above (Table 6.12) and calculate the centred trend, the seasonal-unassignable component and the seasonal index. Adjust the seasonal index if this is necessary. On the basis of your calculations, what would be your forecast for demand over the next five weeks?

Table 6.13

Week	Demand
11	131
12	102
13	118
14	122
15	106
16	143
17	103
18	121
19	126
20	111

Another time series technique is *exponential smoothing*. This method calculates a forecast on the basis of the old forecast plus the actual demand just experienced. The forecaster has to determine how much weight to give to the forecast and how much to give to the actual demand. The formula is

$$\alpha \text{ (most recent demand)} + (1 - \alpha) \text{ (most recent forecast)} \quad (6.9)$$

where α = the weighting factor (known as the smoothing constant). The value of α can vary between 0 and 1.

Example

Suppose that the forecast for the current period was 20 and that the actual demand was 24. If a value of .9 is given to the forecast, then the calculation for the next period becomes:

.9(20) + .1(24)
= 18 + 2.4   (6.10)
= 20.4

Exercise

Sales in week 20 are 35 compared to a forecast of 40. What will be the forecast sales in week 21 using an exponentially weighted average with the actual demand experience being given a weight of .2?

Regression analysis

Regression analysis is a long-term forecasting technique. It is most useful where there are identified influences affecting the demand pattern. For example, where the management are trying to influence demand through advertising, the likely effect of the advertising can be estimated by using regression analysis. Regression analysis may also be used to provide a forecast based upon past data.

The formula for finding the regression straight line of best fit is

$$y = a + b(x)$$ (6.11)

where

y = the amount to be estimated
a = the point where the line intercepts the y axis
b = the gradient of the line
x = the time period.

The value of a is given by:

$$a = \frac{\Sigma Y}{n} - b\left(\frac{\Sigma x}{n}\right)$$ (6.12)

The value of b is given by:

$$b = \frac{n\Sigma xy - \Sigma x\Sigma y}{n\Sigma x^2 - (\Sigma x)^2} \qquad (6.13)$$

In these formulas

x = time, usually denoted by a simple coding system where number 1 represents the first time period, number 2 the second time period and so on consecutively
y = the demand value
n = the number of demand items in the sample.

Example

Suppose that the record of demand is as shown in Table 6.14.

Table 6.14

Year	Quarter	Units
1998	1	4500
1998	2	2400
1998	3	6100
1998	4	2900
1999	1	7700
1999	2	9600
1999	3	6700

The calculations for the regression formula are as shown in Table 6.15.

Table 6.15

Year	Quarter	Code for Time $- x$	Demand y (th.)	xy	x^2
1998	1	1	4.5	4.5	1
1998	2	2	2.4	4.8	4
1998	3	3	6.1	18.3	9
1998	4	4	2.9	11.6	16

Table 6.15 (continued)

Year	Quarter	Code for Time − x	Demand y (th.)	xy	x²
1999	1	5	7.7	38.5	25
1999	2	6	9.6	57.6	36
1999	3	7	6.7	46.9	49
Totals		28	39.9	182.2	140

Substituting gives:

$$b = \frac{n\Sigma xy - \Sigma x\Sigma y}{n\Sigma x^2 - (\Sigma x)^2} = \frac{7(182.2) - 28(39.9)}{7(140) - 784}$$

$$= \frac{1275.4 - 1117.2}{980 - 784} = \frac{158.2}{196} = 0.807 \tag{6.14}$$

Demand will therefore increase by 807 units per quarter.

$$a = \frac{\Sigma Y}{n} - b\left(\frac{\Sigma x}{n}\right) = \frac{39.9}{7} - 0.807(28/7)$$

$$= 5.7 - 3.228$$

$$= 2.472 \tag{6.15}$$

The value of a indicates that the demand line originates at 2472 units.

Using this model to predict the demand for the next quarter, i.e., 1999 Quarter 4, requires the values of a, b and x to be substituted into the formula.

Demand = 2472 + 807(8)

$$= 2472 + 6456$$

$$= 8928 \tag{6.16}$$

Exercise

An enterprising group of students decide to investigate the feasibility of opening a drinks and food bar just for students. As a part of their research they find that the catering services in universities report differing sales levels according to the size of the student population covered. The data is shown in Table 6.16.

Table 6.16

Annual sales (000)	Student population (000)
64	2.2
116	6.6
96	8.8
130	8.8
129	13.2
151	17.7
173	22.0
186	22.0

Using regression analysis, forecast the likely level of sales where the student population is 10 000.

Self Assessment

1 Insert the missing words in the following statement: 'The capacity of the organization may be defined as its _____ to undertake the _____ demanded by its _____.'
2 Plans:
   (a) must be computerized
   (b) never change
   (c) specify how resources will be allocated
   (d) ignore corporate objectives
   (e) balance demand and corporate objectives?
3 Where one process supplies another process this is a situation of independent demand. True or false?
4 The general direction of the demand pattern is called its trend. True or false?
5 In your own words define the meaning of seasonality.
6 Seasonality may only occur at quarterly periods. True or false?
7 Unassignable variations in demand are:
   (a) caused by trends

(b) caused by seasonality

(c) caused by unknown factors?

8 Which mean absolute deviation shows the most accurate forecast:

(a) the lowest mean absolute deviation

(b) the highest mean absolute deviation?

9 Identify the three main features of a good forecast.

10 Organizations should always plan to:

(a) exceed expected demand

(b) keep capacity below demand

(c) match capacity to demand exactly

(d) adopt the level of capacity which seems to best fit the situation?

11 Identify three terms that refer to the basic question of how much of the total task should be performed by the operation.

12 Give at least three ways of increasing human resource capacity in the short term.

13 Name at least three ways that resource usage can be improved in the short-term.

14 Level capacity means:

(a) adjusting capacity to follow demand

(b) keeping capacity fixed

(c) always having too much capacity?

15 Modifying the output has little to offer as a way of managing capacity better. True or false?

16 How can marketing help operations to manage capacity in the short term?

17 All of the following make queuing a more positive experience, except:

(a) entertaining the queue

(b) informing the queue of the duration of the waiting time

(c) allowing 'queue jumping'

(d) avoiding solo waiting?

18 Insert the missing words in the following statement: 'The task of allocating people to processes in order to get the work done is known as _____ _____.'

19 The objectives of scheduling include the following, except:

(a) providing excess capacity

(b) ensuring on-time delivery

(c) providing optimum efficiencies

(d) balancing cash flow?

20 Forward scheduling brings the following advantages, except:

(a) high utilization

(b) preserving future capacity

(c) committing resources until absolutely necessary?

21 List at least two factors to be used in evaluating the best scheduling option.
22 Sketch in outline the basic format of a Gantt chart.

Further reading

Baker, K. R. (1984). *Introduction to Sequencing and Scheduling.* John Wiley.

Fitzsimmons, J. A. and Fitzsimmons, M. J. (1994). *Service Management for Competitive Advantage.* McGraw-Hill.

Lovelock, C. H. (1992). *Managing Service.* Prentice-Hall.

Chapter 7

Planning and control of work: the management of materials

Operations are in most organizations an important factor in both the successful delivery of the basic purpose and the total costs incurred. The purpose of this chapter is to review one particular resource and its links to these two factors. This resource is the material used by the organization. In particular, the chapter addresses the following questions:

Learning Objectives

1 *What do we mean by materials?* The term 'materials' has several meanings. The chapter will describe some of the more important of these definitions. It should become clear that materials are an important resource in all operations, not just manufacturing.
2 *What do we mean by a materials system?* Like many of the resources involved in operations, materials behave in a dynamic way. In other words, the resource changes over time. The chapter outlines some of the important ways in which

materials behave and explores some of the important factors in materials management situations.

3 *What is materials management trying to achieve?* The basic objective has already been indicated, that is, to support the effectiveness and efficiency of the operation. In the context of materials management this overarching objective takes on some more specific meanings.

4 *What are the key questions for managers of materials?* The chapter will explore the key questions in inventory management situations, namely:
   (a) How often should stock levels be checked?
   (b) When should an order for more stock be placed?
   (c) What quantity should be ordered?

5 *What techniques are available to the manager?* In previous chapters techniques have been introduced which can help operations managers to resolve the problems and opportunities facing them. In relation to materials management, there are also some specific approaches that can help to deal with the situations that arise. These techniques will be introduced at a basic level.

At the end of the chapter, the reader will have a sound understanding of the basic factors involved in managing the materials resource and will be prepared for the development of this subject in Chapter 8.

Introduction

In the previous chapter the task of planning and controlling the operation in order to meet the demands placed upon it was discussed. This discussion centred upon how to provide the resources required in a general sense, covering, for instance, facilities, people and materials. This chapter develops the approach by focusing upon one of these resources, namely materials, also called inventory or stock.

All organizations need to acquire and use materials if they are to function properly. This statement is manifestly true for manufacturing organizations. In manufacturing the whole point of the operation is to work on materials in some way so that they are transformed into something of value. A walk around a car factory would make this immediately obvious. The overwhelming impression would be of car components such as chassis, doors and steering wheels being processed.

In the service sector we are perhaps less aware of the role of materials in supporting the service delivered, and yet a small pause for thought reveals that in this sector also materials have a role to play in the smooth operation of the delivery process. This is more obvious in services where materials make up a substantial part of the service package. In the food sector, for instance, a McDonald's restaurant without materials such as burgers, buns, cups and food packaging would be a very ineffective operation. In other services the role of materials is less a part of the service package and yet they still have an important role to play. Universities use a wide range of materials, from paper and chairs to technical equipment like computers. Local authority departments such as building and highway maintenance cannot function without materials such as doors and grit for the roads respectively. Seen in this light, the good management of materials is essential for both the efficiency and effectiveness of a wide range of operations.

This chapter therefore explains what is meant by the term 'materials'. The chapter then goes on to consider the basic aspects of the way in which material systems behave and how they can be managed.

Types of materials

Accountants classify materials as 'raw materials', 'work in progress' and 'finished goods'. These terms are also in common use in the field of operations management.

Raw materials are those items which are stored waiting to be worked on as a part of the delivery processes of the organization. Physically, they can usually be found, therefore, in a warehouse or stockroom from which the operational staff withdraw stock as they require it. Work in progress is material that is being worked as a part of the process. When this work is completed the material will have been transformed into its final state and is ready to move down the supply chain. Inventory in this state is referred to as finished goods.

Case Study

These terms can be illustrated in the context of a McDonald's restaurant. Potatoes, buns and meat etc. are stored in the restaurant unit just beyond the cooking area. At this stage the items are raw materials. When the potatoes etc. are drawn into the cooking area for processing they become work in progress. The notion of finished goods stocks is exemplified by the filled meal containers stacked on the racking behind the counter staff. In this case, of course, the finished goods remain stored for only a very short space of time.

Some other classifications of inventory are also in common use. 'Consumable materials' refers to those materials that are used (i.e., consumed) by the process but which do not form a part of the direct material that is passed down the supply chain. Oil to lubricate the machinery of the process would be an example of this type of material. Another classification is 'service' or 'spare parts'. In some industries the outputs from the process are retained as spare items to provide support for users in the event of future breakdowns or exhaustion. Manufacturers of televisions need to be able to provide replacement on/off switches for the lives of their models for instance.

Case Study

Morgan cars prides itself on being able to provide spare parts for models which it produced over forty years ago. These spares are stored on its main site and are seen as an essential part of the company's commitment to the Morgan car enthusiasts. The availability of spares is perceived to be an important part of the brand image.

One final category of inventory is 'buffer stocks'. Buffer stocks are materials that are being deliberately used to protect the operation from the otherwise disruptive effects of interruptions to supply or sudden increases in demand. Thus, raw materials, work in progress and finished goods might all be used to act as buffer stocks. Raw materials might be stockpiled to protect against possible supplier failures due, for example, to industrial action or extreme weather conditions. Work in progress might be built up prior to a key process so that it can keep on working even if supplying processes breakdown for a period. Finished goods can be built up so that sudden increases in demand can be met from stock so that the process is given time to increase its output in response.

The basic concepts of materials systems

A generalized view of the operation of a materials system is portrayed in Figure 7.1.

At the start of the time period the stock level is high. Over time, however, the usage of this material diminishes the amount available on the site. Clearly, if this trend were allowed to progress unchecked, the result would be that all inventory would be exhausted. In order to avoid this the organization has to decide at some point to request more supplies of the material. The point at which it does this is known as the reorder level. In other words, at some agreed level of stock reduction more stock will be ordered. Stock usage continues so that the amount available on the site maintains its decline. At some time after the request for more material is made the stock will actually be delivered. The time which elapses from the placing

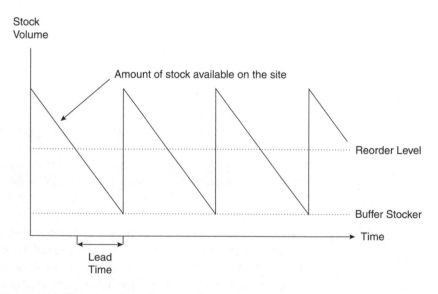

Figure 7.1 The operation of a materials system

of the order for more material to the material actually being delivered is known as the lead time. An organization will know the average lead times of its suppliers and it will therefore try to ensure that it has on hand enough material to cover the longer times that can be expected. In this way continuity of material supply will be maintained to the operation even if the supplier is a little late meeting the order. In Figure 7.1 more material is delivered by the supplier just as the buffer (or safety) stock is about to be called into use. This pattern then continues through the remainder of the diagram. It will be apparent that in addition to the setting of the buffer stock and reorder levels, the system requires someone to decide on the precise amount of stock to be reordered.

Exercise

How far does this description describe the behaviour of domestic household stores of food items?

The aims of materials management

Having set out the basic features of an inventory system, it is appropriate to identify the objectives which managers will bring to bear when they try to plan and control these features. It is these objectives which will guide how the organization uses the techniques covered in the rest of this chapter and also the areas covered in Chapter 8.

One of the main aims is to maintain a steady supply of materials so that the operation continues to run smoothly. A surgical operation that has to stop because of a lack of blood plasma or a manufacturing process which halts because it has run out of a component has a lot of adverse implications. Clearly, the processes are not delivering their primary purpose. This might lead to dissatisfied customers, which in turn can lead to lost support for the organization. The enforced idleness of the operation will probably incur costs associated with staff, equipment and facilities. The very act of stopping a process in an unplanned manner may also incur extra costs for the organization. Moreover, the situation of being out of stock will probably require urgent attention so that the supply is resumed as quickly as possible. This will add to demands on staff time and might incur cost penalties with suppliers for their rapid response.

Given the potential adverse consequences of going out of stock, there is clearly a strong incentive to maintain stock levels at such a high volume that the operation is virtually guaranteed a constant supply, no matter how inefficient the management of stock becomes. This option, however, is not a valid one in most circumstances.

1 Stock levels have financial implications. In terms of cash flow, stock represents money out of the organization. High stock levels can therefore be a substantial brake on the cash flow of an organization, with the material items being paid for long before they are put to use. Moreover, the operation will incur costs in simply managing the stock it has. These costs might be related to the staff involved in stock management, the facilities used to store items and any interest paid on capital borrowed to fund stock purchases.

2 Stock represents certain risks, and by holding large amounts of stock the organization increases its exposure to these risks. Such risks arise from factors such as the likelihood that the stock will become obsolescent or damaged whilst in storage.

3 High stock levels can be a powerful force against improvement. The problems of an inefficient operation can be hidden by customary large amounts of inventory. Poor forecasting, haphazard scheduling, ineffective communication etc., can be accommodated by always having stock on hand to cushion the operation from the adverse effects of such practices (see Chapter 8 also). In the modern environment in which operations function all operations have to continuously improve in order to satisfy their stakeholders and hiding problems is not acceptable.

As a result, the task of managing materials is to achieve a balance between the advantages of maintaining stock and the disadvantages of high stock levels.

Exercise

Formulate a set of objectives that might be appropriate for a manager of materials.

Performance measures for materials systems

Various measures can be formulated to measure both the efficiency and the effectiveness of stock management within an organization. This section covers two main categories of measures.

Customer service level

Case Study

The major supermarket chains, such as Tesco and Sainsbury, usually demand 100 per cent customer service from their suppliers. This means that they expect all their orders for food, for instance, to be met on time all the time. They take a dim view of any supplier who leaves them with empty shelf space.

Customer service is indicated by how often the operation delivers materials exactly when they are needed. Customers, of course, may be internal or external to the organization.

Customer service can be measured either as a percentage figure or as an absolute number. An example of a percentage measure would be:

$$\frac{number\ of\ orders\ met\ on\ time}{total\ number\ of\ orders\ placed} \times 100 \qquad (7.1)$$

An absolute measure would be:

number of orders not met.

Inventory investment

The total value of all inventory (raw materials, work in progress and finished goods) in the operational process is an important measure of efficiency. Once obtained this information can be used to provide a number of absolute and relative measures.

As an absolute figure, the total investment can be compared to budgeted standards in order to allow for any variances to be identified and investigated. If the figure is a projected figure against the forecast levels of activity then it can be used to indicate the future cash flow effects of the inventory required.

Relative measures are also important indicators of how well the inventory is being managed. One such measure is inventory turnover, which is given by a formula such as:

$$\frac{total\ cost\ of\ sales}{average\ inventory\ value} \qquad (7.2)$$

Case Study

IKEA has a higher inventory turnover than its major competitors. This helps to fuel investment in the growth of the organization, which has expanded to cover most of the conurbations in England.

Where sales performance is not relevant, an alternative measure could be:

$$\frac{total\ inventory\ budget}{average\ inventory\ value} \qquad (7.3)$$

The higher the ratio, the more the financial investment in inventory is being worked. High ratios, therefore, indicate better performance. It is possible to generate a wide range of customer service and inventory investment measures. No particular measure will be right or wrong. The important criteria are that the measures employed should be understood, practical and useful to those who manage in the situation in which they are used.

Exercise

Review the objectives that you set in the previous exercise. What measures could you use to monitor performance against those objectives?

ABC analysis of stock

ABC analysis is a very useful tool for understanding inventory management situations. It can help to suggest where the real problems/opportunities lie and what steps should be taken.

ABC analysis is based upon the Pareto principle. This principle is that many situations are dominated by a few key elements. This has been summarized as the 80/20 rule, i.e., 80 per cent of a situation is probably dominated by 20 per cent of its constituent elements. In inventory management terms, we should look at the data on cost and usage to see if a large part of the total inventory budget is accounted for by relatively few of the inventory items. We may not always find such a relationship, but frequently it does hold true. If the 80/20 relationship is found we can then channel our energies to gain the maximum reward for our efforts.

The ABC analysis procedure

The ABC analysis procedure consists of three main steps.

1 Calculate the monetary values of the stock items.
2 Produce a Pareto table or graph.
3 Classify the stock items into ABC categories.

Each of these steps will now be considered in turn. In order to provide a context for the review of ABC analysis, the following data will be used.

Example

The details in Table 7.1 have been taken from a representative sample of stock items held by a local authority distribution warehouse.

From an initial scan of the information in Table 7.1, what problems can you identify which suggest that this inventory control system can be improved? Would computerizing this system help the management task at this stage?

Table 7.1

Item reference	Stock balance (units)	Unit value £	Average usage per month (units)	Reorder level (units)
R175	6 320	17.20	1 920	5 000
R246	5 380	14.40	1 690	5 000
N682	1 840	3.04	5 230	4 000
S220	Nil	10.00	1 210	800
S293	13 590	1.60	4 090	10 000
R401	1 450	14.40	270	1 000
N266	8 075	1.36	2 760	6 000
N630	Nil	4.48	810	900
F101	153	3.60	750	1 000
M385	525	11.20	230	300
F437	1 362	1.60	1240	2 000
S153	3 000	20.00	80	2 500
F197	4 325	0.56	2 460	3 000
D114	2 520	6.48	200	2 000
M225	Nil	1.44	450	400
N422	587	0.12	1 630	2 000

Calculate the monetary values of the stock items

The monetary value of each stock item is given by the following calculation:

$$material\ item\ unit\ value \times usage \qquad (7.4)$$

The result of this calculation is known as the requirement value for the item:

$$requirement\ value = material\ item\ unit\ value \times usage \qquad (7.5)$$

Produce a Pareto table or graph

The Pareto table should rank the items in descending order of value, so that the single largest value item is placed at the top of the table and the lowest value item is at the bottom. Presented this way it is clear where most of the budget expenditure is consumed. Suitable headings for such a table would be: Stock item; Usage; Unit value; Requirement value; Cumulative requirement value; Percentage of total value.

Presented in this way it is clear if a Pareto relationship exists as can be seen in Table 7.2.

Classify the stock items into ABC categories

The reason for the Pareto analysis is to enable the task of managing inventory to be focused so that the maximum reward is obtained

Table 7.2 ABC analysis example

Item reference	Unit value £	Average monthly usage	Monthly requirement value £	Cumulative requirement value £	Cumulative % of total value
R175	17.20	1 920	33 024.00	33 024.00	0.29
R246	14.40	1 690	24 336.00	57 360.00	0.50
N682	3.04	5 230	15 899.20	73 259.20	0.63
S220	10.00	1 210	12 100.00	85 359.20	0.74
S293	1.60	4 090	6 544.00	91 903.20	0.80
R401	14.40	270	3 888.00	95 791.20	0.83
N266	1.36	2 760	3 753.60	99 544.80	0.86
N630	4.48	810	3 628.80	103 173.60	0.89
F101	3.60	750	2 700.00	105 873.60	0.92
M385	11.20	230	2 576.00	108 449.60	0.94
F437	1.60	1 240	1 984.00	110 433.60	0.96
S153	20.00	80	1 600.00	112 033.60	0.97
F197	0.56	2 460	1 377.60	113 411.20	0.98
D114	6.48	200	1 296.00	114 707.20	0.99
M225	1.44	450	648.00	115 355.20	1.00
N422	0.12	1 630	195.60	115 550.80	1.00*
			115 550.80		

Note: * Error due to rounding to two decimal places.

for the effort invested. This focusing is achieved by classifying the items into categories and then managing each category in a different manner. The guidelines for classifying inventory under the Pareto analysis can be stated briefly. A items should be those items which account for the bulk of the total expenditure. In a classic Pareto relationship, the A items will be those accounting for approximately 80 per cent of the value. The B items will be those items that consume around 15 per cent of the total value, with the remainder being classified as C items.

1 *A Items*. Decisions about A items can be crucial to organizational efficiency and effectiveness. It is important that such decisions are made with the involvement of a wide range of the management team. In terms of control, most effort should be expanded on the A items. It is these that will yield the greatest financial payback. Table 7.3 contains appropriate starting point guidelines for A items.
2 *B Items*. For B items the control actions indicated for A items are still appropriate starting points, but the frequency of the activities can be less. Buffer stocks can be allowed to be a little higher than the levels associated with the A class of items.

Table 7.3

Aspect of control	Appropriate actions
Forecasts	Forecasts should be evaluated regularly for accuracy and the forecasting method should be challenged for improvements in accuracy.
Data records	The data records on usage and stock levels should be updated frequently (e.g. daily). Data accuracy should be very high, with 100 per cent accuracy the goal.
Management parameters	All the assumptions underpinning order quantities and safety stock levels should be reviewed under continuous improvement activities.
Inventory tracking	The movement of these materials through the whole supply chain should be monitored closely so that expediting is conducted most effectively to keep workable stock levels low.
Buffer stocks	As these items are of very high value, buffer stocks should be kept as low as is practical.

Table 7.4

Aspect of control	Appropriate actions
Forecasts	Not needed
Data records	Very simple. Count the items annually or half-yearly.
Management parameters	Operate with large order quantities and safety stocks.
Inventory tracking	Minimal.
Buffer stocks	These can be allowed to be higher than in the case of B items.

3 *C Items*. Physical stock checks are not a high priority in this category. A reorder point system based on the principles of the two-bin method (see 'The continuous review fixed reorder quantity system' section in this chapter) should suffice. If periodic stock checks are to be performed they should take place at long intervals. The planning assumptions made about demand, lead times and costs should be reviewed on a far less frequent basis, perhaps half-yearly or annually. Table 7.4 contains appropriate starting point guidelines for C items.

Exercise

Classify the items in the table of local authority inventory (Table 7.1) into A, B and C categories.

Independent and dependent demand

The contents of this chapter so far are relevant to all materials planning and control systems. From this point forward, however, the chapter deals only with techniques applicable to situations of independent demand. This is an important distinction. Situations of dependent demand are dealt with in Chapter 8.

Independent demand is defined as demand that is independent in two senses. First, the demand is independent of the demand for other items. Second, the demand is outside the control of the operation and is usually subject to trends and seasonal patterns. Finished goods are a classic example of independent demand.

In contrast, dependent demand is defined as the demand which results from (i.e., depends on) the demand for other items. In a manufacturing organization, the demand for raw materials and component parts is derived from the demand for the finished goods. These items are, therefore, dependent demand items, whilst the demand for the finished goods is classified as independent.

Belling Cookers suffered from the independent demand for cookers. Sales of cookers are strongly influenced by the economic cycle. In times of recession fewer houses are built and the demand for cookers falls. Against this scenario the factory making Belling Cookers found it extremely difficult to continue in business and the operation was eventually sold.

Techniques for managing materials in cases of independent demand

In the following examples figures are given to a level of accuracy based on individual units. In many situations such a high level of accuracy is not required in practice. Rounding to the next highest hundred is often used where the effect on total costs is negligible. This should be borne in mind when the solutions are considered.

The economic order quantity

Olivetti make and distribute computers. An important part of their business is the ability to repair machines when they malfunction. A speedy response is required by their clients, whose own businesses suffer when the Olivetti computers are down. This after-sales activity of Olivetti relies heavily upon the availability of replacement components for computers that have failed on clients' premises. In Holland, the central store stocking these components holds about 10 000 different items. These 10 000 components account for about 20 per cent of the floor space at the warehouse. The warehouse generates demands for the supply of components from manufacturing by a computerized system that uses exponential forecasting and economic order quantities.

The economic order quantity (EOQ) concept is intended to help managers to decide what amount of materials to order. It does this by a formula that calculates the order quantity that minimizes the total incremental costs of holding inventory and processing orders. Before proceeding further it is worth while mentioning what these different costs might consist of. The costs of holding stock derive from the following.

1 *Interest.* If an organization has borrowed money in order to purchase either the stock or the buildings within which it is kept, then the interest repayments on the loan represent a cash flow out of the organization attached to the stock concerned.
2 *Insurance.* Premiums paid to insure the stock against possible damage from fire etc. are a cost associated with the materials held.
3 *Council tax.* The buildings in which the materials are housed will be rated by the local authority. This again is cash out of the organization.
4 *Deterioration in value.* The value of the stock might decline over time due to several factors, such as obsolescence and theft.
5 *Stock management.* Whilst the materials are in the control of the organization they will require handling, surveillance and data recording.

Case Study

Many foods now use natural or nature identical ingredients. These ingredients tend to be more volatile than the chemicals that they replace. One consequence of this is that they require special storage conditions, with temperature and humidity control being more important. Moreover, once the containers holding these ingredients are opened they also tend to have a shorter life than the older formulations. The net result is that the new ingredients incur extra holding costs.

The costs of placing an order derive from all the activities associated with preparing and processing orders. They include the following activities:

- preparing the order
- preparing the material specifications
- tracking the order
- processing invoices
- receiving and handling the ordered materials when they are delivered.

In these areas the major cost categories will usually be salary and communication costs.

Case Study

Communications between suppliers and vendors are increasingly becoming paperless. Electronic data interchange (EDI) computer systems allow suppliers and buyers to place orders and invoices electronically. Traditionally, such systems have been reserved for large organizations only due to their cost and complexity. Now, however, the Internet is facilitating the spread of these networks to smaller organizations. Chrysler uses TradeWeb to offer EDI to its smaller suppliers. Tesco is experimenting with a similar initiative. These developments offer the prospect of diminishing ordering costs, thereby reducing EOQ levels.

It is often difficult to arrive at exact costings for these various headings of holding and ordering costs, and experience is usually used to estimate them. Holding costs are commonly estimated as a proportion of the purchase price. This proportion can be high, in the region of 25–33 per cent.

The EOQ formula will now be explained. Suppose that we propose to use 1000 units over the next five weeks and that our supplier can be very flexible in terms of what is delivered and when it can be delivered. We clearly have a wide range of options open to us. We could take delivery of the 1000 units in one go, we could take delivery of 200 per week or two lots of 500, to mention but a few. Which would be best? Ordering 1000 would require only one order, which is a saving over ordering more frequent deliveries. However, the cost of holding 1000 items is higher than the cost of holding smaller quantities. The approach of the EOQ is to calculate the best balance between these two sources of cost.

The total holding cost is given by the costs of holding one unit of stock multiplied by the total number of units of inventory. In our example, if the holding cost is £0.40 per unit, then the total holding cost is:

$$Q \times £0.40 \tag{7.6}$$

where Q is the volume of inventory.

In graphical form this gives the line shown as Cost A on the graph in Figure 7.2.

The ordering costs vary in proportion to the number of orders placed per year. A formula for the number of orders to be placed in a year is:

$$\frac{R}{Q} \tag{7.7}$$

where R = the annual number of units to be ordered and Q = the quantity to be ordered.

The fewer the number of orders that are placed, the lower the total costs of placing orders will be. In the case of the example, if the cost of an order is £20, then the graphical line will be as shown in line Cost B as in Figure 7.3.

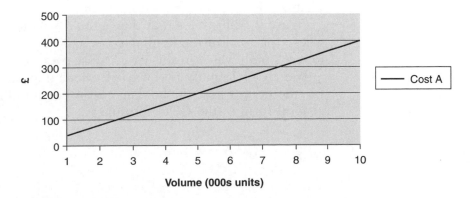

Figure 7.2 Holding costs

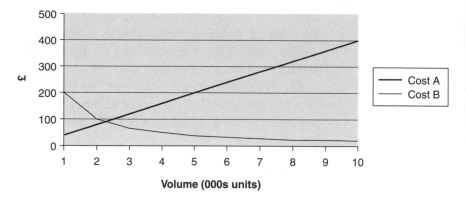

Figure 7.3 Holding and ordering costs

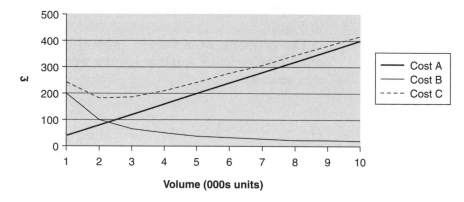

Figure 7.4 Holding and ordering costs summed

The two costs thus behave differently. The larger the size of the order, then the higher the holding costs but the lower the ordering costs. The totals of these two costs are shown as line Cost C in Figure 7.4.

Figure 7.4 illustrates that the optimal volume of units to hold is where the total of the holding costs and the ordering costs is at its lowest point, which in this case is just over 200 units.

The EOQ formula is a way of calculating this optimal volume, i.e., the point where the holding cost is equal to the order cost. The general form of the EOQ formula is:

$$EOQ = \sqrt{\frac{2PN}{IC}} \qquad (7.8)$$

where

P = the ordering cost per order
N = annual usage
I = storage cost per year as a decimal fraction of the purchase price
C = unit purchase price.

A simple example illustrates the application of this formula.

Example

An item used at a rate of 5000 per annum is purchased at a price of £10.00 per unit. The annual storage cost is estimated to be 25 per cent of the purchase price. The ordering cost is £30.00 per order.

$$EOQ = \sqrt{\frac{2PN}{IC}} \qquad (7.9)$$

substituting:

$$= \sqrt{\frac{2 \times 30 \times 5000}{0.25 \times 10}}$$

$$= \sqrt{120\,000}$$

$$= 346.4$$

$$= 346 \text{ (rounded)} \qquad (7.10)$$

Exercise

For each of the A items in the table of local authority inventory (see Table 7.1) calculate the EOQs. The relevant additional information is that:

● the cost of handling a purchase order is, on average, £32.00
● the average holding cost as a decimal fraction of the purchase price per unit is 0.20.

The EOQ model outlined above is the basic formulation. It rests upon some important assumptions and these need to be borne in mind when deciding if the model can be applied in its simple form. The model assumes that:

1 Average demand is at a constant level.
2 Supply lead time is constant.
3 The replenishment of the inventory item is not connected with the replenishment of any other item.
4 The unit purchase price, the ordering cost and the storage cost do not change.
5 The EOQ is equal to the amount which can actually be delivered by the supplier.

If any of these assumptions do not apply then the simple model cannot be used and a more sophisticated version may be necessary. The basic EOQ model is the foundation block for understanding these more complicated formulations. The EOQ model has been modified to fit many situations and this topic is dealt with further in the operations research literature.

Case Study

National Health Service warehouses carry a wide range of items. They cover medical provisions, with items such as syringes, medicines and dressings. Foodstuffs, both fresh and long-life are also included. Consumable items like cleaning agents and supplies of bedding are held as well. These are situations that have been modelled on classic EOQ principles.

There may also be other factors that limit the strict application of the model, even if its basic assumptions are valid. These other factors could include:

1 *The risk of obsolescence.* Items with a limited life need to be consumed before they become obsolete. Moreover, some items might be at the risk of becoming outdated by trends in either fashion or technology.
2 *The risk of deterioration.* Where items are likely to be stored for

some time there is a risk of deterioration, perhaps by changes in the temperature of the storage area.

3 *Limited storage space.* The physical restrictions imposed by the amount of storage space available may limit the amount of stock that can be held.

4 *The availability of money for stock purchases.* Where an organization is short of cash it might not be possible to order the quantity indicated by the EOQ calculation and some smaller amount is therefore required.

Robustness of the EOQ model

For some of the reasons indicated above it may be necessary to order in quantities which vary from the EOQ solution. As the EOQ formula finds the optimal trade-off between the holding and ordering costs any deviation from the quantity will incur a cost penalty. This can be visualized by referring to Figure 7.4. Any variation of the order quantity will move either to the left or the right of the EOQ point on line C.

It is possible to calculate the costs associated with any deviation from the EOQ. (The costs of safety stocks are assumed to be the same under all of the order quantity options and they are therefore an irrelevant cost for the purposes of this analysis.) The total annual holding and ordering cost of an inventory stock level is given by:

$$TC = (median\ inventory \times unit\ holding\ cost)$$

$$+ (number\ of\ orders\ per\ year \times cost\ per\ order) \tag{7.11}$$

where TC = Total annual holding and ordering cost

$$median\ inventory = \frac{order\ quantity}{2} \tag{7.12}$$

This formula can be applied to the same example used in the previous section in order to illustrate the idea.

Example

An item used at a rate of 5000 per annum is purchased at a price of £10.00 per unit. The annual storage cost is estimated to be 25 per cent of the purchase price. The ordering cost is £30.00 per order. The EOQ is 346 units.

$TC = (median\ inventory \times unit\ holding\ costs)$

$+ (number\ of\ orders\ per\ year \times cost\ per\ year)$

$$TC = \left(\frac{346}{2}\right)(0.25) + \left(\frac{5\,000}{346}\right)(30)$$

$TC = (173)(0.25) + (14.451)(30)$

$TC = 43.25 + 433.53$

$TC = £476.78$ (7.13)

Suppose that in this example the company managers are considering order quantities of 300. The effect of this decision can be calculated and compared to the total cost of the EOQ optimal decision.

$$TC = \left(\frac{300}{2}\right)(0.25) + \left(\frac{5\,000}{300}\right)(30)$$

$TC = (150)(0.25) + (16.667)(30)$

$TC = 37.5 + 500.01$

$TC = £537.51$ (7.14)

Thus, the effect of decreasing orders by 46 units is to increase the annual total cost by £537.51 − £476.78, i.e., £60.73.

Exercise

For the major A item in the table of local authority stocks (Table 7.1) indicate the total cost of the EOQ optimum volume and show the effects on the total cost of deviating from the EOQ by 10 per cent in either direction.

These calculations show that the cost of deviating from the EOQ optimal solution increases relatively slowly. Line C in Figure 7.4 illustrates this. Total costs increase gradually around the EOQ point. This feature is one example of the robustness of the EOQ formula. Other sensitivity analyses have shown that the parameters of the model can also vary moderately with only slight effects upon the total cost. Thus, if the estimates of the volume requirement, the cost of placing an order and the holding cost prove to be moderately wrong the effect on the total cost is only slight.

The EOQ model and just in time

Just-in-time costing systems place a higher value on the costs of holding stock than do non-just-in-time systems. Under the JIT approach costs associated with inefficient setup procedures, poor scheduling and poor quality are built into the cost of holding inventory. This practice has the immediate effect of making the holding cost line on the graph in Figure 7.5 much steeper, and the EOQ therefore occurs at a lower volume. The effect of this is shown by doubling the holding cost used in Figure 7.4.

The EOQ point is now around the level of 1000 units instead of just over 2000 units. Just in time's systematic attack on these forms of waste will lead to lower holding costs in the longer term, which has the effect of increasing the EOQ figure. However, as explained in Chapter 8, such an increase in order quantities runs contrary to the philosophy of just in time and is unlikely to be acceptable to the manufacturer.

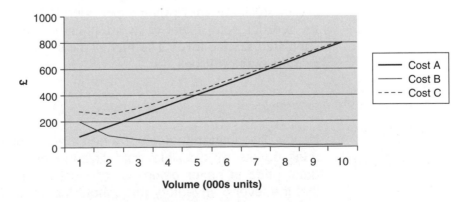

Figure 7.5 JIT costing effects on the EOQ

The reorder point

One of the basic features of an inventory system is the order quantity. Another fundamental aspect is the decision when to place an order. At what level should the existing stocks be when an order is placed? This level is usually referred to as the reorder point.

Situations of known demand

Where the demand for the material is a constant figure, then setting the reorder point is straightforward. Orders should be placed when the existing stock level covers the demand which occurs in the given lead time. Thus, if the known demand is 100 units per week and the known lead time is four weeks, then the reorder point should be set at 400 units.

Situations of uncertain demand

Where the level of demand is uncertain, the operation risks being out of stock on some occasions, whilst on other occasions the stocks will be too high. Both consequences have unpleasant implications for the operation. In the case of out of stocks, the result will be dissatisfied customers. If stocks are unnecessarily high, the organization will be carrying needless holding costs.

One common way of dealing with this situation is for the management of the organization to stipulate a policy that says what percentage of time they are prepared to accept being out of stock. Such a statement will be along the lines of 'we are not prepared to accept stockouts more than x per cent of the time'. In these cases the reorder point is set to avoid stockouts in accordance with the stipulated service level. The higher the service level, the higher the reorder point will be.

Case Study

Double Two shirt manufacturers had a policy of supplying as many retail outlets as possible from finished goods stock. They took great pride in never being out of stock of any item. This meant that the level of inventory throughout the process, from raw materials to finished goods, was very high. After several years of making financial losses the company decided to rationalize its product offerings. The company reduced its product range and thus was able to substantially reduce its raw material and finished goods stock levels.

One way of calculating reorder levels in this situation is by the following formula:

$$M = \overline{D}\,\overline{L} + k\sigma d\sqrt{L} \qquad\qquad (7.15)$$

where;

M = the re-order level
$\overline{D}$ = average usage per unit of time
$\overline{L}$ = average lead-time
σd = standard deviation of demand per unit of time
k = the standard normal deviate.

The standard normal deviate represents the risk of stockout that an organization will accept. The standard normal deviate values can be obtained from tables. As an illustration, values of 1, 2 and 3 correspond to 15.8 per cent, 2.3 per cent and 0.1 per cent risks of stockout respectively.

Example

Assume that $\overline{D}$ = 100 units per month, $\overline{L}$ = 4 months and σd = 10 units per month.
    If a service level of 95 per cent was specified, the risk of stockout that the organization will accept is 5 per cent. The corresponding value of k for 5 per cent is 1.65. The reorder level M is given by:

$$M = 100 \times 4 + 1.65 \times 10x\sqrt{4}$$

$$M = 400 + 33$$

$$M = 433 \text{ units} \qquad\qquad (7.16)$$

Exercise

Returning to Table 7.1 calculate reorder levels for the A items. The additional information you need is that:

● the average lead-time for each item is 1 month
● the standard deviation of usage for each item is 100
● the required service level is 99.9 per cent.

As a result of your ABC analysis and the subsequent EOQ and reorder level calculations, what advice would you offer to the management of the inventory system?

In some situations management might require that the system should never be out of stock. In these cases the reorder point should be set at the estimated maximum possible demand during the lead time.

Inventory control systems

Two basic types of control system are used to help manage the flow of materials. They act as mechanisms to draw the attention of managers to the fact that action is required. These systems help to answer these fundamental questions:

1 How often should stock levels be checked?
2 When should an order for more stock be placed?
3 What quantity should be ordered?

The continuous review fixed reorder quantity system

Under this system the stock level is reviewed very frequently. This high degree of surveillance means that it is soon apparent when the reorder level has been reached. The amount to be ordered and the reorder level are fixed and the approaches outlined above can be used to calculate these.

One simple method of maintaining the high degree of review required is the 'two-bin' system. The inventory is separated into two bins (containers). One of the bins contains an amount of stock equal to the reorder level. The other bin has the balance of inventory above the reorder point. Stock is drawn from the second bin until it is empty. At this point the stock will have to come from the bin containing the reorder level inventory and it is thus made physically obvious that a new order to replenish the stocks should be made.

Continuous review is greatly facilitated by the use of information technology.

Case Study

At all the major supermarkets goods are identified by means of a barcode displayed on the packaging. Each item purchased has its barcode read by a remote computer scanner. As a result, the sale of this item is immediately recorded and it is deleted from the in-stock record. Thus, the stock records provide real-time information all the time.

Downstream from the supermarkets, similar systems are used by the major food suppliers so that they too can keep a live record of their own stock movements.

The periodic reorder system

Under this system stock reviews are not maintained on such a high level and the amount of replenishment stock is not fixed to the same volume every time an order is placed. Instead, the reviews of current inventory levels are conducted at set periods of time and the amount ordered is intended to replenish stock to a planned maximum ceiling. The reorder quantity therefore varies from one period to the next.

The frequency of the review periods can be calculated by using the EOQ. If the EOQ is divided into the total annual usage this will suggest how often reviews should be conducted. The formula for doing this is:

$$\frac{R}{EOQ} \tag{7.17}$$

where R = the annual inventory requirement and EOQ = the economic order quantity.

The maximum stock limit has to be set at a level to accommodate the variability in both demand and delivery lead time.

The main advantage of this system over the continuous review fixed order system is that it takes account of changes in demand. If demand increases above the average, then the amount ordered will also increase. On the other hand, if demand decreases, order sizes will also decrease.

The main disadvantage of this system is that the inventory holding costs will usually be higher than in the case of the continuous review fixed order system.

Summary

Materials, or inventories, form an important resource in most operations, from manufacturing to service. The term 'materials' is very broad and several subcategories of the term have been introduced. Accountants tend to classify materials into raw materials, work in progress and finished goods. Other classifications emphasize the role that the material actually plays in the functioning of the operation. Under this perspective, terms such as consumables, spares and buffer stocks are also very useful.

Inventory, like all resources, is dynamic. The driving forces of all inventory systems are generically the same. Stocks are gathered together and then used. As they are used, they will need to be replaced if a stockout is to be avoided. This general pattern takes on particular characteristics depending upon the exact nature of the situation faced by an organization. The situation is defined by the key variables of supplier lead time variation and demand stability. The less certain these factors are, the more difficult is the task facing the resource manager.

In dealing with the situation, operations managers are trying to balance several competing objectives. First, they want to avoid disrupting the operation by running out of inventory. In extreme cases, stockouts can lead to the loss of goodwill amongst its customers and stakeholders. Second, operations managers need to avoid incurring the disadvantages of excessive stock levels. These disadvantages include negative financial effects on the cash flow of the organization and its stock holding costs. Financial implications are not the only areas of concern however. High stock levels represent increased exposure to the risks inherent in holding inventory. Large amounts of inventory also serves to cover up operational problems, so that they become accepted as the normal way of working.

Given the importance of inventory, it is not surprising that organizations have developed a wide range of measures to monitor the performance of the stock system. Two measures have been indicated. Customer service is the extent to which the customer receives exactly the volume of materials when they are required. Under this measure, delivering too much or delivering too soon would not be good customer service. The level of the financial investment in inventory is a second major category of measures. This provides an indication of the efficiency of the system. Stocks represent money tied up and they should, therefore, be kept as low as is practical so that the money can be put to better use within the organization. Both sets of measures can be formulated in either absolute or relative terms. It is possible to create a large number of such measures. What matters, however, is that the number of measures is manageable, to avoid information overload, and that the measures actually provide information which can be used effectively.

Most inventory situations will be managed more effectively if the operation has a clear understanding of the monetary value of each item of stock and how the values are spread throughout the total stock holding. ABC analysis is, therefore, a very useful method that should be applied early in most analyses, if it has not already been done. The Pareto principle is applied in order to look for a situation where most of the money spent on materials is accounted for by a small range of the total items involved. As a rule of thumb, the relationship sought is expressed as an 80/20 ratio. Producing an ABC analysis is a three-step process:

1 The requirement value of each item should be calculated.
2 The monetary values should be arranged in a Pareto table or graph.
3 The items should be classified into A, B, or C categories according to their values.

The A items are the most valuable and should, therefore, be subjected to the most managerial effort in their control. The B items require less effort and the C items the least effort of all. In many cases the Pareto relationship will be found. When it is found, the operations managers can channel their energies to gain the maximum payback for the organization.

ABC analysis is of general use. The remaining techniques in the chapter are applicable only to cases of independent demand. The distinction between independent and dependent demand is therefore an important one. Independent demand items are independent in two senses:

1 These are materials that are not linked to the demand for other stock items.

2 The major influences upon the size of the demand for such items are external to the organization.

One of the major questions for the manager of materials is how many replacement items to order. The EOQ formula offers some guidance. The formula balances the costs of ordering materials against the costs associated with holding stocks. The optimal volume to order is the volume that produces holding costs and ordering costs which exactly match each other. This the EOQ formula does. The basic EOQ formula is:

$$EOQ = \sqrt{\frac{2PN}{IC}} \qquad\qquad (7.18)$$

Obtaining precise costing information is usually difficult and estimates are often employed. It is usual, for instance, to express the holding costs as a decimal percentage of the unit purchase price. Figures in the region of a quarter to a third are not uncommon.

The basic EOQ model presented here rests upon assumptions that might not apply in practice. If these assumptions do not apply then a more sophisticated version of the EOQ is required. The basic model is the foundation block for understanding these more complicated formulations. Moreover, the resulting EOQ calculation cannot be followed slavishly. The volume ordered may have to reflect other realities such as the amount of storage space available. Fortunately, the EOQ model is fairly robust and departures from the optimal solution incur extra costs only at a slow rate. Similarly, the EOQ formula is fairly forgiving of slight errors in the estimates of costs and demand.

Just-in-time manufacturers increase the costs of holding stock by giving values to the wasteful practices associated with the processing of materials. Poor quality, poor setup procedures and the effects of poor scheduling are all built into the costs of holding stock. The effect of this upon the EOQ calculation is to decrease the figure produced by the formula.

Having decided what amounts to order, the next major question for the materials manager is when to place the order. At what volume of on-site inventory should an order be triggered? The reorder point reflects the attitude of the management to stockouts. The less acceptable stockouts are, the higher the reorder level will be. One way of calculating the reorder point is offered by the formula:

$$M = \overline{D}\,\overline{L} + k\sigma d\sqrt{L} \tag{7.19}$$

K is known as the standard normal deviate and it is set at a value to reflect the risk of stockout which the operation is prepared to accept.

The fundamental questions involved in managing inventory are the same in all organizations:

1 How often should stock levels be checked?
2 When should an order for more stock be placed?
3 What quantity should be ordered?

Over time recognized systems have developed to deal with these recurring questions in different inventory situations. It is outside the scope of this book to detail all of the options, but the basic systems have been outlined. One system is the continuous review fixed reorder quantity method. Using this approach the stock level is monitored continuously, the reorder level is fixed and the amount to be ordered on each occasion is also fixed. The two-bin system is a classic example of this approach. An alternative way of managing is provided by the periodic review system. Here, the review of stock levels takes place at predetermined intervals. When the review shows that stock is below an agreed ceiling an order is placed to bring the on-site inventory up to this ceiling level.

Self Assessment

1 Materials management is only relevant to manufacturing organizations. True or false?
2 Items stored and waiting to be worked on are called:
   (a) finished goods
   (b) work in progress
   (c) raw materials?
3 Insert the missing words in the following statement: '_____ _____ are materials which are being deliberately used to protect the operation from the otherwise disruptive effects of interruptions to supply or sudden increases in demand.'
4 Supplier lead time is
   (a) the time it takes to place an order
   (b) the rate at which materials are used
   (c) the time from an order being placed to the materials being received
   (d) the time it takes to pay for materials?

5 Identify two adverse consequences of running out of stock.
6 Identify two adverse consequences of having too much stock.
7 The customer service level can be indicated by:
(a) the number of orders not met
(b) the percentage of orders met on time
(c) neither (a) nor (b)
(d) both (a) and (b)?
8 Insert the missing word in the following statement: ' The formula

$$\frac{\text{total cost of sales}}{\text{average inventor's value}}$$

is known as inventory _____.'
9 The 80/20 rule is also known as:
(a) Parkinson's law
(b) the Peter principle
(c) Pareto's rule?
10 In an ABC analysis, what percentages of the total value should be represented by the A, B and C categories?
11 Independent demand is demand which:
(a) results from the demand for other items
(b) does not depend on the demand for other items
(c) is controlled by the organization?
12 The costs of holding stock derive from all of the following, except:
(a) interest
(b) insurance
(c) deterioration
(d) stock management
(e) preparing supplier orders?
13 The costs of placing orders derive from all of the following, except:
(a) preparing material specifications
(b) Council Tax
(c) tracking orders
(d) processing invoices
(e) receiving ordered materials?
14 Holding costs are usually under 10 per cent of the purchase price. True or false?
15 As the order size increases:
(a) the ordering costs decrease
(b) the ordering costs increase
(c) the holding costs decrease
(d) the holding costs increase
(e) costs are unaffected?

16 The EOQ formula calculates the point where holding costs are equal to ordering costs. True or false?

17 List three assumptions which need to be borne in mind before applying the simple EOQ formula.

18 Decreasing order quantities from the calculated EOQ will:
 (a) decrease the total holding and ordering cost
 (b) have no effect on the total holding and inventory cost
 (c) increase the total holding and inventory cost
 (d) always radically alter the total cost calculation?

19 Just-in-time costing systems usually have the effect of decreasing the EOQ. True or false?

20 The risk of stockout which an organization is prepared to accept influences the re-order level. True or false?

21 The 'two-bin' system is an example of:
 (a) continuous stock review
 (b) periodic stock review
 (c) no stock review?

22 Under periodic review systems stock levels are:
 (a) monitored very frequently
 (b) monitored at set periods
 (c) replenished by fixed order quantities

23 Under continuous review systems stock costs are usually lower. True or false?

Further reading

Plossl, G. (1985). *Production and Inventory Control: Principles and Techniques*. Prentice-Hall.
Waters, C. D. J. (1992). *Invenory Control and Management*. John Wiley.

Chapter 8

Scheduling batch and flow processes

Chapter 3 outlined the ways in which operations can be organized and introduced various process types. In this chapter two of these types, namely batch and flow, are considered. The main focus of the chapter is to review how the work of these two processes may be planned and controlled, a topic introduced in Chapter 6. Specific objectives for the chapter are outlined below:

1 *Dealing with complexity*. The basic elements of scheduling work are fairly simple. Knowing the date by which the job has to be completed, how long it will take and what resources it will require will enable a schedule to be drawn up. This basic format does not change when scheduling operations. What does change is the complexity of the task, because there will be many jobs requiring a complicated set of resources. The overriding purpose of this chapter is to show how this complexity is dealt with.

2 *Master scheduling*. The main starting point for scheduling operations in batch and flow environments is the master schedule. It is important, therefore, to understand the format

of this planning tool and its role in the overall planning and control process. Such considerations lead naturally to the question of what makes a good schedule.

3 *Differing approaches to scheduling.* Three main approaches have been developed to the scheduling task: Manufacturing resources planning systems, JIT manufacturing and OPT. This chapter provides an overview of all three. MRP is described and the logic of its calculations is explored. An important feature of such systems is the bill of materials, so this is also described. Recent developments of MRP into enterprise resources planning (ERP) are briefly outlined. The meaning of JIT is explained at both the technical and the managerial levels. Just in time goes far beyond the scheduling task and these further areas are explained so that a proper understanding of the concept is possible. Manufacturing resources planning and JIT do not have to be mutually exclusive and some consideration is given to how they might be viewed as complementary in some situations. The approach of OPT is described, with its basic principles outlined for a fuller understanding of its particular perspective on the scheduling task.

4 *Aids to single work station scheduling.* Within the overall frameworks of these three systems there are still occasions when short-term schedules are required for single workstations. Some of the basic guidelines to help in this situation are outlined.

The master schedule

The master schedule is a statement of what output is required in order to meet the short-term known demand plus the short-term forecast. In manufacturing it is usually referred to as the master production schedule. The required output will be expressed as end products or major modules of end products. In the service sector the terminology is less precise. The master schedule might be referred to as an appointment book for instance. In the case of a hospital, the master schedule might be referred to as the planned admission schedule. In the case of personal services, the output might be defined as service personnel time. In the context of master scheduling, short term usually means around three months. The master schedule thus becomes the basis for planning how to allocate the capacity of the organization for this time period. In the case of a hospital, for instance, a bill of resources can indicate the amount and timing of all the resources needed to process particular types of patients during their stays.

Master schedules are normally presented as time-phased documents showing the relationship between output, forecasts and, in the case of manufacturing, inventory balances.

Example

Suppose that the forecast for manufactured items during the next twelve weeks (in units) is 20, 15, 10, 10, 15, 20, 20, 25, 20, 15, 10 and 10. These figures include the known customer orders for this period as well. This information will be shown as in Table 8.1.

Table 8.1

Weeks	1	2	3	4	5	6	7	8	9	10	11	12
Forecast	20	15	10	10	15	20	20	25	20	15	10	10

Any current stocks available to meet this demand would be shown at the beginning of the first period (Table 8.2).

Table 8.2

Weeks	1	2	3	4	5	6	7	8	9	10	11	12
Forecast	20	15	10	10	15	20	20	25	20	15	10	10
Available stocks	20											

Based upon known capacity constraints the schedule for production might be set as 14 per week. The master schedule will show this as in Table 8.3.

Table 8.3

Weeks	1	2	3	4	5	6	7	8	9	10	11	12
Forecast	20	15	10	10	15	20	20	25	20	15	10	10
Available stocks	20											
Production	14	14	14	14	14	14	14	14	14	14	14	14

It is now possible to run the schedule calculations across the time period. In week 1 the forecast is 20 and this can be met from the available stocks. All of week 1's production therefore goes into stock. It is on hand at the end of week 1 and becomes available for week 2 (Table 8.4).

Table 8.4

Weeks	1	2	3	4	5	6	7	8	9	10	11	12
Forecast	20	15	10	10	15	20	20	25	20	15	10	10
Available stocks	20	14										
Production	14	14	14	14	14	14	14	14	14	14	14	14
On hand	14											

The logic of the calculations for each week is thus:

(forecast − available stocks) + production

= on-hand and available inventory   (8.1)

Where the forecast exceeds the total stock this will result in a stock shortage, which is shown as a negative on-hand figure.

Applying this logic yields the final master schedule in this simple example (Table 8.5).

Table 8.5

Weeks	1	2	3	4	5	6	7	8	9	10	11	12
Forecast	20	15	10	10	15	20	20	25	20	15	10	10
Available stocks	20	14	13	17	21	20	14	8	−3	−9	−10	−6
Production	14	14	14	14	14	14	14	14	14	14	14	14
On hand	14	13	17	21	20	14	8	−3	−9	−10	−6	−2

Clearly the inability to meet demand from week 8 will have to be discussed between production and sales.

Exercise

Around what options will this discussion centre?

Case Study

Master scheduling at McDonald's

Each McDonald's restaurant has a record of the pattern of its sales during the months, weeks and days throughout the year. A schedule of demand for the next few weeks and months can therefore be drawn up. The resulting volumes will indicate the number of staff required to maintain the targets of keeping queuing down to two minutes or less and times at the counter to sixty seconds or less.

The role of master scheduling

The role of the master schedule in the capacity planning of the organization is illustrated in Figure 8.1.

Communication between all these different elements is vital and the whole process involves much feedback and iteration. One of the reasons underpinning the importance of communication is that the

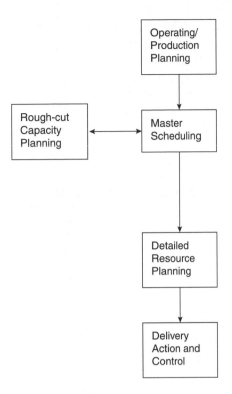

Figure 8.1 The role of master scheduling

people dealing with the customers of the organization use this schedule to make promises of what the operation can deliver and when it can deliver it. The master schedule is thus a key document linking the operation and the customer-facing functions. If the organization is to provide good customer service then internal communication about the schedule must be clear to all concerned, and accepted.

Another reason for sound communication around the master scheduling process is that the finance function will refer to the schedule for projecting cash flow and profits. Clear and accepted communication is not always easy to achieve. Often the real-time demand and supply varies from what was planned in the original schedule. The schedule is only a statement of what is intended to happen, not a guarantee that it will actually happen. For this reason, the schedule needs monitoring on a frequent basis, usually weekly, and amending as necessary. Where the actual situation is worse than the master schedule envisaged there will usually be a debate about available capacity versus demand and trade-off judgements may well be required.

The master schedule is a key input into MRP systems, JIT and OPT. Manufacturing resources planning and OPT take the schedule in the traditional format indicated above. Just in time, on the other hand, requires the master schedule to be broken down so that some of the total demand is produced every day. These distinctions are elaborated below.

Master scheduling at a business school

Case Study

The capacity of a business school could be defined in terms of the time its staff have to support the various subjects, such as finance, marketing, human resources and operations management. This capacity is constrained by factors such as the budget, staff expertise and teaching-room space. Actual demands for this capacity are represented by course registrations. The requirements for the next two semesters can therefore be predicted on the basis of past experience and knowledge. These predictions become firmer as the enrolment process progresses. Forecasts of demand can be compared to the available staff capacity, so that a provisional timetable can be issued for the next two semesters allocating the broad staff groupings of finance etc. At this point the timetable is in fact a master schedule. It requires further, more detailed, working to allocate individual members of staff to particular courses.

Approaches to master scheduling

In manufacturing, there are three basic approaches towards constructing a master schedule: make to stock, make to order and assemble to order.

Make to stock

In the case of make to stock, the manufacturer stores its outputs as finished goods inventories. This means that customers can be supplied from readily available stock and do not therefore have to wait long. The food processing industry largely operates on this basis, thereby giving the supermarket chains a quick service but at the expense of carrying stock.

Make to order

Make to order operations do not carry finished goods. Everything that they make is produced only when there is an order for it. This approach is best suited to organizations where the final product has many possible permutations so that forecasting demand is not realistic. One way of approaching scheduling in this situation is known as consuming the master schedule. This involves the master scheduler recording actual demand against available capacity. The actual demand is viewed as eating into the available capacity and the remaining capacity is allocated as 'available to promise.' This means that the customer-facing staff can promise this available capacity to customers. Fashion clothing items are often made on this basis.

Assemble to order

Assemble to order is a hybrid of the two approaches. Here, basic components and subassemblies are made to stock, but they are only assembled as finished goods when a firm order is in place. Car manufacturers use this strategy, having relatively few basic platform designs from which a large number of final car designs can be made. The master schedule covers the platforms and these are made to stock on the basis of forecast demand. Final assembly occurs only when a dealer order confirms the end item specification. The final assembly schedule states the number of end products to be made over time and it is the lead time to make to the final schedule which determines the speed of delivery.

Measuring the master schedule

The criteria for judging a good master schedule depend on the particular situation of the organization. In general, the criteria will include how effectively it uses the resources of the organization, the level of customer service provided and its effects upon the cash flow of the organization.

Master schedule stability

The master schedule is clearly at the heart of planning and controlling the operation. As explained in Chapter 5, changes in service or product volume and type challenge operations to be flexible and are factors working against high productivity. A master schedule that frequently changes has the same effect. Operations will find it difficult to implement short-notice changes to planned volumes and mixes. For this reason, operations will function better if the schedule is stable. As the actual demand and production will usually vary from the plan, some push for changes to the schedule is inevitable in order to maintain customer service. However, organizations can help to protect their productivity by bolstering the stability of the schedule in several ways:

1 They can insist that all changes are made only with the consent of the person responsible for the master schedule.
2 The organization can stipulate that, within a certain short time before actual production is planned, changes are not allowed except on the authority of the chief executive. In other words, the schedule is treated as frozen. This might be, say, six to eight weeks before the planned production date.
3 The organization can stipulate the times before production in which certain types of changes are allowed. Thus, it could be that twenty-six weeks before production all changes are allowed, scaling down to eight to thirteen weeks where only minor changes are allowed. This practice is known as time-fencing.

Rough-cut capacity planning

This stage of the planning process is concerned with checking the master schedule to make sure that it is achievable within the overall capacity constraints of the organization. It is called rough-cut because the analysis is conducted only at the general level of whether the total output target is achievable. This stage does not analyse capacity availability in detail. Rather, it usually compares the feasibility of the schedule against the scarcest resource, which might be equipment or staff related. If capacity is found to be inadequate at this stage then the master schedule is normally adjusted by moving the demand overload to some other time period.

MRP systems: materials requirement planning and manufacturing resources planning

MRP systems are the first of the three broad scheduling approaches to be considered in this chapter.

Materials requirement planning

An overview of materials requirement planning

Materials requirement planning systems are computer-based programmes which perform all of the calculations needed to order materials for operations which are governed by dependent demand. Dependent demand was explained in Chapter 7. Such programmes are also called MRP 1 to distinguish them from manufacturing resources planning.

The MRP 1 programme relies upon three types of data input as shown in Figure 8.2.

The inventory status records provide information about the levels of stock held on-site, what order quantities the supplier works to, the lead times from order to delivery and safety stock levels. The master production schedule details what products need to be produced in the future and when they are needed by. The bill of materials stipulates what materials are needed to produce particular items and how these materials are assembled. With this basic information the MRP programme can calculate future inventory requirements. The outputs from the computer show what items will

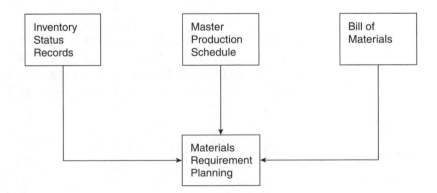

Figure 8.2 Data input for the MRP 1 programme

Table 8.6

Weeks	5	6	7	8	9	10	11	12	13
Gross requirement			100	50		100	50		70
On-hand	100								
Net requirement									
Planned order receipts									
Planned order releases									

Table 8.7

Weeks	5	6	7	8	9	10	11	12	13
Gross requirement			100	50		100	50		70
On-hand	100			100	0				
Net requirement				0	50				
Planned order receipts			50						
Planned order releases	50								

have to be ordered, how many will be needed and when they will have to be ordered. The programme will also highlight outstanding orders that need to be expedited, delayed or cancelled. In performing its calculations MRP uses backward scheduling, which was explained in Chapter 6. This is illustrated in Table 8.6, where the delivery lead time is two weeks.

The first requirement is for 100 units in week 7. The on-hand is projected forward to meet this demand, which results in a net requirement of zero. An order release is, therefore, not necessary. In week 8 the on-hand inventory is zero, leaving a net requirement of 50 units. These will have to be ordered in week 5 for delivery in week 7. The result will thus be as shown in Table 8.7.

Exercise

Complete the MRP table (Table 8.7).

The bill of materials

The bill of materials is a hierarchical list of all the parts needed to make up one end item. It is usually portrayed as a diagram, with the end item at level 0, the next subparts at level 1 and the subparts of the first-tier subparts at level 2 and so on (Figure 8.3).

Items at each level are sometimes referred to as the parent items of those at the immediately lower level. Where the bill of materials shows all the materials, from the end item down to the basic raw materials, it is called an indented bill of material. This is useful to help production managers design how the product should be made or for finance to provide detailed costings. In some situations this is too much detail. A record showing only those materials needed for one level of parent items might be adequate and this is called a single-level bill of material. The data in the bill is fundamental, and it is normal for there to be only one set of bills of material. In this way updates can be managed and everybody is working to the same record. Having more than one set opens up the possibility of inconsistencies. In this area data integrity is very important.

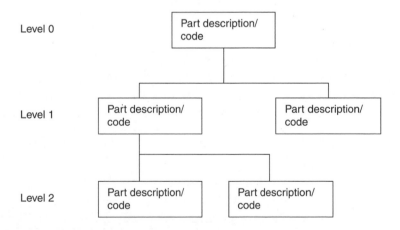

Figure 8.3 Bill of materials hierarchy

Bills of materials in airline catering

Case Study Airline caterers have to calculate their requirements for all the items that go to make up in-flight meals and snacks. When the number and type of passengers for a particular flight is known they can apply the relevant bills of materials to calculate demand. Thus, there might be separate bills of materials for, say, evening meals for children, adults, vegetarians and non-vegetarians.

Exercise

An electrical appliance A consists of three major subassemblies: B, C and D. One unit of A comprises two units of B, three units of C and four units of D. The subassembly B comprises three units of D and two units of E. The subassembly of C comprises three units of E and one of F. The subassembly D comprises one unit of E and one unit of F.

Draw a bill of materials for product A.

Use your bill of materials for item A and the gross requirements schedule below to complete Table 8.9 for item F. The lead time for F is two weeks. It is the policy that all materials should be delivered the week before production is scheduled. Assume that the scheduled receipts and on-hand quantities for B, C, D and E are all zero.

Table 8.8 Gross requirements schedule for item A

Weeks 4–11

4	5	6	7	8	9	10	11
100	0	100	50	100	70	100	0

Table 8.9 Table for item F

	4	5	6	7	8	9	10	11
Gross requirements								
On-hand	100							
Net requirements								
Planned order receipts	200	100	400	100	175	100	150	150
Planned order releases								

Companies have reported that MRP has delivered the following benefits:

- faster inventory turnover
- shorter delivery lead times
- greater consistency in meeting promised delivery dates
- reductions in the number of expeditors.

Manufacturing resources planning

Manufacturing resources planning was developed from materials requirement planning and is sometimes called MRP 2. MRP 2 is a computer-based system that does all that MRP 1 does plus some other program modules.

MRP 2 includes master scheduling, capacity planning, purchasing, finished goods delivery schedules, cash flow forecasting and personnel requirements. The information needs of MRP 2 are thus greater than those of simple MRP. One set of additional information is the bill of labour. This states the labour skills and quantities needed to produce one unit of output. In this way the computer can identify future labour needs to the human resource department. The system can also convert the planned schedules for materials and labour into projected cash outflows, whilst the master production schedule or finished goods schedule can be converted into cash inflows. In this way the finance department has a much better information system for controlling the budget and cash flow management. With all this additional information, and the power of the computer, it is possible for management to run 'what if' plans and to analyse the effects of different decision options. Thus, MRP 2 is a powerful way of uniting production with human resource management, finance and marketing.

Enterprise resource planning systems

Enterprise resource planning is seen as a development of MRP 2. MRP 2 integrated manufacturing with other departments and ERP takes this further. The aim of ERP is to provide one information system for the whole organization, so that there is only one set of common data for the whole workforce to use. The term 'ERP' can, therefore, cover a wide range of activities. It can embrace everything that MRP systems do plus managing warehousing, customer relationships, supplier relationships, accounting, human resources and wider strategic planning. Enterprise resource planning thus offers the promise of up-to-date information that gives a total picture of the organization.

In a university, for instance, the first stage of an ERP system might involve having only one set of data to support departments dealing with finance, human resources, student administration, research and facilities. This would eliminate duplication of data and enable the linkages between the functions to be exploited.

ERP applications

- Borregaard is a Norwegian company operating in Europe, the USA, Asia and South Africa. It deals in the manufacture and distribution of chemicals. The company has implemented an ERP system to integrate finance, manufacturing, purchasing and sales.
- Liebherr are a Swiss engineering group that makes heavy construction equipment. It has fifty-two operational units in seventeen countries. It has implemented ERP and this has enabled it to re-engineer some of its business processes. For example, because of ERP the company was able to create a single order centre to cover activities previously conducted by sales, purchasing, distribution and production.

MRP and ERP systems are computerized solutions to the problems of planning and controlling operations. What problems do you think operations will experience in implementing such solutions?

Optimized production technology

Optimized production technology is an approach to scheduling which places the primary focus upon the 'bottleneck' process or processes. Bottlenecks are an everyday concept. Motorway road works and supermarket check-outs are bottlenecks at busy times of the day. They restrict the flow of people. Similarly, production bottlenecks restrict the flow of work through the operation. Processes may be bottlenecks because either their capacity is less than the level of demand or because their capacity is used in an inefficient manner. Once bottleneck processes are identified, supplying processes are backward scheduled from the bottleneck to keep it busy. The operations fed by the bottleneck, i.e., the downstream processes, are forward scheduled from the bottleneck (see Chapter 6 for an explanation of these terms). At all the non-bottleneck processes, therefore, operations are activated on the basis of delivering products just in time for their linked downstream processes.

Like MRP systems, OPT is a computer-based scheduling system. The more bottlenecks a system contains, the more complex the scheduling task becomes and a computer is essential.

Optimized production technology is based on the view that the goal of the operation is to make money. It was developed for manufacturing; however, some of the principles of OPT are applicable to all organizations.

The ten operating rules

Optimized production technology systems view the overall process according to the ten rules that are outlined below. These rules are intended to achieve the maximum utilization of the bottleneck:

1 Balance flow, not capacity. The non-OPT scheduling approach is to plan for each operation to work to its optimum capacity. Thus, if each stage of the total process is targeted by the organization's policy to run at 90 per cent of its full capacity the schedule will require this level of activity. The capacities will be balanced at 90 per cent. If the total process contains a bottleneck, the net result of such a schedule is to produce more work upstream than can be smoothly processed. Whilst the capacities can be said to be in balance, the flow of the work cannot.

Example

Suppose that 100 per cent capacity utilization yields the following outputs per day on linked processes.

process 1, 100 units
process 2, 100 units
process 3, 90 units
process 4, 100 units.

If the policy is to achieve 90 per cent capacity utilization, a schedule balancing capacity will require the following outputs:

process 1, 90 units
process 2, 90 units
process 3, 81 units
process 4, 90 units.

If applied, this schedule will result in a queue of work in front of the bottleneck process, i.e., process 3, and a lack of work for the downstream process (Figure 8.4).

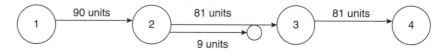

Figure 8.4 Bottleneck process: 1

In contrast, OPT schedules reflect the objective of achieving a smooth flow of work. This might require that the processes upstream and downstream of the bottleneck work at lower levels of capacity.

Example

In the previous example, balancing flow would result in process 3 continuing to run at 90 per cent capacity, but the remaining processes would reduce their capacity utilization to 81 per cent (Figure 8.5).

Figure 8.5 Bottleneck process: 2

2 Bottlenecks govern both throughput and inventory.

3 The bottleneck ultimately determines the utilization of non-bottlenecks.

4 Resources should only be activated to produce what is needed by the bottleneck. As the first rule suggests, the starting point for scheduling is the bottleneck. The output of a whole system of interlocked processes is determined by the rate at which its bottleneck works. Even upstream operations will eventually be forced to slow down when their overproduction meets constraints such as lack of storage space or adverse cash flow implications. Costly resources such as people, technology and materials should only be used when they can most effectively produce items which will soon realize revenue for the organization.

5 An hour lost at a bottleneck is an hour lost for the whole system.

6 An hour saved at a non-bottleneck is a mirage. Rules five and six are useful guides for improvement initiatives. If the aim is to increase throughput, then making a non-bottleneck process faster is wasted effort.

7 Transfer batch sizes can be smaller than production batch sizes. A transfer batch is the number of items moved between operations. A production batch is the number of items produced in one production run. In many operations the transfer batch and the movement batch are the same size. This slows down the movement of inventory through the system. Instead, the schedulers should ask what is the smallest input required to support a succeeding activity and attempt to arrange for this number to be the volume moved between processes.

8 The production batch size should be variable. The task of scheduling to meet variable customer demands is made easier if the operation has the flexibility to vary its volumes. This aspect of flexibility is discussed in Chapter 3.

9 Schedules should be established by looking simultaneously at all of the constraints.

10 The schedule should consider the effectiveness of the operation as a whole. Scheduling is a complex activity and moving away from scheduling each operation independently increases the difficulty of the task. The logic of focusing on bottlenecks, however, demands that such a change in mindset is made. This is why computer power is nearly always necessary.

Buffers

The crucial role of the bottleneck in determining total throughput gives it centre stage in the OPT scheduling process. It is necessary to keep the bottleneck running for as long as possible and yet it might be stopped by problems associated with its feeder operations that interrupt its supply. For this reason it is usual to plan for a stock build-up prior to the bottleneck so that this stock can act as a buffer against upstream problems. In this way, upstream operational problems have a built-in time within which they can be resolved before the bottleneck production is affected. For example, if most disturbances can be resolved within two days, the buffer prior to the bottleneck might be set at three days of production output. Setting the size of the buffer is a matter of trial and error.

Example

If this was the case in the above example, where the bottleneck produces at the rate of 81 units per day, this would give a buffer of 243 units (Figure 8.6).

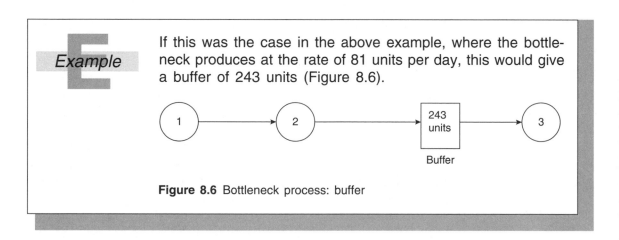

Figure 8.6 Bottleneck process: buffer

Exercise

Next week's schedule for a bottleneck resource is shown in Table 8.10.

Table 8.10

Day	Parts to be worked on	Quantity required	Hours of work
Monday	A	10	2
	B	20	2

Day	Parts to be worked on	Quantity required	Hours of work
	C	10	2
	D	30	2
Tuesday	B	40	4
	C	10	2
	D	30	2
Wednesday	A	10	2
	C	20	4
	D	30	2
Thursday	A	20	4
	B	20	2
	C	10	2
Friday	A	10	2
	B	20	2
	C	10	2
	D	30	2

Management has set the size of the buffer at three days. Before work commences on Monday morning the buffer's contents should be as shown in Table 8.11.

Table 8.11

Monday	Tuesday	Wednesday
A 10	B 40	A 10
B 20	C 10	D 30
C 10	D 30	C 2
D 30		

What should the contents of the buffer be before Tuesday morning production commences?

The buffer is used to control the release of raw materials into the system. Only enough is released to bring the buffer up to its predetermined size.

Using OPT for continuous improvement

By emphasizing the key role of bottlenecks, OPT highlights these as vital areas for improvement. The aim is to challenge and break the bottleneck constraints. Continuous improvement of the whole system can be stimulated by proactively managing the buffer stocks. Once the production system is operating under OPT principles the volume of stock in the buffer can be measured. The following questions will help to guide the improvement initiative:

1 Is the buffer larger than the scheduled target? If the answer is yes, why is this? Has the capacity of the bottleneck been over-estimated? Alternatively, is an upstream operation producing before the schedule says that it should?
2 Is the buffer smaller than the scheduled target? If the answer is yes, which process is underachieving against the plan? Or is the size of the required buffer overestimated?

Ultimately, the challenge is to reduce the size of the buffer. In pseudo-objective terminology, the standard to compare the buffer to is zero inventory. The task for the operation then becomes how to improve so that the buffer moves closer to zero. Challenging the size of the buffer in this way can be based upon JIT principles and techniques.

At non-bottleneck processes full utilization is not envisaged. This offers the potential to use the planned idle times for continuous improvement activities in areas such as quality and working methods.

Just in time systems

Japanese management was discussed in Chapter 5. The aim of this section is to outline the Japanese approach to planning and controlling work in batch and flow environments. This approach is called just in time manufacturing.

An overview of just in time manufacturing

Just in time aims to have the resources of people, technology and materials deployed just when they are needed and to provide only the necessary inventory at just the right time and place. The notion of JIT therefore embodies a set of techniques to achieve this. In addition to this technical aspect, JIT is a management philosophy. The philosophy of JIT manufacturing is that operations should be continuously improving through the elimination of waste, so that overall productivity and quality is improved on a never ending cycle. Forms of waste include not only inventory, but also time, energy and errors.

The idea of continuous improvement is sometimes expressed in terms of absolute goals, such as zero inventories, zero transactions and zero disturbances to the production schedule. Applying this philosophy means that the JIT approach to manufacturing is all embracing, covering the whole of the organization and also its suppliers and customers.

Just in time places great emphasis upon maintaining the even flow of materials through the operation and producing only what is required. Producing more than is required is seen as a major waste of resources and is not to be tolerated.

Case Study

The Toyota Motor Company production system

Just in time was developed by the Toyota Motor Company in Japan. It is generally attributed to the work of two employees, Ohno and Shingo. Ohno developed the production process operating, planning and control systems. He introduced a control method known as a two-card kanban system. At Toyota this system extends to suppliers as well, with the supplier's authority to produce being a kanban. Container kanbans at Toyota are kept small and standard. As a guideline, no container has more than 10 per cent of a day's requirements. The master production schedule is frozen for one month and the daily schedule is identical for each day of the month. Shingo's main contribution was to develop efficient setup procedures.

The Toyota view of inventory is that it is like water covering up rocks. The rocks symbolize the problems of the production system. Just as lowering the level of the water reveals the rocks, so lowering inventory shows the hidden problems. The number of kanbans should, therefore, be reduced over time.

The Toyota system places great emphasis upon smoothing the flow of materials and encouraging all staff to use their judgement in the performance of their tasks and the seeking of improvement.

Just in time systems may involve computers, but not necessarily. Modules can be added to MRP 2 programs so that kanbans are generated electronically. There are also programs that deal with JIT on a standalone basis, covering order entry, scheduling and pull control.

Kanban control

The internal discipline for making sure that there is no over or early production is provided by a system of control known as Kanban. Kanban originated in the post-war years in the Toyota Company. Kanban means card, but it is a term which is used to mean more broadly a signal that authorizes production or movement of product. The signal might be in the form of a card, but other ways of devising kanbans have been developed. For example, kanbans have included empty containers, light signals and computer communications.

The kanban is passed down the line from the end process, so that the pace of production and movement is set by the end process. Only production or movement that is authorized by a kanban is allowed. The discipline, therefore, is that if there is no kanban, then there is no activity. The way that the kanban operates is illustrated in Figure 8.7.

Process 2 will take a container of incoming stock. This container will contain a card (i,e., a kanban) authorizing the movement of one container. This card will be sent upstream to process 1. Each full container at the outgoing stock point has a card authorizing the production of one full container. In response to the transport card from process 2, a production card is removed from a full container and is replaced by the transport card. The full container with the transport card is moved from the outgoing stock point at process 1 to the incoming point at process 2. The removed production card is passed to process 1 as its authority to make another container's worth of product. This process is repeated for every movement and

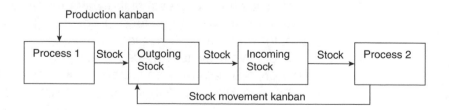

Figure 8.7 The operation of a kanban

production run throughout the whole manufacturing chain. As it utilizes both production and transport cards, this method of control is known as a two-kanban system.

The transport card is sometimes replaced by a kanban square. This is quite simply a square painted on to the floor between the two processes. The square is used to store containers in. When the square is empty this is the signal for the upstream unit to start production to fill the square again.

Kanban at Biosystems

Implementing kanbans requires good communication across the functions of production, purchasing and accounting. Biosystems facilitated this by locating purchasing and accounting near to one another in the centre of the production floor. In this way the needs of the production cells for external supplies are quickly made known to purchasing, and cost information is speedily given to accounting. Accounting can more easily track the progress of purchase orders and arrange for their speedy settlement.

By using kanbans production is pulled through the whole process and JIT systems are called pull systems of production. This is in contrast to MRP systems that authorize production at each work centre against a master production schedule regardless of what the other processes are doing. For this reason MRP is called a push system of production. Single kanban systems are a mix of the two approaches. Under these approaches, a kanban is used only to control movements between the work centres. Production is actually organized on a push basis against a schedule.

The degree to which the independent processes rely upon one another is governed by the volume of kanbans in the system. It is the number and size of the kanbans that sets the level of inventory in the system. If there is only one production and one movement card between processes, then they are virtually synchronous. In this case, if production halts at one work centre then the whole process chain will soon halt as well. Setting the number and size of the kanbans is thus a key activity. The number of kanbans will reflect the policy on safety stock and the level of confidence in the production system to operate without disturbance. The size will be influenced by considerations such as material handling constraints, space availability, production rates and setup costs.

Service sector kanbans

Signals from internal customers to internal suppliers authorizing the activation of resources occur in the service sector as well. In libraries, storage trolleys may be set aside for books to be reshelved. When the trolleys are filled to some agreed level they are then moved to the shelf stock and put back. In some supermarkets, if the line of customers exceeds an agreed number then this is taken as a signal to open another checkout. In hospitals, the pharmacy can be linked to the operating theatres by a cart. The cart is loaded with supplies for delivery to the theatres. When the deliveries are complete the cart is returned to the pharmacy and the empty cart is the signal for another set of supplies to be loaded. In McDonald's restaurants, when the number of food items on the shelving behind the servers falls to a set level this is taken as a signal to make more food.

Just in time production schedules

The master production schedule is arranged so that all the products are made all the time, instead of making single products in very long runs. This means that the inventory holding of each item is reduced. An early step in the master production schedule is, therefore, to convert forecasts into daily requirements for each item.

The high value placed upon even material flow means that the production schedules should be as smooth as possible. The schedule has to balance capacities so that an even flow of material is maintained. Evenness is also facilitated by freezing the schedule against changes within a certain lead time of the planned production run. For example, it might be the policy to prohibit all changes to the plan within one month of its execution.

Other tools and techniques of JIT

Smoothed schedules and kanban are not the only principles of JIT systems. Just in time goes beyond the boundary of schedule planning and control, and other important elements are briefly described here.

Setup reduction

Producing just what is needed at the right time needs flexibility. Individual work centres need to be able to change from one product to another as the demand changes. These changes are called setups. The time of a setup is measured from the moment the last good product of the current run is produced to the time when normal production of the next product is reached.

Lengthy setup procedures are a constraint on flexibility and they are therefore seen as an important source of waste that must be reduced to the absolute minimum. The classic way of reducing setups is to study the current methods of working and to seek improved ways of doing the tasks involved. There are three main avenues to explore:

1 Those activities which take place whilst the production is stopped should be reviewed with a view to transferring as many of them as possible to activities which can be completed whilst the production unit is still running.
2 Those activities which require the operation to stop should have all their associated equipment modified so that it supports the rapid exchange of technology during setup.
3 Effort should be focused on eliminating adjustments made after the setup is complete and production is resumed.

By following this rigorous approach Japanese companies have reduced setup times greatly, often reducing procedures requiring hours of downtime to methods of working involving only minutes of downtime.

Case Study One of the earliest setup reduction successes at Toyota led to setup time for an 800 ton punch-press being reduced from hours to three minutes. Shingo expressed the goal for all setups as being to achieve exchanges of dies (tools for moulding, cutting, stamping etc.,) in minutes. This is frequently referred to as SMED – single minute exchange of dies.

In this way the flexibility of the operation to produce smaller volumes of more products is greatly increased. Simply increasing the number of changeovers without reducing the setup times will increase the product costs, resulting in flexibility being gained but at an anti-competitive premium. This is so because of the economics of setups, which are captured by the economic batch quantity formula:

$$\sqrt{\frac{2CoD}{Ch(1 - [D/P])}} \tag{8.2}$$

where

Co = setup costs
D = demand
Ch = holding costs
P = production rate.

This formula gives the production volume with the optimum overall cost balance. Reducing the setup time reduces the costs of the setup, by lowering the amount of lost capacity and the labour hours needed to effect the changeover. This has the effect of reducing the economic batch quantity. Attacking setup time, therefore, enables the operation to lower its batch sizes without incurring cost penalties. Thus, flexibility is gained without any additional product costs. This does not mean that some investment is not required. New equipment may be needed and this should be treated like any other capital investment.

Achieving setup reduction requires cross-functional teams, drawing together engineering, production and quality personnel.

Problem solving

Inventory is seen as a way of hiding problems in the functioning of the operation. For example, excess stock can help buffer the production system from the effects of poor work scheduling and control. Just in time tries to deliberately find these 'hidden' problems and address them so that the buffer stock is not needed. One way of doing this is through forced problem-solving. This involves the level of inventory in the system being deliberately reduced until a problem is revealed. The reduction is achieved by lowering the number of kanbans in the process. The inventory is then restored until the problem is resolved. At this point the inventory is again reduced until another problem emerges. This cycle is repeated as a part of the effort to continuously improve the operation.

Employee involvement

Just in time places great emphasis upon all the employees of the organization being involved in decision-making and improvement. This is achieved through team-based structures and empowerment.

Cellular layout

This topic is dealt with in Chapter 3. The advantages of cellular manufacturing greatly support JIT. The wastes of travel distances, materials handling and inventories between machines are reduced. Cells also facilitate the formation of teams.

Quality improvement

Quality improvement helps to reduce the size of planned batches and also protects the process from disturbances caused by quality failures. As a result JIT is greatly assisted by attacks on quality forms of waste. This topic is dealt with in Chapter 11.

Exercise

If the level of quality failures reduces from 10 per cent to 5 per cent, what is the effect on the planned volumes needed to support the master production schedule? What does this do to the level of inventory in the system?

Product design

The complexity of the materials planning and controlling task is seen as a key driver of transaction costs. Transaction costs arise from ordering, tracking materials through the process, storage, handling, data entry and data processing etc. Designs that emphasize commonality across the product range are one way of reducing the complexity of this task. Modular designs, delaying variety until the end processes nearest to the customer, are thus an important part of JIT.

Housekeeping

This is described in Chapter 5.

Supplier relationships

This is dealt with in Chapter 10.

Just in time at Harley Davidson

One of the most notable success stories in the USA was the turnaround of Harley Davidson, the motorcycle manufacturer. Following intense pressure from Japanese competition, the company implemented a highly effective turnaround plan with JIT at its heart. The organization moved from producing in large batches to what it called the 'jelly bean' system. This meant that it made every model, in different colours, every day. The company focused its efforts on waste reduction, employee involvement and cellular layouts.

Compare MRP systems to the JIT approach.

Hybrid systems

Some organizations successfully use MRP and JIT systems together. For example, MRP can be used to prepare the forecast for production and to provide a schedule for suppliers so that materials are always ready to be called off just in time. MRP can also be used to plan and control products that occur very infrequently. Just in time can then be used to control the flow of all regular products through the system. In addition, the wider aspects of JIT associated with continuous improvement can be used to take the operation towards better levels of performance in terms of quality, flexibility and cost. Which approach is best for an organization is a complex decision. Just in time is easiest to achieve where the product structure is relatively simple and the production process fairly straightforward. Where these factors are very complex then MRP may be the better approach. Hybrid systems may be viewed as the compromise solution suitable where product structures and processes fall somewhere between the simple and the complex.

Other aids to scheduling

In this section we consider three particular aids to detailed scheduling. The first of these is a technique called Johnson's rule. The second is two scheduling heuristics, namely the runout and critical ratios. Thirdly, some priority rules for single workstations are outlined.

Johnson's rule

This technique applies only to situations where two (and in special circumstances three) workstations deal with jobs sequentially and in the same order. Thus, the situation is of the type where the jobs to be done pass from process A to process B and process B starts to work on the jobs in the order in which they come from process A (Figure 8.8).

Process A		Job 1	Job 2	Job 3	
Process B			Job 1	Job 2	Job 3

Figure 8.8 Johnson's situation

Johnson's rule finds the shortest overall time for the total job load to be completed. This maintains good delivery speeds and high levels of utilization on the two processes concerned. The rule may be stated as follows: 'If the shortest time for a job is on the first facility, schedule the job start time for as early as possible. If the shortest time for a job is on the second facility, schedule its start time for as late as possible.' In order to apply Johnson's rule it is thus necessary to rank the job times in terms of their completion times on each process and to apply the rule to each job in turn. A simple example will make this clearer.

Example

Suppose that seven jobs have to be allocated to two processes, A and B. Each job has to be completed on process A before it can be dealt with by process B. The process times (in hours) for each job are given in Table 8.12.

Table 8.12

Job number	Process A	Process B
1	2	8
2	4	2
3	6	10
4	5	3
5	7	6
6	3	4
7	1	2

The first step is to find the shortest processing time. This is one hour for job number 7 on process A. This is the shortest job time and it is on the first process, therefore the start time for this job should as early as possible. Job 7 thus becomes the first job to be undertaken (Table 8.13).

Table 8.13

Job 7					

The next shortest processing time is two hours. Job 1 requires two hours on process A, whilst job 2 takes two hours on process B. As the two hours for job 1 is on the first process it takes the earliest possible start time (Table 8.14).

Table 8.14

Job 7	Job 1				

The two hours for job 2 occurs on the second process, so it starts as late as possible in the schedule (Table 8.15).

Table 8.15

Job 7	Job 1				Job 2

The next shortest processing time is three hours by job 6 on process A and by job 4 on process B. As the three hours for job 6 is on the first process it takes the earliest possible start time (Table 8.16).

Table 8.16

Job 7	Job 1	Job 6			Job 2

The three hours for job 4 occurs on the second process, so it starts as late as possible in the schedule (Table 8.17).

Table 8.17

Job 7	Job 1	Job 6			Job 4	Job 2

Job 3 takes six hours on process A and job 5 uses six hours of process B's capacity. As the six hours for job 3 is on the first process it takes the earliest possible start time, leaving only one slot in the schedule for job 5 (Table 8.18).

Table 8.18

Job 7	Job 1	Job 6	Job 3	Job 5	Job 4	Job 2

This then is the schedule resulting from the application of Johnson's rule.

Exercise

Draw a Gantt chart showing the schedule which results from completing the jobs in the order: job 1, job 2, job 3, job 4, job 5, job 6 and job 7. Then draw a Gantt chart for the order given by Johnson's rule, i.e., job 7, job 1, job 6, job 3, job 5, job 4 and job 2. What is the overall completion time for each Gantt chart? How much quicker is the schedule resulting from Johnson's rule than the schedule resulting from just doing the jobs in the order first listed?

Heuristics for scheduling

These guidelines are useful where the process is making to stock and the objective is to schedule jobs so that the stock does not run out. Unlike Johnson's rule, for instance, the guidelines are not trying to find the shortest overall processing time.
The runout ratio is:

$$\frac{inventory\ remaining}{demand\ rate} \qquad (8.3)$$

The logic of the runout ratio is that the next item to produce should be the one for which the stock will be exhausted first.

Example

Suppose that the decision to be made by a manufacturer of instant desserts is which product to make next. The basic information is shown in Table 8.19.

Table 8.19

	Dessert A	Dessert B	Dessert C
Current stock	12 000	15 000	10 000
Demand rate(per week)	2 100	3 000	1 700

The corresponding runout ratios are:

Dessert A, 5.7 weeks
Dessert B, 5.0 weeks
Dessert C, 5.9 weeks.

The schedule for production would therefore be Dessert B, A and C.

The critical ratio compares processing time to runout time and gives priority to those jobs with the lowest ratios. The ratio is:

$$\frac{runout\ time}{processing\ time} \qquad (8.4)$$

Example

In the above example for the runout ratio, suppose that the processing times are as follows:

Dessert A, 3 weeks
Dessert B, 2 weeks
Dessert C, 1 week.

The critical ratios are:

Dessert A

$$\frac{5.7 \text{ weeks}}{3 \text{ weeks}} = 1.9 \qquad\qquad (8.5)$$

Dessert B

$$\frac{5.0 \text{ weeks}}{2 \text{ weeks}} = 2.5 \qquad\qquad (8.6)$$

Dessert C

$$\frac{5.9 \text{ weeks}}{1 \text{ weeks}} = 5.9 \qquad\qquad (8.7)$$

The schedule for production would therefore be Dessert A, B and C.

Exercise

In the situation of the food manufacturer which schedule would you follow and why? Is there any other information you would need to help determine the final schedule?

Sequencing guidelines

In situations where several jobs are waiting to be scheduled on to a single workstation there are many priority rules that can help to decide the best order in which to schedule these jobs. There are over a hundred such rules and a few of the most common are briefly outlined below.

1 *First come, first served.* Here the order of undertaking jobs follows exactly the same order in which the jobs arrive at the operation. This rule is usually seen as fair and is thus the most common one used in personal services.
2 *Due date.* Under this rule the jobs are ranked according to their target completion dates, with the nearest due date job scheduled first, the next nearest date scheduled second and so on.
3 *Least slack time first.* Slack time is the difference between the target completion time and processing time. Thus, the jobs with the most slack are delayed in the schedule.
4 *Smallest operation times first.* This rule maintains a fast flow of work through the operation. As a consequence it helps to maintain the cash flow of the organization.
5 *Most profitable jobs first.*

What is the best schedule is a matter of judgement and depends upon the particular circumstances of a given situation. Usually, the concern will be to achieve the optimum balance between the competing demands of delivering the work on time and maintaining productivity. Following one rule all the time is not feasible. For instance, applying rule 4 logically means that the longer jobs will probably never be scheduled.

Summary

The master schedule
The master schedule shows the output required over the short term. It is normally presented as a time-phased plan and the logic of time-phased calculations has been explained as:

(forecast − available stocks) + production

= on-hand and available inventory   (8.8)

Master scheduling is a key activity in effective capacity planning and control. As the real experience of production against forecast unfolds the master schedule will require updating, and good communication across operations, finance and customer-facing staff are required to make sure that this is handled in a professional manner. The master schedule is the basis for all three scheduling approaches, i.e., MRP, OPT and JIT. The schedule can be drawn up in order to make to stock, make to order or assemble to order. A good schedule is one that is efficient and gives good customer service. The effect upon cash flow is usually also important. A stable schedule helps operations to achieve these three objectives.

Rough-cut capacity planning is a first-look check on the feasibility of a proposed master schedule. It compares the schedule to its demands upon the scarcest resource.

MRP systems

Materials requirement planning schedules materials to be delivered in situations of dependent demand. Like the master schedule it is a time-phased plan and the logic of its calculations has been explained. A key document is the bill of materials. This is a hierarchical parts list that forms the foundation of the calculations. The link between the bill of materials and demand has been explained. Basic materials requirement planning has been developed into manufacturing resources planning. This enhances MRP to integrate operations scheduling with functions like finance and personnel. More recent advances take this integration further by using a common set of data for all the organization's planning and control. These systems are called enterprise resource planning.

OPT systems

The term 'bottleneck' has been explained. It is a key concept for OPT. In scheduling operations OPT takes the bottlenecks as its starting point and utilizes these to drive the total plan. It applies ten principles to scheduling and these have been listed and expanded upon. The concept of a buffer has also been explained. Management of the buffer is key to using OPT as a driver of continuous improvement.

Just in time manufacturing

Just in time means both a technical solution to the scheduling task and a managerial approach to the complete operation. Both meanings have been explored. Kanban control is a cornerstone of JIT control. The two-card and single systems have been explained. Setting the volume of kanbans is a vital task and some of the factors influencing this have been raised. Just in time schedules require daily production of all items in the forecast. Stability is essential to the smooth flow of materials in such a system and freezing the schedule is an important concept.

Other important features of JIT in its widest sense include:

1 *Setup reduction.* This is vital to the flexibility needed to produce a wide variety of products each day. Identifying the internal and external components of setup is achieved by a classic method study approach. Following this route means that the economics of setups are dealt with in a responsible manner. The economics rest upon the economic batch concept that is embedded in the formula:

$$\sqrt{\frac{2CoD}{Ch(1 - [D/P])}} \qquad (8.9)$$

2 *Problem-solving.* Reducing the kanbans in the process is practised in order to force problems into view. These problems are addressed and the kanbans are then reduced again to expose more problems. This cycle of kanban reduction is continued indefinitely and helps to drive continuous improvement.

Employee involvement, cellular layout, quality improvement, housekeeping and supplier relationships complete the wider view of JIT.

Hybrid systems
MRP and JIT can be run in a complementary manner. This is most appropriate when the product designs and processes are of medium complexity.

Other aids to scheduling
Scheduling work on to single or dual workstations can be helped by:

1 *Johnson's rule.* The rule may be stated as follows: 'If the shortest time for a job is on the first facility, schedule the job start time for as early as possible. If the shortest time for a job is on the second facility, schedule its start time for as late as possible.'
2 *Heuristics.* Two rules have been mentioned. The runout ratio is:

$$\frac{inventory\ remaining}{demand\ rate} \qquad (8.10)$$

The critical ratio compares processing time to runout time and gives priority to those jobs with the lowest ratios. This ratio is:

$$\frac{runout\ time}{processing\ time} \qquad (8.11)$$

3 *Sequencing guidelines.* Five simple guidelines have been mentioned. They have to be used with care and will not automatically resolve the problem in the best manner.

1 Master scheduling is performed in manufacturing organizations only. True or false?
2 In a master schedule, on-hand stocks are those stocks:
   (a) available at the start of the week
   (b) required by the forecast
   (c) left at the end of the week?
3 The master schedule is a key document because:
   (a) it forms the basis of promises to customers
   (b) it is used by finance in profit and cash forecasts
   (c) it forms the basis of detailed resource plans
   (d) of all of the above?
4 In make to order operations:
   (a) stock is stored as finished goods
   (b) orders precede the master schedule?
5 State two criteria by which a master schedule might be assessed.
6 Time-fencing means:
   (a) changes to the schedule are not allowed at all
   (b) changes to the schedule may be made at any time
   (c) changes to the schedule may only be made by the chief executive
   (d) time limits are applied to schedule changes?
7 What does MRP 1 stand for?
8 Identify two types of information contained within the inventory status records.
9 MRP uses:
   (a) backward scheduling
   (b) forward scheduling
   (c) mixed scheduling?
10 Insert the missing words in the following statement: 'The _____ of _____ is a hierarchical list of all the parts needed to make up one end item.'
11 Data integrity is vital in MRP systems. True or false?
12 An indented bill of materials;
   (a) shows only materials needed for one level of parent items
   (b) is formatted to be right justified
   (c) shows all of the materials needed to make one end item?
13 What does MRP 2 stand for?
14 Identify two program modules which MRP 2 uses but which MRP 1 does not possess.

15 What does ERP stand for?

16 Insert the missing words in the following statement: 'The aim of ERP is to provide one _____ _____ for the whole organization.'

17 What does OPT stand for?

18 Insert the missing word in the following statement: 'OPT is an approach to scheduling which places the primary focus upon the _____ process or processes.'

19 Recall three of the ten operating rules of OPT.

20 What does JIT stand for?

21 Under JIT waste can mean:
    (a) overproduction
    (b) errors
    (c) waiting time
    (d) storage space
    (e) all of the above?

22 Insert the missing word in the following phrase: 'The JIT system of control is known as _____.'

23 A single kanban system is:
    (a) a pull system
    (b) a push system
    (c) a mix of both pull and push systems?

24 Under JIT systems the economic batch quantity formula does not apply. True or false?

25 Fill in the missing words in the following statement: 'Under Johnson's rule, if the shortest time for a job is on the first facility, schedule the job start time for as _____ as possible.'

26 The

$$\frac{\text{inventory remaining}}{\text{demand rate}}$$

formula is known as:
    (a) the runout ratio
    (b) the critical ratio?

Further reading

Goldratt, E. M. and Fox, R. E. (1986). *The Goal: Beating the Competition*. Creative Output Books.

Harrison, A. (1992). *Just-in-Time Manufacturing in Perspective*. Prentice-Hall.

Vollman, T., Berry, W. L. and Whybark, D. C. (1992). *Manufacturing Planning and Control Systems*. Irwin.

Chapter 9

Project planning and control

Chapter 8 highlighted some of the problems associated with batch and flow scheduling. This chapter deals with the successful management of projects in order to enable organizations to meet the completion time within the constraints of the available resources and the allocated budget for the project. In particular, the chapter addresses the following questions:

Learning
Objectives

1 *What is project management?* Projects can be large or small. The bigger the project the more complex it will be to plan and control. To appreciate this, the meaning of a project and the concept of project management are considered.

2 *What are the characteristics common to all projects?* Regardless of their types and sizes, all projects have similar characteristics. An understanding of these common elements helps in planning of the work content and the resources needed by the project. These common characteristics are identified and explained.

3 *What is the role of a project manager?* Project managers play a crucial role in the success or failure of projects in terms of their time, costs and quality. They need to be competent in resource management and the relevant technical and interpersonal skills. The managerial qualities required by an effective project manager are explored.

4 *What are the key stages in project planning and control process?* For a project to be successful it requires that the people involved should understand the environmental factors which can directly or indirectly influence the project completion time. Also, a project needs to have clear goals and objectives, be well planned and controlled. The different stages in project planning and control are discussed.

5 *What are the tools and techniques used in project management?* Several graphical representation techniques are available in the planning and monitoring of projects. They can help in the visual display of the activities involved, showing their dependencies in the form of a chart or a network diagram. The diagrams can then be used for time, costs and resource analysis. These techniques are described and their practical applications are demonstrated by the aid of various examples.

The nature of project management

To understand project management we need to know first what is meant by a project. A project is a set of activities that has a definable start and a definable end. It can be large or small in size, for example, building the Millennium Dome, or painting a room. Other examples of projects include:

- developing a new software package
- relocating an office
- implementing a new information system
- opening a new hospital
- setting up a new business.

Planning and control of projects can be complex, especially those with large number of activities. To reduce confusion and avoid any delays, project management is used for planning, scheduling, budgeting and control of the activities involved in order to achieve project objectives in terms of time, cost and quality.

Case Study

Pdd is a design and development company specializing in ergonomics of user interfaces such as keyboards and displays. The company believes that to embark on a new project people involved need to have a clear sense of all aspects of the project. In a business climate where getting better products out more quickly is a major concern, the ability to manage project time is a key competitive factor for a supplier company. Once a project is under way, clients prefer to have and respond to a single point of contact such as a product or project champion. So, to spark new ideas the company encourages and plans for contact between different specialists internally and between client representatives and its own people at various levels. It is the view of the company that spending more time and getting things right at an early stage of a project development may add to its initial costs but saves the clients money in the longer run by eliminating rework and delays.

Project characteristics

All projects have some common characteristics. These include:

- A well-defined objective in terms of the end result, the work content and the project strategy.
- Most projects are usually a one-of-a kind undertaking.
- Relationships between project activities can be complex.
- Because of changes that may occur in the environment and the client expectations, all projects carry a certain amount of risk in terms of their time, cost and resources.
- Once a project achieves its specific objective the resources used on the project are usually abandoned.
- All projects go through different stages.

The role of a project manager

Project managers' jobs can be both complex and challenging. They need to posses effective interpersonal and negotiation skills in addition to detailed technical knowledge of the project, in order to motivate and influence the team who perform the work. In particular, project managers should address the following management activities:

- manage the project's work content to define the goals and the work to be done in detail
- manage the people involved in the project
- manage information and channels of communications within the project
- manage time by planning and meeting a schedule
- manage quality so that the project outcome is satisfactory
- manage costs so that the project is performed within budget.

Exercise

Comment on the importance of communication and feedback capabilities in the successful management of a new airport project.

Stages in project planning and control

Effective planning and control of projects depends on clear understanding of the following stages in project management:

- project environment
- project definition
- project planning
- project control.

Project environment

This relates to factors which may influence the project during its life cycle, such as; supplier's reliability, political instability, local laws, national culture of the host country, other projects currently using the company resources and so on. An understanding of the project environment can help in achieving the project goals and objectives.

British Airways employs 62 000 people, 9000 in offices outside the UK. In November 1997 it announced the launch of Go, a new 'budget' airline carrying passengers between the UK and cities in two European countries for less than half the price of its regular economy services. The company believes that because of its overseas operations, British Airways management should be aware of the local laws and the cultural differences when undertaking international projects.

In the light of the above issues, outline three additional environmental factors that can influence the project completion time in developing a new training programme for a company.

Project definition

This is to do with being clear as much as possible about what is going to be done. A new one-of-a kind project is more difficult to define in advance than a repeat project that has been completed before. A project can be defined by its objectives (the end result), its scope (the work content) and its strategy (the way the organization is going to achieve the project objectives and set milestones to review project time, cost and quality as it progresses towards its completion).

Nexar specializes in leading edge electronic messaging and directory software. The company targets the large enterprise market, and has a niche in the defence industry with contracts to supply to the UK, USA and Canadian armed forces. Other key customers include Philips, BT, BASF and the World Bank. It is the view of the company that all projects should be well defined and one should not embark on a new project just for the sake of it. Hence, the feasibility study should be focused, and the quality objective should not be compromised just because the project or the product is the first of its kind.

Project planning

Project planning determines the duration and cost of the project. It also assists in the allocation of work to people, monitoring progress and assessing the impact of any change on the project. The process of project planning may repeat itself as circumstances, such as customer needs, change during the life of the project. The selection of a dedicated project team is essential at this stage in order to stay focused and maintain efficiency.

Case Study

The Northern Ireland Civil Service (NICS) is organized across six departments. These are agriculture, economic development, environment, finance, personnel, and health and social services, including those working for security, law and order and political development issues. As a diverse traditionalist organization it has been involved in planning and executing different projects. However, they acknowledge that in order to have achieved success they had to choose their early projects more carefully. In the past, most projects were chosen by senior and top management who were rather remote from the processes involved. They allowed this ad hoc identification of projects to go on far too long, without using any analytical tools such as cost of poor quality outcome etc. The Northern Ireland Civil Service was too slow in setting up targets and goals for their projects in terms of quality and efficiency that could have increased the momentum. Some projects were under-resourced by reducing work-scheduled dedicated time for team members.

In recent years the NICS has taken the initiative to create a dedicated unit from the start of the project which has helped to maintain focus and build momentum during the life of the project. Also, at corporate level, they have provided the financial, human resources and other systems that will support the successful implementation of various projects at local level.

Project control

This relates to management activities that take place during the execution of the project. It deals with decisions on how to monitor the progress, measure the performance (in terms of time, cost and quality), and how to intervene to make necessary changes in the project to bridge the gap between the actual performance and the original plan.

Case Study

Bombardier BN is one of four operating divisions of Bombardier Eurorail, itself a wholly subsidiary of Bombardier Inc., the Montreal, Canada, based rail transport manufacturer. The company is involved in a consortium building wagons for Le Shuttle, the channel tunnel rail service, as well as making passenger cars, light-rail guided transit vehicles familiar around Brussels, Vienna, London, Amsterdam and Paris. Its headquarters are in Brussels, employing 1750 people in two factories at Bruges and Manage in Belgium.

Bombardier BN has successfully created cross-functional teams for its projects. The working party members come together as a team around the project goals and do not consider themselves representatives from different places. The company believes that for a project to be successful the project team should meet regularly. The rolling forty-eight hours project meetings will generate achievable targets and discourage leaving anything until tomorrow; tomorrow can be too late. Also for project teams to do their jobs they need to have the necessary tools. Obstacles can be overcome if the necessary resources are seen to be available without constraint. It is the BN view that targets to achieve must be tough but realistic. If people involved in a project believe that the target is too high, they will not even try, but if it is too easy it is not worth doing.

Project management techniques

Several techniques are used for project planning and control. These include:

- Gantt chart
- critical path method (CPM) – widely used in UK and European industry
- performance evaluation and review techniques (PERT) – widely used in American industry.

The above methods, though different in their approaches, all serve the same purpose. The Gantt chart technique has been covered in Chapter 6. The remainder of this section deals with CPM and its differences to the PERT approach when it comes to estimating the duration times of project activities.

The critical path method

The critical path method, sometimes called the critical path analysis or network analysis, is a management technique developed for planning, scheduling and controlling any kind of project. It takes a project of any size and breaks it down into a set of activities and places them in a logical network or diagram by working out their interdependencies. The primary aim is to complete the project in the shortest possible time, whilst making the most economic use of available resources.

The network diagram shows the complete picture of the project indicating the jobs to be done and the sequence in which they should be carried out. Other information about timing, costs and activities that are critical to the project can also be included.

Drawing the network

Once the project's work content or activity list is produced, the relationships between jobs to be done can be established by taking each activity and asking the following three questions:

- Which job should follow the activity?
- Which job should precede the activity?
- Which job(s) can run concurrently with that activity?

When the relationships between activities are identified, we can use one of the two methods available to draw the network. These are the activity on arrow and the activity on node diagrams.

The activity on arrow network

This type of network diagram uses the symbols shown in Figure 9.1.

Using these symbols we can now draw an arrow diagram or a 'network' as shown in Figure 9.2. The diagram displays the relationships between activities, where job B depends on the completion of activity A and D depends on completion of activity B. These are called 'dependent' activities. It also shows that activities B and C can start concurrently, whilst activity F cannot begin until both activities D and E are completed. The broken arrow in the network is a dummy activity which means that activity D needs some information from activity C and it cannot start until both activities B and C are completed. We can see from the diagram that job A depends on nothing, and therefore known as an 'independent activity'.

Basic symbols	Name	Purpose
—————→	Arrow	Represents an activity
◯	Event	Represents a point in time when an activity starts or ends. Sometimes called a junction
- - - - - - →	Dummy Activity	Represents a time constraint on a particular activity

Figure 9.1 Network symbols

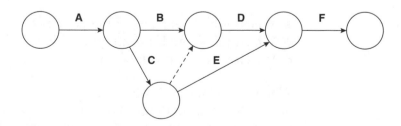

Figure 9.2 A simple network

What is the implication of 'dependent' activities on the completion time of a project?

It is important to note that all activity on arrow networks have a point of entry and a point of exit. In this type of convention each activity requires a starting event number and a finishing event number. These are shown inside the circles representing the events in Figure 9.3.

The network diagram in Figure 9.3 shows that activities B, C and D are both using the same event numbers. To eliminate this problem, dummy arrows can be used as shown in Figure 9.4. Remember that dummy arrows carry zero resources in terms of time, people, materials etc. They only represent time constraints.

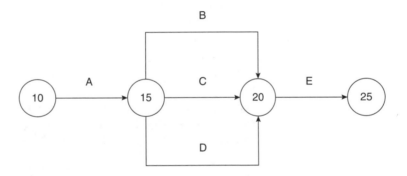

Figure 9.3 Starting and finishing event numbers

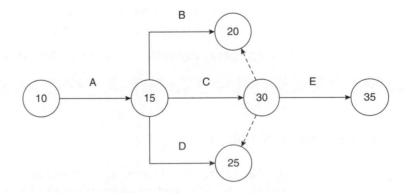

Figure 9.4 Use of dummy arrow

Exercise

Draw a network diagram to represent the following dependencies:

● activity B follows activities C and D
● activity E and F must follow activity H.

Example

The following activities are planned for building a house. The work content for this project together with interdependencies between the activities are shown in Table 9.1.

Table 9.1

Code	Stages or activities	Immediate predecessors
A	Digging foundation	B
B	Plan or blueprint	–
C	Carrying out painting	J
D	Building roofs	E
E	Building walls	F
F	Pouring concrete for foundation	A
G	Fittings	C
H	Windows	I
I	Doors	E
J	Plastering	L, D, H
K	Provision of services such as gas	B
L	Distribution work within the house	E

The complete network is shown in Figure 9.5.

Activity on node network

Another method of drawing networks is the activity on node diagram. In this system activities are represented as rectangular boxes or nodes, and arrows are only used to show the dependencies.

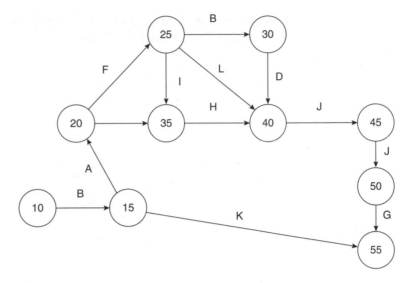

Figure 9.5 Network diagram for the 'house' project

The advantage of using this type of convention is that it will completely eliminate dummy activities and hence make the network diagram look simpler. Figure 9.6 shows both the activity on arrow and the activity on node networks for the following dependencies:

● activity C depends on activity A
● activity D depends on activities A and B.

Draw an activity on node diagram for the dependencies in Table 9.2.

Table 9.2

Activity	Depends on
A	–
B	A
C	A
D	C
E	B
F	E
G	B, D
H	F, G

In activity on node diagrams, each box or node is divided into a set of information as shown in Figure 9.7.

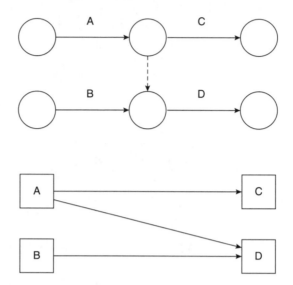

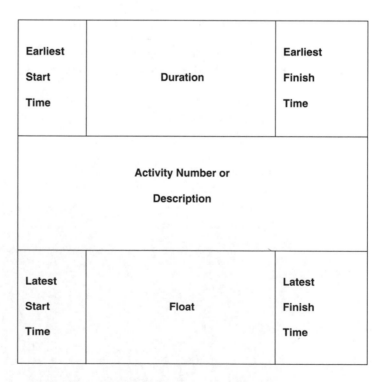

Figure 9.6 Activity on node network

Earliest Start Time	Duration	Earliest Finish Time
	Activity Number or Description	
Latest Start Time	Float	Latest Finish Time

Figure 9.7 The node information

Time analysis

Having produced our network the next step is to work out the times. There are a number of times that need to be determined for each activity of the project. These include:

- activity duration time
- earliest start time
- latest finish time
- total float
- free float.

By calculating and analysing the above time elements, the project management team will be able to identify the activities that are critical and those with spare time.

Duration time

This is an estimate of the time required to complete each individual activity in a project. In activity on arrow diagrams, the duration time for each activity is simply shown below its arrow in a convenient unit, say, days, weeks or months (see Figure 9.8). It is important to use the same unit of time throughout the network.

The times used for the duration of activities must always be realistic estimates. Unlike CPM, which adopts single time estimates, the PERT approach uses three time estimates:

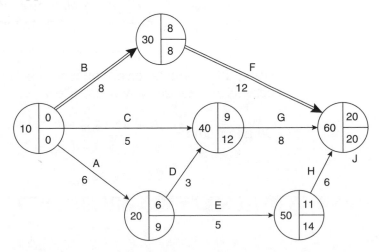

Figure 9.8 The earliest and latest event times

- the optimistic time – the time it will take to complete the activity when everything runs smoothly (the best time)
- the most likely time – the time it will take to complete the activity when there are minor problems
- the.pessimistic time – the time it will take to complete the activity when almost everything goes wrong (the worst time).
- The above times are estimated by consensus and through consultation with the project team. The following formula can then be used to calculate the activity duration time;

Duration time =

$$\frac{\text{the best time} + 4* \text{the most likely time} + \text{the worst time}}{6} \tag{9.1}$$

Example

Let us consider a simple project of changing a car tyre at night. Supposing that:

1 There is plenty of light and good weather together with easily removed nuts and bolts. In this situation the optimistic time to complete the task may be around ten minutes.
2 There are usual small problems but no major disasters. The most likely time in this situation may be around fifteen minutes.
3 It is raining, there is poor lighting, nuts and bolts are hard to remove, and everything else around us goes wrong. In this situation it may take up to sixty minutes to change the tyre.

Using the formula given above, the duration time for this activity can be estimated as follow:

$$\text{Duration time} = \frac{10 + 4* 15 + 60}{6} \tag{9.2}$$

$$= 22 \text{ minutes.}$$

Earliest start time

It is important to calculate the earliest an event can start. This is usually done by performing a 'forward pass' through the network and shown in the top right-hand sector of its circle (see Figure 9.8). Remember that for the 'start activity' in a project, the earliest event time is usually assumed to be at a zero time period.

The process of calculating the earliest start of any activity involves taking the earliest start time of the preceding activity and adding to it the duration of the preceding activity. Where there is more than one preceding activity, then we always choose the latest of their earliest finish times. The earliest start time of the last event is the earliest completion time of the project. This can also be determined by the sequence of activities that take the longest time to complete (i.e. the critical path). For example, in Figure 9.8, the possible paths are:

10–20, 20–50, 50–60
10–40, 40–60
10–20, 20–40, 40–60
10–30, 30–60

The corresponding times are:

6 + 5 + 6 = 17 days
5 + 8 = 12 days
6 + 3 + 8 = 17 days
8 + 12 = 20 days

Therefore, the longest path in Figure 9.8 includes activities 10–30 and 30–60. This means jobs B and C are the critical activities and that the project time = 20 days.

Exercise

Duration times for activities in the example shown in Figure 9.3 are as in Table 9.3.

Table 9.3

Activities	Duration (days)
A	12
B	2

Activities	Duration (days)
C	7
D	5
E	8
F	3

Determine the critical path and the project completion time. State the critical activities.

Latest finish time

This is the latest possible time by which all activities arriving at an event can finish in order not to delay the completion of the project. It is also the latest possible time any activity leaving an event can start. This process is done by starting from the end event and performing a 'backward pass' through the network, as shown in the bottom right-hand sector of the circle in Figure 9.8. Where there is more than one activity leaving an event, then we always choose the earliest of their latest start times.

Total float

In CPM the spare time in a network is called float. Total float is the amount of time a non-critical activity may expand without extending the project completion time. It is the difference between the time available and the time required to complete an activity. This can be shown as:

Total float = maximum time available − duration time   (9.3)

The maximum time available for any activity is the difference between the earliest start and the latest finish times for that activity. So we now have:

Total float = Latest finish time − earliest start time

− duration time   (9.4)

Joan 414

10 bks stamps given
to Boston Mobule

cost £17.80

for Transfer please

Pure

9141600

POF.

y C in Figure 9.8 is $12 - 0 - 5 = 7$

activity can be extended without
d without extending the project
ns means that all activities should
nd the free float is normally found
. This is shown below:

eeding activity

$y -$ duration   (9.5)

ty H in figure 9.8 is $= 20 - 11 - 6$

can be identified as the path taken
float. This means that these are
latest start times are the same.
no spare time and delays on these
le project being late (see the top

ur available resources on a project,
ish times of certain activities once
unts of float in the network. This
thing. The example in Table 9.4 is
at in resource levelling.
above project is shown in Figure
begin at their earliest start times, a
ow the combination of these activ-
ect. This is shown in Figure 9.10. A
ts per day can be now produced as

Table 9.4 Data for resource smoothing example

Activity	Depends on	Duration (days)	Labour
A	–	3	6
B	–	4	2
C	–	2	4
D	A	4	3
E	A	2	5
F	B	1	3
G	D	3	4
H	C, D, F	3	6
I	E, G	4	2
K	I, H	1	5

We can see from Figures 9.10 and 9.11 that by delaying the start of certain non-critical activities such as C, E, F and H, we can reduce the labour resources required to the level of the resources available. This is shown in Figures 9.12 and 9.13.

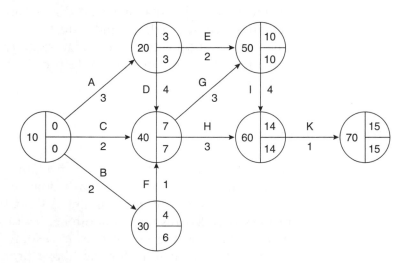

Figure 9.9 The network diagram for Table 9.5

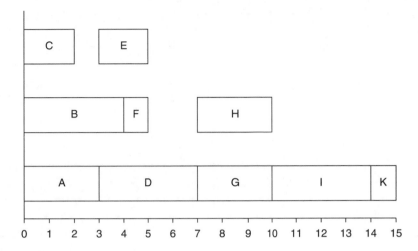

Figure 9.10 Gantt chart of labour requirement when activities begin at their earliest start times

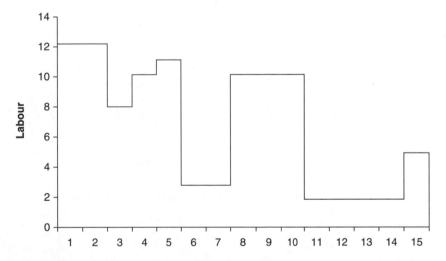

Figure 9.11 Histogram of labour requirement when activities begin at their earliest start times

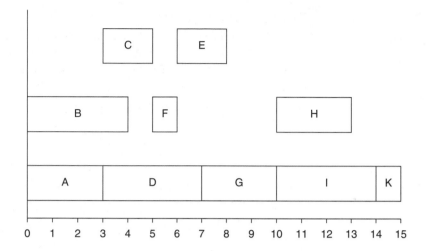

Figure 9.12 Gantt chart of smoothed resources

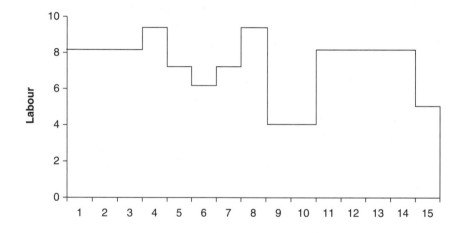

Figure 9.13 Histogram of smoothed resources

Summary

The nature of project management

A project is a series of activities that have defined start and defined end dates, using a defined set of resources. Projects come in all sizes. Those with large numbers of activities tend to be more complex. To reduce this complexity the project management concept is used in planning and monitoring activities involved in order to achieve the project objectives in terms of its time, costs and quality. Today the project management techniques are applied in a variety of organizations, such as banking, hospitals, construction and advertising operations.

Project characteristics

All projects have common characteristics. They all have a defined objective and a certain degree of complexity. In most cases they are unique and carry some degree of risk or uncertainty in terms of time and resources. They all go through different stages and are temporary in nature. This means resources that are used on a project are usually abandoned once it is completed. Projects with high degrees of complexity and uncertainty are usually difficult to plan and control.

The role of a project manager

Successful project management means achieving the project objectives in terms of the completion time, costs and quality standards, whilst making optimum utilization of the available resources. Project managers play an important role in fulfilling these objectives. In doing so, they need to posses the relevant technical and personal skills to effectively manage the people, technology, time, performance standards and, in particular, the channels of communication within a project on a day-to-day basis.

Stages in project planning and control

There are four stages related to the project planning and control process:

1 *Project environment.* This refers to factors present in the project environment which can influence the way it is being completed. These include factors such as the current projects using the company resources, reliability of the suppliers, the local laws and so on.
2 *Project definition.* A project can be defined by its outcome, the work content and the way the company is going to achieve the project objectives.
3 *Project planning.* This helps to determine the duration and cost of the project as well as the amount of resources that will be required. It also assists in the allocation of work and in assessing the impact of any change on the project.
4 *Project control.* This stage deals with decisions on how to monitor the project's progress, measure its performance and how to intervene to make the necessary changes in order to bring it back on schedule.

Project management techniques

There are three graphical representation techniques that are used for project planning and control. These are called; the Gantt chart, the CPM and PERT. Network diagrams can be produced using either the activity on arrow approach or the activity on node format. In both methods the project is divided into a set of activities which are transferred on to a network diagram after working out their dependencies on each other.

Time and resource analysis

There are a number of time elements that need to be determined for each activity of a project:

1 *Duration time.* This is an estimate of the time required to complete individual activity in a project. In estimating this time the CPM uses a single time estimate, whereas the PERT approach uses three time estimates (optimistic, most likely and pessimistic times).
2 *Earliest start time.* For any project activity this can be calculated by taking the earliest start time of the preceding activity and adding to it the duration of the preceding activity. This is usually done by performing a 'forward pass' through the network diagram.
3 *Latest finish time.* This refers to the latest possible time by which an activity arriving at an event can finish. This is determined by performing a 'reverse pass' through the network diagram.
4 *Total float.* This is the amount of time a non-critical activity in a network may expand without expending the project completion time.
5 *Free float.* This refers to the amount of time an activity can be extended without rescheduling other activities and without extending the project completion time. The free float is usually found at the end of a non-critical path.

The critical route in a network can be identified as the path taken by those activities that have no spare time or float. It can also be determined by the sequence of activities that take the longest time to complete.

When we have calculated the amount of spare time on activities within a network, we can then alter the start and finish times of certain non-critical activities in order to make best use of our resources. This process is called resource smoothing.

Self Assessment

1 Define a project.
2 List four examples of a project.
3 What are the main goals of project management?
4 Describe three characteristics common to all projects.
5 A project manager has to manage the following, except:
   (a) people involved in the project
   (b) marketing of the project
   (c) channels of communications
   (d) costs of the project
   (e) duration of the project?
6 Following are the main stages in project planning and control, except:
   (a) project strategy
   (b) project environment
   (c) project definition
   (d) project planning
   (e) project control?
7 List four factors related to the environment of a project that can have implications for its completion date.
8 A project can be defined by the following, except:
   (a) the project outcome
   (b) the project work content
   (c) the project network
   (d) the project completion time
   (e) the project costs?
9 Project planning involves the following activities, except:
   (a) calculating project duration time
   (b) allocating work to people
   (c) assisting in the monitoring of the progress
   (d) evaluating the environment of the project
   (e) determining the costs of the project?
10 Project control relates to the following management activities, except:
   (a) monitoring the quality standards of the project
   (b) controlling the actual costs of the project
   (c) monitoring the actual time of the project
   (d) deciding how to intervene in order to make the changes required
   (e) all of the above?
11 List three graphical techniques that can be used for the planning and control of projects.
12 In an activity on arrow diagram, differentiate between a full arrow and a dummy arrow.

13 Differentiate between the activity on arrow and activity on node diagrams.

14 In an activity on node diagram the node includes the following information, except:
(a) the critical activities
(b) the float
(c) the activity number or description
(d) the earliest start time
(e) the latest finish time?

15 List three time elements that are required to describe each activity of a project.

16 In CPM differentiate between total and free float.

17 In PERT what are the three time estimates used in calculating the duration time of an activity.

18 The latest finish times for a project activities can be calculated by performing a 'forward pass' through the network diagram. True or false?

19 The earliest start times a project activities can be determined by performing a 'reverse pass' through the network. True or false?

20 In CPM spare time in the network is called float. True or false?

21 Differentiate between the critical and non-critical activities in a project.

22 Table 9.5 shows the data collected about a project.

Table 9.5

Activity	Immediate predecessors	Estimated time (days)	Cost per day
A	B	2	£50
B	–	3	£60
C	B	4	£70
D	C, A	2	£40
E	D	3	£30
F	E	1	£75
G	B	15	£20
H	G, H	3	£50

For the above project:
(a) draw an activity on arrow diagram, showing the duration of each activity, the earliest start and latest finish times

(b) draw an activity on node diagram
(c) determine the completion time and the project cost
(d) identify the critical activities
(e) calculate the total and free floats.

Further reading

Burke, R. (1993). *Project Management and Planning and Control.* John Wiley.
Gilbreath, R. (1986). *Winning at Project Management.* John Wiley.
Harrison, F. (1981). Advanced Project Management. Gower.
Lock, D. (1997). Project Management. Gower.
Locker, K. and Gordon, J. (1996). *Project Management and Project Network Techniques.* Pitman.
Maylor, H. (1996). *Project Management.* Pitman.
Reiss, G. (1995). *Project Mangement Deymstified.* E. and N. Spon.

Chapter 10

Purchasing and supply chain management

Chapter 7 described the importance of materials as one of the key input resources for operations and discussed the various concepts and techniques that can be used for planning and control of inventory to produce goods and services both efficiently and cost effectively. This chapter deals with purchasing and supply chain management, which is the management function concerned with the purchasing of materials and developing a reliable and close relationship with the operations external suppliers. In particular, the chapter addresses the following questions:

Learning Objectives

1 *How important is the purchasing and supply function?* The purchasing and supply function is very important to the efficiency and effectiveness of any organization because of its financial, operational and strategic implications. These aspects of purchasing and supply activities are being described.

2 *What is the link between purchasing and operations?* For a company to be successful in its delivery performance, cost and customer satisfaction, it is essential that the purchasing function communicates and integrates with other departments such as design, production and marketing. The relationship between

purchasing and these internal functions in a firm are explored and their benefits to the end products are highlighted.

3 *What are the main responsibilities of the purchasing function?* The purchasing department has a variety of objectives in order to locate the right suppliers and provide goods and services that meet the needs of the organization. The nature and importance of these responsibilities are explained.

4 *What are the key steps in purchasing?* Material resources bought by the purchasing department can be of two types: the transformed and transforming resources. Both are essential purchases for operations. The activities involved in the effective purchase of these materials are outlined.

5 *What are the elements of a purchasing mix?* There are several factors involved in providing the best purchasing mix for materials and services bought for a company. These elements are identified and their affects on the organization's efficiency and effectiveness are discussed.

6 *What is meant by supply chain management?* A company may have to depend on many suppliers for it materials and services. Selecting the right vendors and developing and maintaining close working relationships with them are crucial to all types of business. Strategies that can be used to select and evaluate suppliers are investigated. Partnership with vendors and its advantages to both buyers and suppliers are considered.

The importance of purchasing and supply

To any business, purchasing and supply of materials, products and services is important in financial, operational and strategic terms. The cost of materials purchased is normally a large proportion of an organization's spending. In addition, the quality of input resources can affect the quality of operations outputs. Running out of materials and dealing with suppliers who fail to meet the purchase specifications will result in delays and reworks that can have serious implications on the efficiency with which goods and services are produced. Hence, strategically it is important to a firm to get its suppliers involved in planning and understanding the organization's long-term goals and, in particular, the company's quality objectives.

The interface between purchasing and operations

Chapter 2 briefly deals with the link between purchasing and the operations function. In this section we consider the wider implication of the interaction between purchasing and the various internal functions in an organization:

Design

The integration between design function and purchasing is essential. There is no point including a given material in a new product if it is not available in the market or is available at high cost or at high risk. This interaction with the design team provides the purchasing staff with more scope through understanding the required performance specifications for purchased materials, including the emphasis that they will need to place on the environmental performance. On the other hand, involving the purchasing department allows design function more time to plan for future requirements.

Production

The relationship between purchasing and production management is an important one. An operation can create several advantages by integrating the day-to-day activities of buying, transporting, and sorting materials and goods, with the process of adding value to them through manufacturing. These benefits are to do with the operation meeting its performance objectives in the area of delivery, quality, dependability, flexibility and cost.

Finance

The purchasing department is involved in negotiating payment arrangements with suppliers. Therefore, its relationship with the finance function can be particularly important. For example, purchasing staff are able to ease cash flow problems by negotiating longer-term payment, or smaller, more frequent delivery.

Marketing

By being well informed and proactive, purchasing and supply can make suggestions to the marketing department to exploit the capabilities of new or changing suppliers. By knowing future product lines, purchasing and supply can develop new sources of supplies in good time and avoid overcommitment in areas having little future.

Sales

Interaction between sales and purchasing is also important. Purchasing department can help sales to know about the cost make-up of a product. This in turn helps sales staff to protect margins when dealing with customers.

Exercise   Explain how a purchasing department can contribute to the efficient and effective operation of a company.

Purchasing responsibilities

As described in Chapter 2, there are two types of materials and services that are bought by the purchasing function. The first group comprises those items that are used directly in producing the goods and services for customers, and the other group comprises those items such as stationery, oil, catering materials and services which help to run the business and are regarded as essential purchases for operations. Some of the objectives and responsibilities of purchasing department includes:

1 Selecting, evaluating and developing sources of materials, supplies and services required by the firm.
2 Maintaining and developing close relationship with suppliers in terms of quality, delivery, payments and returns.
3 Seeking new materials and products, and new sources of better materials and products, for possible future use by the company.
4 Negotiating and acquiring raw materials, capital equipment, consumer goods and services at prices that represent the best

value for money and consistent with the quality requirements. It is important to note that the best value does not always mean the lowest cost so, when purchasing, factors such as the product expected life, serviceability and the maintenance cost should be considered.

5 Co-operating in cost reduction activities such as value analysis, make or buy studies, long-term planning and so on. Purchasing must be aware of trends and projection in prices and the availability of the resources that a company must have in order to meet the clients' expectations.

6 Maintaining an effective communication system and regular consultation with the organization's internal functions such as design, production and marketing, and with the company's external suppliers.

Case Study

Barclays Direct Loan Services (BDLS) is a successful customer-sales focused operation. The company has a mission to 'exceed customers service expectations'. Creating an innovative integrated culture that challenges current business practice has been a major success factor for BDLS. New initiatives have been introduced as a result of sharing ideas from staff, customers and suppliers. This has led to many improvements in areas such as quality, information flow and lead times.

7 Keeping the company's senior and top management informed of the purchasing costs and any changes in the market that can influence the firm's profits or growth in the future.

Exercise

Describe three categories of purchases that a company may make.

Purchasing process

Some of the steps in the purchasing process include:

- receiving the formal request from other functional departments
- defining the product and or purchase specification
- grouping items that can be supplied by the same vendor
- sending formal request to potential suppliers
- evaluating quotations submitted by various suppliers
- selecting preferred supplier(s)
- preparing the purchase order
- checking with supplier(s) to see whether the order will arrive on time
- following up with the operation to see that the order has arrived and its quality on delivery is satisfactory
- keeping information on supplier(s) price, quality, and delivery performance for future evaluation.

Single and multisourcing

Before processing orders for the purchase of materials and services, it is important for the purchasing staff to decide whether to use a single source for the product or more than one source. Some of the advantages of single and multisourcing are shown in Table 10.1

To select a vendor as the sole provider of an item, a firm needs to have a great deal of trust and confidence in the supplier. If the relationship between the buyer and the supplier is not good, then it is better to have more than one source. The trend is for a firm

Table 10.1 Advantages of single and multisourcing

Single sourcing	Multisourcing
Bargaining power and the likelihood of quantity discount are increased	Risk of interruption in supply is reduced
Paperwork and co-ordination effort are reduced	Competition for future business is stimulated – a single supplier may develop a monopoly.
The number of sets of special tooling required for production is reduced	New supplier can be evaluated and may become a superior source

to have fewer suppliers and work closely with them. Supplier relations will be discussed in more detail later in this chapter.

There are two more purchasing activities that involve other functions in order to reduce the cost of materials and supplies: value analysis and the make or buy decision.

Value analysis

The concept of value analysis is usually applied by a multidisciplinary team that comes together from different departments, such as purchasing, design, marketing, finance, production, etc., to review an existing or a new product, with the aim of reducing the expenditures involved in producing the product without reducing its value. To achieve this the value analysis team seeks to answer questions about the product, such as:

● What is the function of the product?
● Is the function necessary
● Are all of its features necessary?
● Can a standard part that will serve the function be found?
● What does the item cost?
● What else will perform the equivalent function?
● What does this substitute cost?

Exercise

Explain why the purchasing function should be involved in value analysis exercise.

Make or buy decision

The decision whether to make an item or buy it from outside, has implication on the in-house capacity planning system and as explained in Chapter 6. A service company might have to decide whether to try to do a job using full-time staff, employ freelancers or by contracting it out. Similarly a manufacturing company might have to decide whether to make or subcontract a batch of components. This requires a well-prepared and well-informed purchasing and supply function, good capacity planning systems and inputs from other departments such as finance and marketing. The key questions that should be asked by the purchasing and supply function are:

- Could we buy it from outside at less cost and in similar or greater quality and reliability?
- Could we buy it from outside and maintain or improve on the flexibility and responsiveness that we get from our in-house capacity?
- What about the future? What are the technology trends and investment implications? If we go for an outside supplier now, will we be able to buy it easily in five years time?

Case Study

As the second largest bicycle producer in the UK, Falcon Cycles makes about 300 models of cycle for a fashion-led, price-competitive market. In the past, Falcon used to import 40 per cent of its bicycles from the Far East. The disadvantage of importing is that the lead times are longer, so it is hard to respond quickly to changes in customer demand. In recent years home-based production has been made 30 per cent more efficient owing to significant improvements in manufacturing techniques, the introduction of quality systems (BS EN ISO 9000) (see Chapter 11), capital investment and improved buying techniques. As a result Falcon plans to produce its entire future sales requirement in-house. By eliminating the need to import, Falcon can eliminate the problem of lead times. Also, because home-based production now competes favourably with Far Eastern producers in terms of cost, the improvements in Falcon's flexibility and competitiveness are paying dividends.

The purchasing mix

The purchasing manager is responsible for obtaining the best purchasing mix for different operations. To achieve this goal he or she should be able to buy all the materials and services needed at the right price, in the right quantity, to the right quality and for delivery at the right time. The main elements of the purchasing mix are explained below.

Price

Purchasing at the right price can have a significant impact on the operation's costs and on the overall profitability of an organization. For most companies, a 1 per cent cut in purchasing spending has about the same effect on profit as a 10 per cent increase in sales. Favourable short-term trends may influence the buying decision, but it is important that purchasing staff keep an eye on the best value and negotiate the best overall price deal over a period of time. In doing so, they should consider factors such as quality, delivery, urgency of order, stock holding requirements and so on.

Quantity

Chapter 2 describes how the operation's performance can be affected by the ability of the purchasing department to provide the required materials and services at the right time and in the right quantity. Chapter 7 considers the stock control methods that can be used to determine the volume and timing decisions for operations purchases such as the optimum reorder level, and the economic batch quantity (EBQ). It is important here to remember that the quantity and timing of purchase orders will be influenced by the balance between the delays in production due to shortage of materials, and the costs associated with such factors as stockholding, storage space, tied up capital, deterioration, insurance and so on.

Quality

Purchasing materials and services at the right quality will improve the operation's delivery speed and reliability. To provide an operation with a quality advantage, purchasing staff need to consult with other departments, in particular with the production department about the quality of goods required for the manufacturing process, and with marketing department about the quality of goods acceptable to customers. There is no doubt that buying poor quality components and services can increase operation's costs. To prevent this and the late delivery of finished products, many companies in recent years are helping their suppliers with training programmes such as the supplier quality assurance (SQA) scheme, to reach the quality levels that are expected of them (see 'Quality assurance of suppliers' section in this chapter).

Delivery

The lead time between placing an order and receiving the materials in store can be critical to efficient stock management and to the overall performance of an operation. In arriving at a reliable lead time it is important to consider and evaluate the reliability of the supplier's delivery performance in an ongoing basis. If the materials are to be purchased from the overseas market (global sourcing), then more time should be allowed for delivery to their required destinations.

Case Study

Sainsbury's supermarkets deliver to its 402 stores through a network of twenty-two distribution centres. Stores receives daily deliveries of goods they require, ordering many perishable commodities today for tomorrow. The short lead times and volatile demand patterns require sophisticated systems to ensure customer demand is being met. Inventory and stock rotation are controlled through central mainframe computer systems. Store deliveries are planned at each distribution centre using local systems which optimize vehicle loads and schedule.

Supply chain management

Since the late 1960s there has been a transition from the old concept of purchasing to a newer concept of materials management. This normally includes activities such as inventory control, materials logistics, distribution and purchasing. Since 1980s companies such as Ford, IBM and Hewlett Packard have enhanced the role of materials management and called it supply change management. These companies have been developing a supply chain management process and an integrated procurement system that uniquely fits their own culture and business needs.

Slack et al. (1998, p. 474) define supply chain management as the process of 'managing the entire chain of raw material supply, manufacture, assembly, and distribution to the end customer'. This also involves supplier quality assurance, and the supplier and the buyer working together from the start in order to achieve mutually set goals. The overall objective here is to develop and apply strategies that can satisfy and retain the end customers.

Case Study

Oldrid and Company Limited is a retail department store, selling all household and clothing needs with specialist out-of-town furnishing superstores. The company believes that efficient supply chain management and vendor motivation are required to run a retail business with over fifty departments covering everything from buttons to three-piece suits, hairdressing and restaurants. Logistically, the company have built the most efficient goods-receiving bays and stockrooms, as well as marshalling areas and goods-outs bays to route planning.

Exercise

Why is purchasing such an important part of material management?

Supplier selection

It is important to spend more time early on in order to choose the right suppliers. A firm should look for the best purchasing solution which, amongst other things, should include the best products or services for its needs, at a price that is consistent with the company's demands for quality, quantity, delivery and flexibility. Some of the available tools and techniques that can be used to achieve this goal are outlined below.

Supplier appraisal

Successful businesses make sure that they know about the abilities of their existing and potential suppliers to do what is expected of them. A company needs to ask questions in the following areas before purchasing anything significant from a new supplier:

1 *Financial stability*. Can they finance the working capital needed to carry out the order? Might they go out of business before delivering the goods? Usually a copy of the supplier's last annual report can help to answer these questions.

2 *Ability to do the job*. Are they capable of providing the agreed product or service? What method or systems are used by the supplier to manage its product process? Finding out about the supplier quality assurance systems and talking to one of their satisfied customers can help to get an insight to these questions.

3 *Capacity constraint*. Do they have the capacity to do the work? To find an answer to this question can be rather difficult as suppliers are hesitant to show their order books to potential customers and the order levels can change quickly. A visit to their sites and a walk around their plant and office can be helpful here.

4 *Clarity of purchase specification*. Do they fully understand the product specification? Purchasing staff should make all the relevant details absolutely clear in the product specification and ensure that supplier also understand and acknowledge this information. Misunderstanding in this area can be the biggest cause of delay and extra costs.

5 *Ease of access*. Are they easy to deal with? Are they near and approachable if things go wrong? Do they return phone calls promptly? Do they speak the same language? It is easier to get on with suppliers who share the same business approach and philosophies.

Quality assurance of suppliers

Suppliers who consistently fail to get their quality right can be very expensive. Quality assurance of suppliers means doing anything a buyer's firm should do to be confident that it will receive from its suppliers the goods required, with the same specification, and at the time the company wants them. Establishing quality assured suppliers will involve time and cost. There is a set of quality tools that can be used to achieve this (see Chapter 12). The best evidence a company can look for is a certificate awarded by an accredited certification body that the supplier's systems comply with the relevant part of BS EN ISO 9000. This shows the supplier has a documented quality system to ensure that its products and services conform to specified requirements.

Supplier rating

A firm should review the performance of its vendors to find out how good its existing suppliers are. The measurement system used is called vendor rating. Devising a supplier rating system involves the following steps:

1 List the qualities expected from a supplier.
2 Record supplier's performance against a maximum weighing.
3 Take the necessary actions.

Table 10.2 shows an example of a supplier performance against some measurable and some hard to measure qualities.

Of course, the problems faced by different organizations are what criteria to include, how to measure them objectively and how to weight the results. Subjective criteria such as co-operation, communication and efficient paperwork are hard to measure and will require a subjective assessment of their contribution to the overall performance of the supplier in that field. The balance with each company will depend on the particular needs of the business.

Other criteria are easier to measure. For example, quality achievement can be measured using records of scrap, rework and returns from customers. Price can be measured using competitive tendering, and delivery from delivery notes. A business can buy an off-the-shelf vendor rating system. To develop a custom-made system that is relevant to its particular needs may take longer and is usually more expensive.

It is essential for a firm to evaluate its suppliers' performance at least once a year and give them feedback as to what is being measured and how. Furthermore, time should be set for suppliers

Table 10.2 An example of supplier rating

Criteria	Maximum weighting	Achieved weighting
Quality achievement	20	20
Price	20	8
Delivery performance	20	20
Co-operation in design	20	12
Efficient paperwork	10	7
Good communication	10	7
Total	100	74

to improve their performance. It is also important that small companies should not be afraid of criticizing their large suppliers. Large companies often take customers' views seriously and use them as a way of improving their own performance.

Case Study

With a little help from their computer system, buyers at Lucas's brake factory have secured a major improvement in their suppliers' quality levels. They developed a system on an IBM relational database in order to monitor their suppliers' performance. The computer system can generate a wide range of comparative reports. It can compare one supplier against another, one supplier against the commodity or industry standard performance, suppliers by a particular item. It can immediately generate virtually any report a buyer wants, covering any time period required. The company believes that the system is providing them with the type of information that they and their suppliers need to achieve zero defects. It helps Lucas and their quality department to focus on the real problem areas.

Supplier relations

In today's competitive and complex business environment a firm may be dependent on many other companies for its product and services. Some of these suppliers may be remote and even located in other countries. Also there are many retailers and wholesalers who have no production operations. Service organizations may use supplies that are purchased from other companies. This means that maintaining a good relationship with suppliers is ever more important in all types of operations. To achieve this goal, the purchasing and supply department must ensure that product specifications are sufficiently clear and accurately communicated to vendors in order to obtain the desired performance from suppliers. We have seen in the last section that vendors' performance can be measured using some type of vendor rating system and suppliers should be immediately informed of any deviation from the agreed performance standards. A company needs to establish close relationships with its suppliers by sharing the organization's long-term business objectives and, if necessary, provide suppliers with the required technical support in order for them to meet the product specification. Some of the policies that can be helpful here are described below.

Suppliers' commitment

Care should be taken in selecting suppliers and adopting a vendor rating system that suppliers can understand. To obtain further commitment a company should integrate suppliers into its business by involving them and making them aware of its business plans. This step and some other initiatives are explained below.

Sharing business objectives

Vendors need to know, as far as possible, about the company they supply to in order to plan their own future. Using an 'external' version of the business plan a company should share the following information with its suppliers:

- the past and current company performance in the key markets
- the plans for new markets and investment
- the targets for the year ahead.

Working closely together means that, in a similar way, a firm needs to know about its suppliers' business plans. This enables the company to help vendors by feeding into their investment planning process through informing suppliers about what their markets wants and when it wants it.

Sharing purchasing and supply plans

It is increasingly common for the purchasing and supply department to share information with vendors about its purchasing plans and priorities for the coming months and years. This includes information about the volume of purchases planned in each key area and the target the department has been set by the business. The result of this type of co-operation is that the purchasing and supply function can see from their vendor ratings how they are performing, and the suppliers can see from the company business plans where it is going. The vendors can also identify from the purchasing plans their future opportunities and challenges.

Case Study

Electrolux is a consumer goods producer. The company prefers to 'pull' rather than to 'push' suppliers towards their targets, which include zero defects, improved delivery and a more committed approach. For those suppliers who respond the carrot is greater share of Electrolux's business. The company wants to be a very important customer to their key suppliers, with both sides benefiting from a close relationship. The company believes that the co-operation between buyer and supplier is crucial. They have reduced half their supply base by dropping those suppliers that did not respond to company targets. Using a comprehensive supplier audit and approval exercise, coupled with monthly performance reports, the company identifies those suppliers with which Electrolux wants to continue doing business. The company supports quality improvement programmes with all its suppliers and monitors their attitudes as well. They want proactive suppliers who can come up with good ideas as well as good products.

Encouraging participation

Many companies today are moving away from centralized purchasing and supply. They are encouraging direct communication between suppliers and their users. This means that people from every function should be able to talk and work closely with staff in supply companies and vice versa. This does not eliminate top-level liaison between buyer and supplier companies, which is essential in order to build confidence and develop shared objectives. Some of the ways to motivate suppliers and improve communication are:

1 *Prizes*. For example, 'supplier of the month', and 'supplier of the year' awards. These are usually given by large companies to those suppliers that perform well in their vendor rating system
2 *Supplier newsletter*. This is suitable for companies with enough suppliers. The occasional newsletter or magazine can be used to publicize the supplier of the year and to give a summary of the company business plans, purchasing forecast and some of the advances made by the company.
3 *Supplier open day*. Usually most day-to-day contact between buyer and supplier is between operational people. The supplier

open day provides an opportunity to establish contact between senior management on both sides. It allows exchange of information and, more importantly, it demonstrates to senior people in supply companies that top management in buyer companies sees supplier development as a strategic part of its business planning.

Case Study

Coventry-based Dunlop Aviation Division believes in giving credit where it is due. Through its Supplier of the Year award, the company sends a clear signal to suppliers that their performance affects its bottom line. According to the company's Head of Purchasing and Supply, 'At a time when the market is becoming increasingly competitive, and customers are demanding reduction in unit price, and improvements in quality and delivery performance, the company needs support from key suppliers in order to achieve these goals'. The first of such awards went to California-based International Light Metal Corporation. The second award went to Spencer Clark of Rotherham for their service and delivery, quality, reliability, cost control and flexibility of response to new requirements. The company believes that when they introduced these awards, they hoped that the award would raise the profile of Dunlop Aviation and give their suppliers something to strive for. All those suppliers who have won the Supplier of the Year Award have seen it as a big moral boost.

Advantages of partnership

Working closely with suppliers in a climate of trust and co-operation can lead to mutually beneficial improvements both in the buyer and supplier businesses. Some of these include the following improvements.

Improved information flow

Generating and transferring information between buyer and supplier costs money. By working with suppliers a company can concentrate on really important information and automate their transfer. Electronic data interchange can be used for exchange information on orders, delivery and invoices. Stockholders and distributors allow customers into their stock records electronically. The process can be cheaper than the traditional methods used and it will help to reduce inventory level and improve delivery performance.

Case Study

Forms UK Plc specializes in print management, combining its core skills of print procurement with other value-added activities such as storage, distribution and information management. The company believes that getting its database system right is of major importance. They use electronic commerce/Internet for purchasing enquiry, order processing and transaction records. The company view is that using multimedia helps in the selling process. Also, generating quality information can enhance operational efficiency. This, in turn, will provide additional capacity and a reduction in operating costs.

Improved quality

Quality assurance involves everyone inside a business and those among its suppliers in the elimination of errors. This means that attitudes both in-house and amongst suppliers must change if a company aims at providing its customers with quality every time. In building a quality improvement programme among suppliers a firm should:

● identify quality priorities by analysing the supplier's quality performance
● review its performance and reporting systems to make sure that they are providing the purchasing department with what it needs
● develop jointly agreed targets with suppliers and build jointly managed improvement programmes
● use joint approaches to deal with the rest of the supply chain.

Improved design

Companies need to provide suppliers with clear functional specifications and, where possible, let vendors design the products they will have to make, in materials that are cost-effective and with processes that are quality assured. This means that they should include suppliers' representative in their design and value analysis teams and incorporate their suggestions if the ideas are useful. Equally, it is useful for a buyer to get involved in the supplier design process. This will help to focus on problems that matter, as well as learning about vendors' methods and technologies.

Improved materials flow

As co-operation between buyer and supplier companies increases they will see each other more as partners. Hence, inventory management extends down the supply chain. The two inventory managers can work together and concentrate on stocks that are really needed at the most cost-effective place in the supply chain, while working to reduce queues and buffer stock everywhere else. This approach requires the supplier to have detailed information about the buyer's sales or production plans, and for the buyer business to know about the supplier's response capability. The result will be lower stocks and therefore lower costs.

Improved financial co-operation

As buyers and suppliers get to know and trust each other better, they will find out more about their financial positions and will be able to save oneanother financially. Electronic data interchange can be used between buyer and supplier to pay on an agreed date. This can save both sides a lot of money, time and paperwork. Furthermore, suitable payment terms can be negotiated to help both businesses by using different terms at different times of the year to meet particular seasonal cash flow variations.

The importance of purchasing and supply

The purchasing and supply function plays an important role in all types of business. Financially, a large proportion of a company spending is usually taken up by the cost of materials purchased.

Operationally, the quality of materials as input can influence the quality of the outputs. Furthermore, shortage of stock and dealing with inadequate suppliers will affect the efficiency by which products and services are produced. Strategically, getting suppliers involved in planning the corporate goals can help the buyer business to meet its long-term objectives successfully.

The interface between purchasing and operations

Effective and regular communication between purchasing and other departments in a company can significantly improve the quality and delivery of goods and services produced. These internal functions include:

1 *Design*. This gives purchasing department more scope to establish the required performance specifications for materials.
2 *Production*. Integration between purchasing and production departments can lead to delivery, quality and flexibility advantages.
3 *Finance*. Communication with the finance department enables purchasing staff to ease cash flow problems through negotiating longer terms for payments or smaller but frequent deliveries.
4 Marketing. A good relationship between purchasing and marketing functions can help purchasing people develop new sources of supply in good time.
5 Sales. Interaction between purchasing and sales departments enables sales staff to know about cost make-up of products and take care of margins when dealing with customers.

Purchasing process

The purchasing function is responsible for buying both the transforming and the transformed resources that are needed by operations to provide goods and services required by the end customers. In order to satisfy this important responsibility both efficiently and cost-effectively, purchasing staff are involved on a day-to-day basis in activities such as defining the purchase specifications, selecting preferred supplier(s), placing orders and so on. The purchasing department is also involved in activities such as value analysis and make or buy decisions in order to reduce the cost of materials and supply.

Purchasing mix

The key elements of purchasing mix are price, quantity, quality and delivery. To obtain the best purchasing mix for materials and services required by different operations, the purchasing manager is responsible for making goods and services available at the right price, to the right quantity, in the right quality and for delivery at the right time.

Supply chain management

Supply chain management deals with the entire chain of raw materials, manufacture, assembly and distribution to the end customer. To manage this chain efficiently and effectively the following concepts should be understood:

1 *Supplier selection*. This refers to making every effort early on to select the right suppliers.
2 *Supplier appraisal*. This is to do with the ability of a company to evaluate performance of its existing and potential suppliers. A firm needs to question its suppliers' financial stability, their ability to do the job, their available capacity, the clarity of the product specifications and ease of access.
3 *Supplier rating*. Organizations need to review their suppliers' performance at least once a year to find out how good they are performing. A vendor rating system involves listing the qualities expected from a supplier, recording the supplier's performance against a maximum weighting, examining the results and taking any necessary actions.

Supplier relations

Close relationships between buyers and suppliers are essential in today's competitive business environment, especially when some suppliers may be remote or located overseas. To obtain the desired performance from suppliers, the purchasing department should make product specifications sufficiently clear and communicate them accurately to their vendors. Close partnership can be achieved through:

- obtaining suppliers' commitment
- sharing business objectives
- sharing purchasing and supply objectives
- encouraging participation.

Advantages of partnership

Working with suppliers in a climate of co-operation and trust will lead to many improvements in the buyer and supplier businesses. These benefits include:

- improved information flow

- improved quality
- improved design
- improved materials flow
- improved financial co-operation.

Self Assessment

1 Differentiate between the financial and operational importance of the purchasing and supply function.
2 List four functions whose interaction with purchasing will enhance customer satisfaction.
3 List four advantages gained by a firm when there is frequent communication between its production and purchasing departments.
4 List three factors that should be taken into consideration when purchasing materials and products that represent the best value.
5 The following are part of purchasing function responsibilities, except:
   (a) selecting and evaluating sources of materials
   (b) developing and maintaining close relationship with supplier
   (c) co-operating in cost reduction activities
   (d) negotiating sales of goods and services to the end customer
   (e) seeking new materials and products from new suppliers?
6 The purchasing process include the following, except:
   (a) designing product and service specifications
   (b) sending request to potential suppliers
   (c) evaluating quotations
   (d) selecting preferred supplier(s)
   (e) placing purchase order?
7 The following information about suppliers should be kept for their evaluation, except:
   (a) financial health
   (b) organizational structure
   (c) quality of supplies
   (d) delivery performance
   (e) price level?
8 State different ways by which materials can be sourced by a buyer business.
9 The following are the benefits of multisourcing, except:
   (a) risk of interruption in supply is reduced
   (b) competition for future business is stimulated
   (c) can switch sources in case of failure
   (d) easy to encourage commitment by suppliers
   (e) access to wide source of expertise?

10 Advantages of single sourcing include the following, except:
(a) bargaining power is increased
(b) paperwork is reduced
(c) less vulnerable to disruption
(d) strong and long-lasting relationship
(e) better communication?

11 In addition to the purchasing department state four other departments that could be involved in a value analysis exercise.

12 List four questions that may be asked by a value analysis team about a product.

13 List three questions that should be asked by the purchasing and supply staff when involved in a make or buy decision.

14 The make or buy decision needs input from marketing and finance functions. True or false?

15 The make or buy decision has no implication on the in-house capacity. True or false?

16 The purchasing manager is responsible for the following elements of the purchasing mix, except:
(a) delivery
(b) distribution
(c) quality
(d) quantity
(e) price?

17 When negotiating the best overall value deal, purchasing department should consider the following factors, except:
(a) supplier location
(b) delivery of supply
(c) urgency of order
(d) stockholding requirements
(e) quality of supply?

18 Supplier SQA is a programme devised by vendors to help them reach the quality levels expected by the buyer's business. True or false?

19 Global sourcing means to look nationally for suitable suppliers. True or false?

20 Purchasing management is the same as materials management. True or false?

21 Supply chain management is to do with managing materials in the following areas, except:
(a) raw materials supply
(b) manufacturing
(c) assembly
(d) selling

(e) distribution to end customer?

22 A company needs to ask the following questions about its suppliers' characteristics, except:
(a) capacity constraints
(b) ability to do the work
(c) financial stability
(d) ease of access
(e) all of the above?

23 List three steps that are required in devising a supplier rating system.

24 The following criteria are subjective in evaluating a supplier, except:
(a) quality achievement
(b) delivery performance
(c) co-operation in design
(d) efficient paperwork
(e) good communication?

25 Quality achievement of a supplier can be measured by collecting the following data, except:
(a) scrap record
(b) rework record
(c) investment record
(d) returns from customers
(e) number of complaints?

26 Commitment from suppliers can be enhanced by getting them involved in the buyer's business plan. True or false?

27 List three types of information from a buyer's business plan that can be shared by suppliers.

28 The following ways can be used to motivate suppliers, except:
(a) supplier of the month award
(b) supplier of year award
(c) supplier newsletter
(d) supplier open day
(e) all of the above?

29 Quality assurance involves those inside a business and amongst its suppliers. True or false?

30 Close relationship with suppliers can be achieved through the following, except:
(a) merging with supplier's business
(b) sharing business objectives
(c) sharing purchasing plans
(d) encouraging participation
(e) getting suppliers committed?

31 Working closely with suppliers can lead to the following improvements, except:
   (a) improved information flow
   (b) improved design
   (c) Improved quality
   (d) improved materials flow
   (e) all of the above?

References and further reading

Baily, P., Farmer D., Jessop, D. and Jones, D. (1994). *Purchasing Principles and Management*. Pitman.

Burt, D. N. (1984). *Pro-active Purchasing*. Prentice Hall.

Gattorna, J. and Walters, D. (1996). *Managing the Supply Chain*. Macmillan.

Lee, L. and Dobler, D. (1977). Purchasing and Materials Management. McGraw-Hill.

Saunders, M. (1994). Strategic Purchasing and Supply Chain Management. Pitman.

Slack, N., Chambers, S., Harland, C., Harrison, A. and Johnston, R. (1998). *Operations Management*. Pitman.

Chapter 11

Quality management

This chapter is concerned with quality – its relevance and definition, its measurement, control and improvement. Among the topics considered are:

Learning Objectives

1 *Relevance*. Why is quality an issue? Quality is seen as an order winning or entry criterion in most product and service markets, but it is also increasingly seen as important in public service and not-for-profit organizations. It is also an important contributor to cost.

2 *Definition*. Everyone knows what they mean by quality. Unfortunately one person's definition does not necessarily agree with the next person's. Quality is multifaceted and complex, and a clear definition is essential for measurement and control.

3 *Cost*. There are costs associated with poor quality, of which the cost of rejected goods is perhaps the most obvious, but quality management and improvement also involve cost. The classic case for an appropriate cost balance is presented.

4 *Measurement*. Neither control nor improvement is possible without measurement. Various means of measuring quality in both manufacture and service are discussed.

5 *Control and improvement*. Control implies improvement, since if quality declines then control demands that it be restored.

> Increasingly, as a result of the total quality movement, quality is being seen as a journey rather than a destination. The idea of an acceptable level of quality is no longer necessarily acceptable itself. Some of the methodologies and techniques of the total quality movement are outlined.
>
> 6 *Standards*. The increasing emphasis on quality in all areas has led to an increasing prominence for quality standards. Two of the most widespread quality standards are discussed.

Why quality?

In Chapter 2, the concepts of entry and order-winning criteria were introduced. In order to trade at all an organization must satisfy the entry criteria of the market. In order to prosper it must match and exceed the competition in performance on order-winning criteria. In many situations some sort of quality certification is essential, and the ISO 9000 certification scheme, which was once seen as an order-winning criterion, is now increasingly an entry criterion. Even in the public and not-for-profit sectors, where competition is not usually present, attempts have been made, in the UK in particular, to make quality of service an issue.

Quality is only one aspect of the product or service that might be an order-winning or entry criterion, but it is invariably present and is frequently promoted by suppliers in an attempt to gain competitive advantage.

Quality itself is an abstract concept so most examples are of particular aspects of quality. Two that are well recognised are shown below.

Case Study

In the 1960s, corrosion resistance was an important order-winning criterion in the UK car market, and many manufacturers performed quite badly. Substantial improvements in corrosion resistance, partly forced by competitive pressure, have since occurred with the result that it is no longer a major consideration in car purchase. It has become an entry criterion and is taken for granted.

A chain of car maintenance workshops promotes itself under the motto 'our aim is 100 per cent customer delight'.

Quality of the operation itself can have a direct impact upon costs and hence on profitability. A poor quality process will lead to high reject and rework costs – an unnecessary waste of material and capacity. If this is the best that can be achieved then the market may be prepared to pay the necessary price, but in a competitive market a poor quality process has an adverse effect upon profitability.

Flat-screen liquid crystal displays (used mainly in portable computers, but increasingly in flat-screen television receivers) require several electronic components to drive each pixel. A moderate resolution 25 cm screen might contain more than 1.5 million pixels. If they do not all work perfectly the display is unacceptable. A 75 cm display of acceptable resolution may require 3 million pixels or more. Process technology can now make small screens with an acceptable reject rate, but the reject rate rises rapidly with size, hence the very high cost and limited availability of large flat displays at the time of writing.

In public sector and not-for-profit organizations, the impact of quality is less obvious since competition and profit are not obvious issues. It has been argued that quality in not-for-profit organizations is a moral issue; poor quality is a waste of an invariably limited resource. The UK government, in particular, has sought to raise the profile of quality by introducing performance targets. A form of competitive pressure is introduced in the form of published league tables, and these are being applied in education, health care, local government services, etc. User expectations are raised by the development and publication of 'charters', and performance targets are specified. Penalties varying from public censure to the complete replacement of the management team are imposed for failure to perform. The measures and targets are often simplistic, and open to manipulation and abuse, but do serve to concentrate the minds of both suppliers and consumers.

Case Study

In health care within the UK National Health Service, targets for maximum waiting times for hospital treatment are set. This is, at present, a blanket target and has led to the belief that hospital admissions are sometimes prioritized on the basis of speed of treatment, thus maximizing throughput, rather than on clinical needs. In any case, waiting time, from the point of view of the hospital, does not begin until the first consultation. The patient may wait up to eighteen months for this consultation.

Even in administrative functions and internal services (data processing for example) poor quality has an impact on the costs not only of the function concerned, but also of those other departments dependent upon that function. With the increasing trend towards outsourcing, almost any internal function could be seen as subject to competition as well.

Exercise

How does the quality of service differ between a self-service supermarket and a department store?

Quality is an issue of universal relevance, which, rightly or wrongly, needs to be addressed in all operations.

What is quality?

While seven or more definitions of quality can be found fairly easily in the literature, three definitions cover all the issues of relevance to operations.

Design quality

This represents the degree to which the design of the product or service meets the requirements of the market. Satisfactory design quality requires a clear understanding of the requirements of the customer, and a product or service specification that matches this. Design quality is not specifically an issue for operations, since the task of operations is to deliver to specification. If the specification is wrong, the problem rests with design. This quality is frequently described as meeting customers needs.

Case Study

Design quality failure is not always immediately obvious, but is usually the most expensive to correct if not detected until after the product launch. The Ford Pinto was a popular American car that seemed adequately to meet customer needs. It became apparent after its launch that the petrol tank was very vulnerable to rupture in a collision, because of its location – a design fault that meant the car did not satisfy the market requirement for safety. The cost of redesigning the vehicle, re-engineering the production process and withdrawing all existing vehicles was such that the company seriously considered the trade-off between this investment and simply paying compensation and legal costs as and when accidents occurred.

Exercise

Automated teller machines are designed to meet certain customer requirements in retail banking. Identify the key requirements that ATMs meet, and any that they do not satisfy. Would the perception of quality of service vary with different sectors of the market?

Conformance quality

This represents the degree to which the product or service delivered to the customer matches the specification. Conformance quality is clearly an operations issue since operations is responsible for producing to specification, however, 100 per cent success may be an unrealistic expectation. This is usually described as conformance to specification.

ATMs fail to provide the specified service for a variety of reasons. Identify these, and consider how a bank could reduce or eliminate them.

Operations quality

Delivery to specification can be achieved either by getting things right first time, or by inspecting out defects. The quality of the operations process will be reflected in the number of defects produced, but inspection can still ensure that conformance quality is satisfactory. Defects and inspection have an adverse effect upon costs, but it may still be more cost-effective to use an inferior process followed by inspection than to invest in a process capable of perfection. This quality corresponds to the well-known exhortations of right first time and zero defects.

A bank centralized its main supplementary services (insurance, loans, mortgages, etc.) at a number of specialized service centres. Customers took requests and queries to their local branch, which forwarded them to the appropriate enquiry centre. The system was intended to provide a same day reply for morning enquiries and a following morning reply for afternoon enquiries. While replies were usually received on time, they were frequently incomplete or erroneous.

What advantages to the bank are there in this arrangement, and how should it address the quality issues arising from the failure of the operation?

It should be noted that the distinction between these three qualities is very real in manufacturing, but rather less clear in services. The ultimate judge of quality in services is always the customer – a dissatisfied customer has had a poor quality service regardless of the cause – and the customer is not particular interested in whether the service was poorly specified or poorly delivered. Service specifications are frequently vague compared with product specifications, so it might be difficult for a service provider to convincingly argue that the service met specification. A further problem arises because of the presence of the customer during service delivery confuses conformance quality and operational quality. The strategy of inspecting out defects can realistically only be used when the customer is not present. This is one of the reasons for the preference for a high back shop content in service design – it increases the proportion of the service that can be quality assured before delivery.

Cost of quality

Two costs associated with quality have already been identified – the cost of failure to compete effectively in the market and the cost of rejects. Most authorities identify two classes of cost, each with two major components, which include these.

Cost of conformance

The term 'conformance' is sometimes used here to mean conformance to customer/market requirements, rather than the narrower conformance to specification. The components are prevention and appraisal.

Prevention

All costs associated with the prevention of failure and, in the wider definition, improvement of quality. These include:

- training of staff and customers
- sourcing of quality components and maintenance of supplier relations
- sourcing of quality plant, maintenance of plant and appropriate set-up of plant (see 'Statistical process control' section in this chapter)

- redundancy in the product and the process
- design and redesign of product and process.

ATMs beep and refuse to dispense cash until the card is removed. This greatly reduces the risk of a quality failure caused by customers forgetting to remove their card.

Appraisal

All costs associated with monitoring performance and detecting failure. These include

- inspection
- testing
- the stock costs of holding goods for inspection or test
- the materials tested if the test is destructive.

A great deal of electronic equipment is 'burned in' before being shipped to the customer. This greatly reduces the likelihood of early failure, but can add a week or more to the production cycle. If the normal assembly time of a product is two weeks this would represent a 50 per cent increase in work in progress stock.

Cost of failure

Failure to meet the required level of quality will always result in a cost penalty. It is usually convenient to divide these costs according to where the failure occurs.

Internal failure

All costs associated with quality failures detected prior to contact with the customer fall into this category. They include:

- cost of scrap
- cost of rework
- cost of stock held in anticipation of, or as a result of, failure
- cost of idle capacity – this may be held to allow for the variability caused by failure, or it may simply result from a delay in the process caused by an earlier failure
- damage to plant and equipment caused by processing defective materials
- loss of motivation – no one gets job satisfaction from producing rubbish.

Appraisal costs are sometimes included in the list of internal failure costs, since appraisal is only necessary when production is less than perfect.

External failure

The boundary between internal and external failure is not always clear-cut, particularly in services, but, in general, external failure costs arise when a quality failure is apparent to the customer. The main sources are:

- costs of rectifying problems on site
- costs of handling returns from the customer
- costs of providing customer support
- costs of processing complaints
- compensation payments
- loss of goodwill, possibly the most important since it has a long-term effect on future custom and profitability, but is the most difficult to quantify.

Case Study

A city centre regeneration scheme depended in part upon a new road bridge. As the scheme was intended as a showpiece of urban design, the bridge design was chosen to be aesthetically pleasing.

A result of this was that it involved some slender high technology steel supports. When these were delivered, one was found to be defective. The whole project was delayed by six months while a replacement was made.

Cost balance

Quality failure is not necessarily undesirable. Perfection may be unattainable in practice, and even if attainable may not be economically viable.

At any given stage in the development of a product or service, it can be argued that there is an optimum level of quality that balances the costs of conformance and failure. This is illustrated in Figure 11.1.

It is clear however that, as quality increasingly becomes an order-winning or entry criterion for more markets, the balance point is moving inexorably to the right.

Measurement of quality

Control requires measurement and a standard of performance with which to compare the measurement. Improvement requires diagnosis of the cause of failure to meet the performance standard and

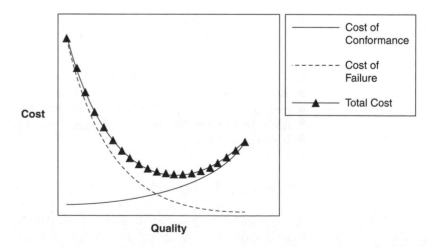

Figure 11.1 Optimal quality level

some capacity for action to improve the situation. For this reason it is never enough to simply say 'quality is poor', information must also be present on which aspects of quality are poor, and to what extent. It is usually also necessary to know when and where the problem arose in the process. It is not enough to simply measure quality, it must be measured in context and in a way that allows interpretation.

Measurement of design quality

Design quality is concerned with meeting the needs of the market. Therefore, its measurement must depend upon customer perception. In general, failures of design quality will only become apparent through customer dissatisfaction. In much of manufacturing, clear specifications are agreed between supplier and user, frequently enshrined in industry or international standards, and there is little opportunity for design quality failure.

When dealing with consumer goods, or services, the situation is less clear-cut. A product may match its specification perfectly, but fail to satisfy the customer – this is a design quality failure. In services the specification is rarely as unambiguous, there is much more scope for customer dissatisfaction and this may be a design quality failure. However, in services the customer is present during some, if not all, of the operation, so customer dissatisfaction may be generated by conformance and operational quality failure.

It should not be forgotten that there are service issues even in industrial product supply. It is not enough that the product meets specification, it must also be correctly supplied.

Design quality measurement is an inexact science belonging to the field of market research rather than operations. The methods used include:

- monitoring complaints
- satisfaction surveys
- focus groups
- mystery shoppers.

All have their merits and their disadvantages. From an operations viewpoint, the important issue is the identification of the source of the failure. If it really is a design quality problem then there is little that operations can do to correct it.

Measurement of conformance quality

Conformance quality is probably the easiest quality to measure, at least for products. It involves measurement of any property, characteristic or dimension of the product or service and comparison of this with the specification. This inspection may be indistinguishable from the measurement of process quality and the same process is often used for both, but the intentions are different. Measurement of conformance quality is directed towards the output from the whole operation, while measurement of process quality is concerned with the means.

The output of conformance quality measurement is a record of failures or defects that reach the customer.

Measurement of process quality

Any measure of failures or defects is a measure of process quality. This may take place during processing, after completion but before delivery to the customer or, even, after delivery to the customer. Generally, however, it is intended to prevent failures reaching the customer.

The inspection process

Measurement may take place through a 100 per cent inspection process or through a sampling scheme. The advantages of sampling are:

1 *Lower cost.* Only a small proportion of items needs to be measured, so the cost in terms of labour and time is lower.
2 *Thorough inspection can take place.* It may be necessary to dismantle or even destroy the product to check quality. Checking a can of beans for foreign bodies, or a bolt for breaking strain, destroys the product and could only be done on a sample basis. If every customer in a service were a mystery shopper there would be no service capacity to offer the genuine customer.

However, sampling has one major disadvantage: it will not detect all failures. The fact that all items in a sample are perfect does not mean that the rest of the batch is necessarily acceptable.

One hundred per cent inspection does not guarantee perfect quality, the inspection process itself can fail, and if inspection involves dismantling a product, faults could be introduced during reassembly. Despite this it is widely used for complex products and for safety-critical products.

In washing machine manufacture, each machine is tested at the end of the assembly process to ensure that the basic functions operate, without leaks.

Cars are usually driven from the end of the assembly line to the local storage area, thus ensuring a basic functionality. Neither of these are exhaustive tests of course, but they are considered adequate in addition to the various inspections which take place during the process.

The fact that product recalls are not unusual indicates the trade-off between quality and cost that is always present.

Electronic equipment, in particular, tends to follow the bathtub curve. A relatively high number of faults occur very early in life, then there is a relatively trouble free period of operation until the product begins to wear out.

In order to eliminate the early failure element and ensure that reliable goods are shipped to the customer, manufacturers may 'burn-in' the product. This involves operating it for several hours or even days to allow early faults to arise and be corrected. This is a high cost strategy, and tends to be used only at the high quality end of the market.

A personal computer assembler is concerned at the high number of early warranty and service claims it is receiving. Specifications of machines have increased and prices reduced dramatically over the past year and during this time claims in the month after shipping have increased from 7 per cent to 20 per cent. A typical machine now costs £1000, and the average warranty/service claim costs the company £100.

What is the economic case for adopting a twenty-four hour burn-in period if this would reduce claims in the above case study to 5 per cent?

Methods of measurement

Measurement must suit the characteristics of the product or service being measured, but it should also provide the necessary diagnostic information for identification of the source and nature of the quality failure. Simply knowing that there were twelve customer complaints last week is of little value, even if put in context that the average number of complaints is fifteen a week. The nature of the complaints must be defined so that the causes of failure can be identified.

It is much easier to measure the physical characteristics of products. For the control of conformance and operations quality, these characteristics must be compared with specification. More subjective elements of products (aesthetic elements, for example) and most aspects of services that involve customer contact are far more difficult to deal with and will be considered later.

Specification usually has dimension and is objectively measurable. Examples include:

- physical size – length, thickness, volume (for example a two-inch number 6 wood screw)
- weight (200 mg penicillin tablet)
- density (90 gm photocopying paper)
- electrical specification (60 watt light bulb)
- viscosity (lubricating oil)
- colour density (paint, fabric, paper)
- time (time to failure, waiting time – maximum waiting time for hospital admission of eighteen months – service time).

The choice is between measuring the particular characteristic or merely checking it against specification. For example, the weight of a bag of flour can be checked by putting it on a set of scales where the maximum and minimum weights are marked on the dial. It is enough that the weight lies between these limits. Alternatively the precise weight of the bag could be noted and recorded. Recording the precise weight requires more skill and takes more time – it is more costly – but it gives more information (such a process would almost certainly be automated, but it is still simpler to check to a tolerance rather than record a precise weight). Attribute inspection (simply checking that the product is within specification) is most often used for measuring conformance quality. Actual measurement is more often used in measuring process quality since the additional information is needed for process control.

Statistical quality control

Statistical quality control is the approach used when it is reasonable to define an economically acceptable level of defectives in the output from an operation. It is used both by producers, who will sample batches to ensure conformance, and by customers, who sample consignments as they are received. The theory and practice of acceptance sampling were fully worked out in the 1930s, and are mainly concerned with large batches where some defectives are acceptable. This is frequently the case with such things as electronic components, fastenings, i.e., low value mass-produced items in general.

Case Study

Capacitors, in common with many electronic components, are sold to a specified tolerance rather than a precise value. For example, a particular product may have a capacitance of 100 picofarads +/− 5 per cent. The manufacturing process generates output that follows the normal distribution. If the standard deviation is 1.25 per cent, then there would be about two defectives per batch of 10 000 components. A standard deviation of 1.5 per cent, however, would give twenty per batch. This assumes that the process is producing to a mean of precisely 100 picofarads. If the mean is only 1 per cent off, then, with a standard deviation of 1.25 per cent, the mean defects per batch would be nineteen, and with a standard deviation of 1.5 per cent it would be seventy-seven.

No matter how small the standard deviation and how precise the production set-up, it is statistically impossible to guarantee perfect conformance since, under the normal distribution, any value has a finite probability of occurrence.

The common problem with statistical sampling is generated by the type I and type II errors. In quality measurement, a type I error is generated when the sample indicates that the batch is not within specification when it actually is, i.e., we wrongly reject an acceptable batch. The type II error is, of course, just the opposite: a sample that is deemed acceptable from a batch that is not.

Case Study

A company buys electronic components in lots of 10 000 and tests a sample of 100 from each consignment on receipt. If more than four defectives are found in the sample, the consignment is rejected. A type I error would arise if a consignment had only six defectives, but all happened to be in the sample. A type II error would arise if a consignment had 1000 defectives but only two were picked up in the sample.

Generally, a rejected batch will be 100 per cent inspected. The cost penalty of a type I error is the cost of inspecting the batch when it is not necessary to do so. This cost is borne by the supplier of the product, so is sometimes called the producers risk. The cost of a type II error is more difficult to determine, since it involves the cost penalties of using an excessive number of defective components. It is borne by the customer, so is called the consumers risk. The objective of the sampling scheme is to balance these costs.

Figure 11.2 shows the ideal operating characteristic for a sampling scheme where the acceptable maximum defects per batch is 1 per cent. All batches with 1 per cent or fewer defects are accepted, while all batches with more than 1 per cent defects are rejected. This is obviously unattainable in practice, but the larger the sample the more nearly an ideal characteristic is approached.

Sample schemes are usually expressed as 'N, n, c' schemes, where N is the batch size, n the sample size and c the maximum permitted defects in a sample. The nearer a scheme comes to the ideal operating characteristic, the more it is able to discriminate between batches which should be accepted and those which should be rejected. Schemes are chosen on the basis of a balance between discrimination and cost.

Figure 11.3 shows the operating characteristics for three sampling schemes with a batch size of 10 000.

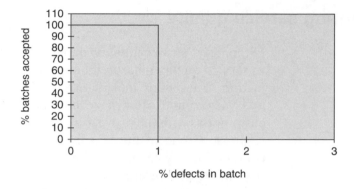

Figure 11.2 Ideal operating characteristic for a sampling scheme

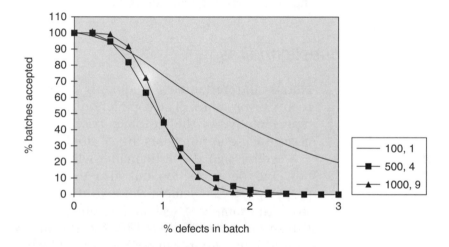

Figure 11.3 Operating characteristics of three sampling schemes

   As might be expected, the larger the sample size the more discriminating the scheme. The scheme based upon a sample of 100 is of very little value and would probably not be considered under any circumstances. The 500-sample size is reasonably discriminating and may well be acceptable. Whether or not the additional discrimination of the 1000-sample size was justified would depend upon a close consideration of the costs.

In practice it is only necessary to determine the relative costs, the acceptable level of defects, and the average level of defects produced by the process. The best sampling scheme can then be found in published tables. It is, of course, necessary that the average level of defects produced by the process is less than the acceptable level of defects.

Measuring service quality

Ultimately, service quality depends on the customer's perception, so service quality measurement reduces to measuring customer satisfaction. The issues that determine customer satisfaction are many and varied, and often have as much to do with the mood of the customer as with the provision of service. This variability of customer response is one of the reasons for seeking to maximize back shop content in service design. The back shop content can be quality controlled as a product.

The measurement of customer satisfaction is more appropriate to marketing than operations, so only a brief review of the more important methods is given here.

Satisfaction questionnaires

Hotels and restaurants frequently leave these questionnaires in rooms or on tables. The completion rate is low and is probably not representative of the customer base, and the design is frequently poor. Such questionnaires are of doubtful value.

A well-designed questionnaire, which not only identifies satisfaction and dissatisfaction but also their causes, administered to a properly selected sample can give reliable data but is quite expensive. An example of such an instrument is SERVQUAL (Zeithaml, Parasuraman and Berry, 1990)) but this involves fifty questions and therefore represents a major investment by both the service provider and the customers surveyed.

Feedback

All organizations should monitor customer feedback, whether praise or complaint. If serious about quality, they should actively encourage it. Again, the problem is that the feedback will not be representative of the general run of customers. Only the really delighted customer is likely to comment on the positive side. On the negative side, it is widely accepted that a disappointed customer is likely to tell ten other people, but not the service provider.

Focus groups

Panels of customers are set up and meet periodically, with a professional facilitator, to discuss issues. The issues may be raised by the panel members or by the service provider. These are more usually used to deal with identified problems or new developments than to monitor ongoing quality.

Mystery shopper

A more or less typical customer is recruited to use the service and complete reports on performance. Mystery shoppers may simply monitor performance, or may be commissioned to look at some particular issue (i.e. how the service deals with a difficult customer). The mystery shopper can give valuable information, but should not be confused with the typical customer. The act of recruitment sensitizes the individual to failure.

Control of quality

The control of quality ultimately reduces to establishing an appropriate balance of the costs of conformance and of failure (see Figure 11.1).

Perfection is considered to be economically unattainable so quality control implies meeting predetermined targets. Acceptance sampling depends on targets like 'mean defect rate of 1 per cent'. Provided this is achieved quality is presumed to be acceptable. If the target is not achieved then investigations will be carried out to find the cause, or at least to apportion the blame.

This tends to lead to a very reactive attitude; problems are solved when they arise, but a degree of complacency is often found. Because quality control is usually the province of the quality department, and dedicated inspectors do the measurement, the normal process operator may not see quality as an issue. This attitude is sometimes seen even with operations managers who might actually blame inspection for quality failures.

Case Study

All is not well at Bloggs Components. Staff absences due to the 'flu epidemic, and a number of inconvenient machine breakdowns have led to delay in the production of a number of orders. Now a batch of fasteners, destined for Apex Engineering, has been rejected at final inspection. Apex Engineering is, unfortunately, a major customer, and the order is already a week late. Only this morning John Morris, the Sales Director, promised that the order would be shipped by tomorrow at the latest. A crisis meeting is in progress in the boardroom, and tempers are becoming frayed.

Bill Jones (Production Manager): 'I really don't see how you can blame me. With half my staff off sick, and a factory that should have been re-equipped five years ago, I think it's a miracle that we get anything made. If Inspection weren't so nit-picking, this order would have been sent two days ago. As it is we are going to have to waste three days inspecting every item and we'll still be short.'

Gordon Brown (Chief Inspector): ' So it's our fault now! My inspectors didn't make the faulty components; they just detected them – and protected the customer from them. We, at least, are concerned about the reputation of the company.'

John Morris: 'I don't care whose fault it is, I just want to know what we are going to do about it. If we don't ship something today we might lose Apex altogether.'

Bill Jones: 'The batch is only 2 per cent over the permitted defect level – according to inspection – and the faults are very minor. I think we should ship it. Apex won't even notice.'

Gordon Brown: 'The batch is substandard. It clearly fails our specification. Once we start saying "it nearly meets specification so it's OK" we might as well give up on quality altogether. We cannot ship this batch.'

Bill Jones: 'You need to get back into the real world and remember who pays your wages.'

Exercise

What should John Morris, in the above case study, do?

Such an attitude is clearly not appropriate when quality is an important market criterion. The pressure for improvement has led to the development of a number of alternative approaches that can be collectively described as total quality management. This sees perfection as the ultimate, if unattainable, aim – 'Quality is a journey, not a destination' – and perceives quality as relevant to all interaction with the customer. The two main targets are *zero defects* (or *right first time*) and *maximize customer satisfaction*. Essentially the organization as a whole should be focused on continuous quality improvement.

Quality improvement

Quality improvement must begin with diagnosis. Without a clear idea of what the problems are, their causes cannot be identified. In the longer term the aim is to ensure that faults do not arise, and to continuously improve the effectiveness and efficiency of the operation, but the short term requires information. Much of the work on diagnostic aids came from Japan where the total quality movement began and, because this depended very heavily upon the involvement of all staff, the techniques tend to be fairly simple.

Total quality management

Total quality management is a philosophy rather than a technique, but its perceived impact upon Japanese industry is so great that almost any organization professing to be 'world-class ' must adopt it. Like just in time (see Chapters 5 and 8), it is difficult to define precisely, and reduced to the essentials there may seem to be very little difference between JIT and TQM. Both aim for the elimination of waste through continuous improvement.

A reasonably comprehensive definition can be derived from the name.

- *Total* – involving every person in the organization and every aspect of its operation (the definition of organization may be extended to include suppliers and customers)
- *Quality* – a customer-centred definition is usually employed, with the ultimate aim of maximizing customer benefit.
- *Management* – although everyone is involved, the role of management is paramount. The senior executive must be fully committed, and this commitment must flow down the hierarchy.

Total quality management is concerned with allowing those in the best position to see improvement potential to implement improvements. The knowledge and experience of the shopfloor operatives are harnessed to drive the improvement process, while the experience of all customer-contact staff is used to identify, develop and satisfy needs.

There are many descriptions of TQM but one of the clearest is that of Nicholls (1993) who identified four phases through which an organization passes to achieve total quality:

- *Phase 1.* The target here is conformance to specification and the systems used include quality assurance, statistical process control and ISO 9000. This is essentially a product- and cost-focused orientation seeking to identify what is currently being correctly carried put.
- *Phase 2.* This uses a quality definition based on fitness for purpose. It achieves this by beginning to develop a team focus and involvement. Systems are more concerned with function and with ideas such as right first time, but the focus is still essentially inward.
- *Phase 3.* The aim now is meeting customer requirements. Systems based upon value chain and customer satisfaction are added. The team focus develops into wide interdepartmental co-operation. The viewpoint is now outwards and the whole organization should be customer focused.
- *Phase 4.* This carries customer focus to its limit, with a quality definition such as 'maximizing customer value'. Organizational re-engineering brings about an integrated partnership focus, and maximizes staff empowerment. Systems will be transparent to the customer, and control will be based upon value added measurement.

Organizations do not necessarily go through these phases in a sequential manner, and they were intended as a classification of development rather than a methodology for implementation. As an approach to implementation, however, it does have the merit of suggesting that an organization should start by clearly identifying what it is actually doing now, the specification, getting that right.

When Girobank introduced TQM in the late 1980s, it achieved an 80 per cent reduction in internal errors. This led to the following improvements:

- a 40 per cent reduction in inventory
- an increase in same day service from 57 per cent to 94 per cent
- a 66 per cent reduction in customer complaints
- a 12 per cent reduction in operations staff
- a £4 million saving in 1990.

Quality improvement tools

Pareto analysis

Pareto analysis is widely used for classifying faults or defects. As with so many other things, it is frequently found that 80 per cent of failures are due to 20 per cent of the possible faults. These are therefore the faults to tackle first. All that is required is a comprehensive record of the reason for each failure. In moving from a quality control approach to a TQM approach an organization may need to change systems to allow this. A system that simply logs whether an item is defective or not must be changed to include a record of the type of fault.

Exercise

A hotel monitors customer satisfaction using a questionnaire completed by guests on departure. The reasons for dissatisfaction (Table 11.1) have been recorded:

Table 11.1

Area	Reason	Number
Reception	Slow	36
	Rude	1

Area	Reason	Number
	Wrong booking	16
	Bill wrong	25
	Messages not received	9
	Messages not passed on	4
Room	Too hot	16
	Too cold	9
	Noisy	9
	Dirty	4
	Too small	9
	Television not working	4
Room service	Slow	4
	Incorrect	4
	Poor quality	4
Restaurant	Slow	9
	Rude	4
	Noisy	1
	Poor quality food	4
Bar	Slow	9
	Rude	4
	Noisy	1

Construct a Pareto curve and identify the main reasons for customer dissatisfaction. Would classification by area, or by fault type, change your conclusions about which to tackle first?

Cause-effect diagrams

These are also known as Ishikawa diagrams, after the Japanese quality guru who popularized them, or fishbone diagrams after their characteristic shape.

They would normally be used after the Pareto exercise as an aid to diagnosing the causes of the main problems. Initially, possible causes would be brainstormed to produce a diagram. This would then be used to investigate the true cause(s). The four main 'bones' of the diagram are sometimes set in advance. This can help get the process started, but can also inhibit the development of ideas. Possible starting points include:

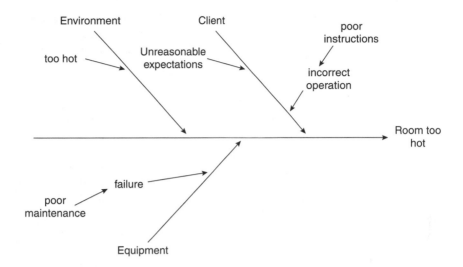

Figure 11.4 Cause-effect diagram of causes of 'room too hot' complaint

● 4Ms – men, machines, materials, methods
● 4Ps – people, policies, places, procedures
● 4Ss – skills, suppliers, systems, surroundings.

Figure 11.4 shows a possible cause-effect diagram for the 'rooms being too hot' problem above.

Exercise

Construct a cause-effect diagram for Reception being too slow in the previous question.

Process charts

Process charts, described in Chapter 4, are a useful way of identifying potential causes of failure. In manufacturing they can highlight vulnerable stages in the operation, as well as causes of inefficiency and delay. In services the use of flow charts which discriminate between the operation of the server and of the customer, can indicate areas where the service would appear to be functioning correctly but is not actually working well from the customer's viewpoint. Flow-charting the customer can also indicate procedures that are unnecessarily complex. Figure 11.5 shows the procedure for ordering, an admittedly obscure, book in a university bookshop. Note that while

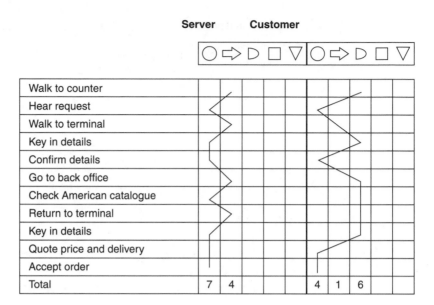

Figure 11.5 Ordering a book: server/customer process chart

the server is productively occupied in seven of the eleven activities, the customer is only productively occupied in four.

Design issues

If quality is to be improved, then generally both component and process quality must be improved. Process quality improvement is implicit in both statistical process control and in quality circles, which are discussed later. Improvements in component quality are usually achieved through developments such as benchmarking and partnership sourcing (see Chapter 10). An important contribution to quality can often be achieved, however, by design simplification.

A product will fail to meet quality criteria if any component in the product fails. It may fail, or perform inadequately, before shipment to the customer or it may fail in use, i.e. be unreliable. Reliability is simply the degree to which the product continues to function to specification. The more complex the product, the more opportunity for component failure and therefore, potentially, the lower the reliability.

If p is the probability of failure of an individual component, and n is the number of components in a product, then the probability of failure of the product is given by:

$$1 - (1 - p)^n \qquad\qquad (11.1)$$

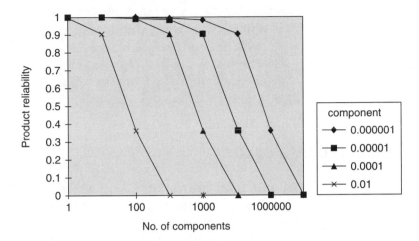

Figure 11.6 Product reliability and complexity

Products such as airliners and cars have many millions of components, so very high levels of reliability are required.

Figure 11.6 shows the relationship between product failure,
component failure and reliability. It is apparent that even with
component failure rates of only 1 in 1 million quality deteriorates
rapidly as product complexity exceeds 10 000 components.

The whole aim of recent developments in microelectronics has
been to overcome this problem through miniaturization. A modern
processor chip contains the equivalent of several tens of millions of
individual electronic components. If a personal computer were to
be assembled from individual components (assuming this was physically possible) then it would probably contain upwards of 1 billion.
Given the reliability of electronic components it would simply not
work.

The same logic applies to processes. Every process has a finite
probability of failure, and therefore the more complex the process
sequence, the higher the probability of that it will not be successfully completed. In manufacturing this means that simple processes
with few stages will produce more consistent quality products. In
services the simple process with few stages is more likely to lead to
a satisfactory outcome.

Exercise

A package holiday is a very complex service process involving
travel, hotel accommodation, services of courier or representative,

as well as the resort facilities and environment. Identify the key steps in the package holiday process (from a customer viewpoint). How many are there? How frequently are they repeated? How many opportunities for quality failure are there?

Statistical process control

All processes are variable, and while variability may be reduced, it can never be completely eliminated. Variation is, of course, the ultimate cause of conformance and operational quality failure. A completely consistent process will produce consistently 'good' output. Walter Shewhart (see Wheeler, 1993) identified two sources of variation, the purely random and that which was due to some change. These are often described as follows:

- *Common cause variation* is intrinsic to the process. Whilst it might be reduced by improving the process design, it cannot be controlled.
- *Special cause variation* is brought about by some influence external to the process. If the cause can be identified then it can be reduced or eliminated. Special cause variation can be controlled.

Case Study

A press, producing 500 mg vitamin C tablets, is capable of operating to a tolerance of +/− 5 mg. This is common cause variation and, short of investing in a better press with a tighter tolerance, nothing can be done about it. Since it is impossible to know if the press is set to produce with a mean of precisely 500 mg, a tolerance must be allowed for the setting. If this is also +/− 5 mg then the total common cause variation is +/− 10 mg. If tablets are found with weights outside this range (say 530 mg for example) then this must be special cause variation. Possible causes include that the press was incorrectly set, the setting has drifted out, tool wear, changes in the powder characteristics, etc. Most likely it is a setting problem, and the press can be stopped and adjusted to bring it back to specification.

Statistical process control is concerned with detecting special cause variation when it arises, and distinguishing it from common cause variation. Change can then be made to the process to bring it back to specification.

The procedures are very similar to those of statistical quality control, but the following are important differences:

● Sampling is carried out at the beginning of the process.
● Sampling is usually carried out by the process operator.
● The objective is to prevent rather than detect faults.

The objective is to ensure that all output is within tolerance. For this to be possible without 100 per cent inspection, it is essential that the process tolerance (the tolerance the process is capable of producing) is tighter than the design tolerance (the tolerance that can be allowed in the product). Taking the example of the 500 mg tablet, if the design tolerance is +/− 10 mg or less then the process will inevitably produce rejects, however well it is set. The ability, or otherwise, of the process to meet requirements is sometimes called the process capability. A simple measure of process capability is given by:

$$PC = \frac{\text{Product Tolerance (Upper limit − Lower limit)}}{6s} \qquad (11.2)$$

where s is the standard deviation of the normal process output, and 6s represents the normal maximum range of output.

A process is deemed to be capable if PC > 1, though a figure of 1.3 or more is preferable. This tolerance safety margin is essential if inspection is to be avoided and zero defects achieved. It can be obtained by improving the process or by relaxing the product tolerance. The product tolerance should always be considered first – is it really necessary that vitamin C tablets should be within +/− 10 mg?

Exercise

Consider the implications of relaxing the tolerance requirements on the following:

● the thread pitch on nuts and bolts
● the weight and thickness of mint sweets
● the pigment content of paint
● the portion size in a restaurant.

Statistical process control uses a regular, usually small, sampling regime. A sample of ten may be taken every fifteen minutes from the output of a process. The sample will be measured and the result plotted on a control chart near the machine. Any measurable parameter can be controlled for. It is frequently physical dimension or weight, but could be other mechanical or electrical characteristics.

Measurement may be by attribute, i.e. the item is within or outside tolerance, or by actual dimension.

Attribute sampling

In statistical process control (SPC), attribute sampling depends upon a definition of defective that reflects the process rather than the product. For example, a tablet may be 'defective' if it lies outside 500 +/− 10 mg even though the product tolerance is +/− 20 mg. The tolerance safety margin allows the process to be adjusted before it starts producing real defects. Attribute sampling usually uses sample sizes of 100 or more, and defines an upper and lower limit for the number of rejects in the sample. If the upper limit is exceeded, the process is stopped and adjusted. If the result lies below the lower limit (always assuming this is not zero), then the implication is that the process is performing better than normal. It should be investigated to determine what lessons can be learned for future improvement.

The limits are set at +/− three standard deviations, the standard deviation being calculated as follows:

$$s = \sqrt{(np(1 - p))} \tag{11.3}$$

where n is the sample size and p is the mean proportion of defects from the process.

Example

A tolerance of +/− 10 mg is applied to the process for producing 500 mg vitamin C tablets. It is found that the average proportion rejected to this tolerance when the process is correctly set is 0.02. If a sample of 100 is taken then:

$$s = \sqrt{(100 \times 0.02 \times 0.98)} = 1.407 \tag{11.4}$$

The upper control limit would now be the mean (p) plus 3s = 2 + 3 × 1.407 = 6.22. The lower limit in this case would be zero. The control chart is shown in Figure 11.7, with some sample results plotted. The machine would be stopped and adjusted after sample 8, which is above the upper control limit.

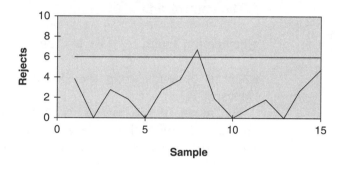

Figure 11.7 Attribute control chart

Sometimes additional warning limits are set at +/− 2s. A result above the warning limit would trigger a second sample immediately, and if the second sample were also above the warning limit the process would be stopped and adjusted.

Case Study

A computer software service department wishes to respond to customer telephone calls within five minutes. Past records show that it fails to achieve this with 5 per cent of calls on average. A sample of 100 calls is monitored each day and the number answered after over five minutes' wait counted. Calculate the upper and lower control limits, and produce a control chart so that the company can detect any deterioration in service.

Dimension sampling

Because measurement gives much more information than simply counting acceptables or rejects, much smaller samples can usually be used. Control charts can be constructed in exactly the same way as for attribute sampling, with limits at +/− three standard deviations, but it is more normal to set the limits using the average range since this is easier to calculate. The average range is derived from a large number of samples and may be periodically updated as further samples are taken.

The control limits are:

specification mean +/− Fx average range   (11.5)

where F depends upon the sample size. Table 11.2 shows some values of F.

The mean of the sample is plotted on the chart, and if it lies outside the limits, the process is adjusted. Unlike attribute control a low value is usually just as much a failure as a high value.

Exercise

Set up a control chart for the weight of 500 mg vitamin C tablets, given that the average range is 12 mg and the sample size is ten.

The general principle of control charts for SPC is that variation within the limits is common cause variation, while variation outside

Table 11.2 Factors for dimensional control charts

Sample size	F
2	1.880
4	0.729
6	0.483
8	0.373
10	0.308
15	0.223
20	0.180

the limits is special cause. In simple process control the special cause is usually simply a need to adjust the process.

In the service sector the cause of variation may be less obvious, and the outcome is more likely to be an investigation to determine the cause and to correct it. In the example of the computer service company quoted above, a deterioration in telephone answering capability could be due to a variety of causes including an increase in calls, absenteeism, high staff turnover, a change in the nature of the help being sought, etc.

Control charts can be applied to one-off measurements as well as sample data. The control limits are based on the mean moving range, and are usually set at +/− 2.66x mean moving range. The moving range is the difference between values in each time period. The calculation is best illustrated by an example.

Example

A company monitors the percentage shipped on time on a monthly basis. This naturally varies (common cause variation) so control limits are required to determine when the variation has become unacceptable. Data for the past six months is shown in Table 11.3.

Table 11.3

Month	1	2	3	4	5	6	Mean
% late	5.4	6.5	8.7	6.6	6.3	6.7	6.7
Moving range		1.1	2.2	2.1	0.3	0.4	1.22

The control chart is shown in Figure 11.8. This indicates that the superficially exceptional figure for month 3 was simply part of the background variation.

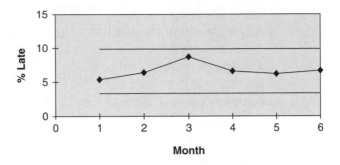

Figure 11.8 Control chart for percentage shipped late

Fitwell Modes, a clothing retail chain, monitors goods returned by customers on a weekly basis. You are the manager of the South-mould branch, and your figures for the last twenty weeks are shown in Table 11.4. Head office is demanding an explanation for the figures for week 20. Construct a control chart to indicate whether or not the figure is exceptional.

Table 11.4

Week	1	2	3	4	5	6	7	8	9	10	11	12	13	14	15	16	17	18	19	20
Returns	5	6	4	5	2	5	1	3	4	5	3	4	0	1	4	1	3	5	2	7

Quality circles

Quality circles are an example of the participatory problem-solving approach also found in kaizen and JIT. Small groups (five to fifteen individuals) of employees from a particular area meet regularly to identify problems with quality. They then analyse the problems and produce proposals for their resolution. This is an aspect of the general TQM philosophy that quality is everyone's business and that teamwork is the best way of solving problems.

The introduction of quality circles may require substantial changes in attitude. Shopfloor operatives, used to thinking of quality as being the province of the quality control department and problem-solving as being the province of management, are often resistant to this extension of their responsibilities. Management often finds difficult the need to delegate responsibility and authority to the shopfloor since it can seem to be a surrender of power and authority. However, if this is not done quality circles will fail since there is little motivation in producing proposals only to see management reject them. Successful implementation requires commitment from management in the form of facilities, training, technical support and a willingness to implement proposals. If proposals cannot be implemented then a reasoned explanation must be given. Within the context of a TQM programme these attitudinal problems should not arise, but implementation of quality circles in isolation rarely succeeds.

While developed initially in manufacturing, quality circles have proved a useful device for harnessing the insight of customer service personnel into customer perceptions in service industries.

Service quality

While much of the foregoing is applicable equally to products and services, some of the specific characteristics of services require additional consideration.

Product quality is usually defined as conformance to specification, and provided the specification meets or exceeds the customer needs then all is well. Even those organizations striving to maximize customer benefit are, in product terms, seeking to ensure that the customer fully realizes the benefits of the specification.

Service quality is entirely in the eye of the customer. A dissatisfied customer has had a poor quality service regardless of the cause of the problem.

Case Study

There has been a great deal of publicity about the poor service provided by the privatized passenger railway companies in the UK, punctuality being a particular issue. The companies, rightly or wrongly, have set some of the blame at the door of the company operating and maintaining the railway tracks, but this is no concern of the passenger who is late. They will inevitably blame the carrier.

Unambiguous specifications are difficult to produce for services, and will not necessarily be accepted by all customers. Many fast food chains (McDonald's for example) seek to control waiting time as a quality indicator, and objective measurable standards can be specified. However, while a three-minute wait might be acceptable or even desirable for someone who is out for the day and not familiar with the menu, it may be far too long for someone on a thirty-minute lunch break who knows exactly what they want.

Services are multifaceted and complex. The criteria that determine quality vary from service to service and person to person. The SERVQUAL model identifies five dimensions of service quality

- tangibles
- reliability
- responsiveness
- assurance
- empathy

and the SERVQUAL questionnaire subdivides each of these into four or five elements. Despite this the model is sometimes criticized for not being comprehensive enough.

Generally, the perception of service quality is seen as being linked to the gap between the customers' expectations and the actual experience. This is illustrated graphically in Figure 11.9, and suggests that a good quality service will always exceed a customer's expectations.

Different aspects of the service will be more or less important to the customer and it is important that the service provider devotes improvement effort to the areas that matter. Customers are also more or less tolerant of variation in different aspects of the service.

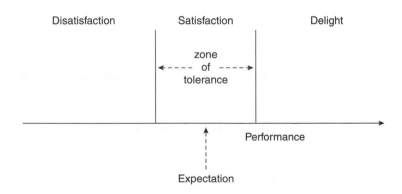

Figure 11.9 Gap between performance and expectation

This zone of tolerance is shown in Figure 11.9, but it may be quite wide for some issues and very narrow for others. It may also change over time.

Exercise

> Competition among roadside rescue services for motorists frequently stresses speed of response. Up and Running Rescue promises a thirty-five minute response but only achieves this in 65 per cent of cases. Roadside Rescue Unlimited only promises a forty-five minute response, but achieves this in 90 per cent of cases. Which gives the 'better' service?

The SERVQUAL model also proposes a number of different causes of any gap between customer expectation and experience, as shown in Figure 11.10. This can be seen as a model for the design of a good quality service, in that it shows all the steps necessary for ensuring that customer expectations are met. It also shows that customer expectations can be managed to ensure that quality is perceived as good. Communication with the customer, through advertising, literature or contracts, establishes a set of expectations. Over-promising will inevitably lead to disappointment and dissatisfaction.

Other influences upon expectations include:

- past experience
- press and television reporting
- the experience of friends and relatives
- general background expectations.

These may be so strong that nothing a company can do will override them. A service encounter that greatly exceeds expectations may not be seen as good, but merely a temporary aberration.

The strength of background expectations, almost folklore, can be so great as to overcome almost anything the service provider can do. Retail banking is one area where this is well established. Fifty-four per cent of dissatisfied bank customers in the UK will not contemplate changing accounts because it is seen as too difficult. A further 27 per cent see no point in changing since all banks are the same (*Observer*, 20 September 1998). Under these circumstances one might ask how important quality of service actually is.

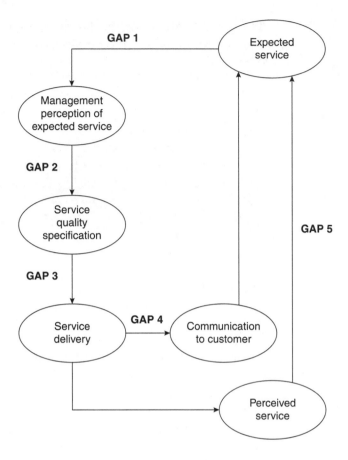

Figure 11.10 The SERVQUAL gap model of service quality

Quality standards

Quality standards for products have a long history, but usually have been designed to ensure that the product actually functions. The pitch and depth of the thread on a nut must be a reasonably close match to that on the corresponding bolt for the pair to function as a fastening. The demands of mass assembly also require that all bolts of a specific size should fit all nuts of that size. Such basic standards are found in most industries and have existed for 100 years or more.

More recently concern has moved from goods to procedures. The capability of organizations to produce consistent quality is recognized, rather than the quality of the output itself. Again this is not new, supply partnerships (see Chapter 10) frequently depend upon the customer validating the suppliers' capability, but the practice has developed to the point where global standards are now required.

It should be stressed that these standards are not about the quality of the product in any absolute sense, but about the capability of the organization to meet its own claims.

ISO 9000 series

The International Standards Organization quality standards require conformity to documented practices. Certification requires that the company produce a comprehensive documentation relating to areas of activity that have a bearing on quality. The company must then demonstrate conformity to this documentation. In other words it must have appropriate quality procedures which it follows.

Continued certification requires periodic third party inspection to ensure that the procedures are still current and still being applied. The ISO 9000 portfolio of standards includes guidance on what standards are appropriate for the activity in question, and what documentation should be produced.

ISO 9000 does not guarantee quality. If the declared objective of an organization is to produce rubbish, then all ISO 9000 certification does is show that the organization is capable of doing this consistently. It has been argued that ISO 9000 is too complex and bureaucratic for small firms, but against this it can also be claimed that all the standard demands is evidence of good practice. Any competent organization should be able to produce this. Whatever the arguments it is now widely demanded and has become an entry criterion for many markets.

The Baldridge award

The Malcolm Baldridge National Quality Award was instituted in USA in 1987. Unlike ISO 9000 it is intended to encourage improvement and reward excellence. Companies enter the award contest for the considerable prestige that winning brings, but even entry itself is seen as a sign of good quality and achieving the site visit stage gives substantial market advantage.

Entering requires completion of a self-assessment and a seventy-five page case study. The discipline of carrying this out is seen as a major stimulant to quality improvement, and the instrument is often seen as a vehicle for self-evaluation outside the USA. Consideration of the documentation by a panel leads to a shortlist of companies which chosen for a site visit. Finally, awards are made in the three categories of manufacturing, service and small business. The European Foundation for Quality Management (EFQM) developed a European version of the Baldridge award in 1991, and this has since become the basis for national awards in most European countries. This model is rather more focused on general business excellence rather than quality, but quality is still the most important element.

Summary

Relevance

1 *Survival* – quality is one of the most important order-winning criteria in many markets, and is an entry criterion in many others.
2 *Cost* – poor quality has a direct impact on cost, again damaging competitive advantage.
3 *Effectiveness* – in not-for-profit organizations, and internal services, poor quality wastes resources that might be devoted to achieving organizational objectives.

Definition

Quality is complex and multifaceted. Three classes of quality are identified:

1 *Design* – the extent to which the product/service design meets customer needs – fitness for purpose.
2 *Conformance* – the extent to which the process delivers a product/service which meets the design specification, i.e conformance to specification.
3 *Operational* – the extent to which the process produces conforming output without inspection/rejection, i.e. right first time.

All three must be correct to produce excellent output.

Cost

The costs of prevention, appraisal, internal failure and external failure have been identified. These may be classed into costs of conformance and costs of failure. There will be some ideal point at which these two costs are in balance, representing the optimum level of quality. In practice this might not be identifiable, and is always changing under the influence of competitive pressure.

Measurement

Measurement of design quality depends on the measurement of customer needs and perceptions, and is more an activity of marketing than of operations. Measurements of conformance and process quality are frequently carried out using samples and the techniques of statistical quality control. These methods always imply that some defects are acceptable. When this is not the case, 100 per cent inspection or even 'burning in' may be used.

Service quality poses particular problems since it cannot be inspected prior to delivery. Again, the methods used are usually those of market research.

Control and improvement

Control alone is rarely seen as an adequate response to quality issues. The total quality movement has led to an almost universal stress on continuous improvement.

Total quality management implies a total commitment of the whole organization to continuous improvement of quality. The ultimate stage is described as an organization totally committed to maximizing customer satisfaction.

A number of TQM tools are described:

- *Pareto analysis*, for classification of problems to establish improvement priorities
- *cause-effect diagrams* to establish problem causes, and process charts to determine their origin
- *design* and the contribution it can make to reliability
- *common and special causes* of variation, and their use to ensure that what is investigated is a problem that it can be dealt with
- *statistical process control* and the concept of *process capability*, intended to ensure that all output is to specification
- *quality circles* as a means of harnessing the skill and knowledge of the whole workforce
- the particular problems of *service quality* and some approaches based on the modelling the gap between expectations and experience.

Standards

The ISO 9000 series of standards is intended to certificate organizational capability rather than quality of product/service, and ensures that the organization is able to, and continues to, meet its own standards. The Baldridge award, and its European derivatives, encourage and reward best practice. Both are seen as important order-winning criteria, and ISO 9000 is, in many markets, an entry criterion.

Self Assessment

1 List four reasons why quality is important in manufacturing.
2 List four reasons why quality is important in services.
3 List four reasons why quality is important in not-for-profit organizations.
4 Design quality is:
   (a) output meeting specification
   (b) specification meeting customer requirements
   (c) process producing to specification?
5 Conformance quality is:
   (a) output meeting specification
   (b) specification meeting customer requirements
   (c) process producing to specification?
6 Operational quality is:
   (a) output meeting specification
   (b) specification meeting customer requirements
   (c) process producing to specification?
7 List four costs of conformance.
8 List four costs of failure.
9 Quality is always measured through inspection. True or false?
10 Quality is always measured using samples. True or false?
11 Statistical quality control aims for:
   (a) zero defects
   (b) minimum defects
   (c) optimum defects?
12 'Burning-in'
   (a) damages products
   (b) increases costs
   (c) prevents early failure?
13 Service quality:
   (a) cannot be measured
   (b) is a matter of opinion
   (c) is not important?
14 TQM is about:
   (a) management being concerned about quality
   (b) getting the right quality level
   (c) trying to avoid customer complaints
   (d) involving everyone in quality
   (e) moving towards perfect quality?
15 Pareto analysis is used to:
   (a) find out who is to blame
   (b) identify the commonest faults
   (c) find what causes faults
   (d) find where faults arise?

16 Cause-effect diagrams are used to:
   (a) find out who is to blame
   (b) identify the commonest faults
   (c) find what causes faults
   (d) find where faults arise?
17 Process charts are used to:
   (a) find out who is to blame
   (b) identify the commonest faults
   (c) find what causes faults
   (d) find where faults arise?
18 Fewer components mean:
   (a) fewer suppliers
   (b) lower costs
   (c) fewer failures?
19 Statistical process control is concerned with:
   (a) controlling process variability
   (b) ensuring output is within specification?
20 Control charts can only be used with samples. True or false?
21 Control charts can only be used by specialists. True or false?
22 List four influences on perceived service quality.
23 List the SERVQUAL dimensions.
24 ISO 9000 ensures:
   (a) high quality
   (b) consistent quality?

References and further reading

Bicheno, J. (1998). *TheQuality 60*. Picsie Books.
Cole, W. E. and Mogab, J. W. (1995). *The Economics Of Total Quality Management*. Blackwell.
Caplan, R. H. A. (1982). *Practical Approach to Quality Control*. Business Books.
Crosby, P. (1979). *Quality is Free*. McGraw-Hill.
Gaster, L. (1995). *Quality in Public Services*. Open University Press.
Ho, S. K. (1995) *TQM: An Integrated Approach*. Kogan Page.
Nicholls, J. R. (1993). Customer value in four steps. *TQM Magazine*.
Oakland, J. S. (1992). *Statistical Process Control*. Heinemann.
Wheeler, D. J. (1993). *Understanding Variation*. SPC Press.
Zeithaml, V. A., Parasuraman, A. and Berry, L. L. (1990). *Delivering Quality Service: Balancing Customer Perceptions and Expectations*. The Free Press.

Chapter 12

Strategic issues in operations management

This chapter is in part intended to highlight some of the key issues developed elsewhere in the book, and in part to look forward to further development and/or study of operations management. It is, therefore, somewhat eclectic. The chapter is mainly concerned with the strategic nature and importance of operations, and develops this through a brief discussion of some of the more important current issues in the subject:

Learning Objectives

1 *The operations environment*. An overview of material already covered, looking at issues of organizational competition, survival and success and the contribution which operations has to make in achieving this.
2 *The product/service dichotomy*. In particular the servicization of manufacturing, and the cross-fertilization of ideas from both manufacturing and service operations.
3 *Productivity, responsiveness and quality*. The continuing development of globalization and technology are increasing the competitive pressure on both cost and responsiveness. The same forces seem to put ever more pressure upon quality of product and service.

The operations environment

Operations is the core activity of any organization. It defines and determines the transformation process that is the organization's *raison d'être*. In the marketplace, operations defines the 'product' which the organization is selling.

Trends influencing operations

Operations has not always had such a central role, and many organizations still behave as if the situation is the same as it was fifty or even a hundred years ago. Operations has always served the marketplace; without demand there is little point in making a product or offering a service. Admittedly, demand can be stimulated artificially, and even perhaps be created from nothing, but this rarely leads to real growth.

Throughout most of the history of industrialization, however, markets for goods in particular have been characterized by under-capacity. The general manufacturing base has been too small to satisfy the market demand. This results, of course, in a situation where most of what is made will sell provided the price is not too excessive and the quality/performance not too poor. Manufacturing organizations certainly competed, but mainly to increase profits, and rarely to survive.

Case Study

An exception to this fairly cosy scenario is the impact of technological development. The gunpowder manufacturing industry saw a significant slump at the end of the Napoleonic wars. Many gunpowder mills went out of business, but some forward-looking owners, seeing the future development of the railways as a source of new business – gunpowder was used in tunnelling, for example – kept their mills operational, and during the middle of the nineteenth century did very good business. Unfortunately dynamite was invented, and gunpowder manufacture disappeared in a very short time.

This situation continued until the 1950s but, thereafter, postwar reconstruction and the increasing industrialization throughout the world began to change the balance. The current situation is characterized by over- rather than undercapacity.

The second major influence is the development of globalization. It is easy to forget that rapid movement of goods, people and information are very recent developments. Until quite recently sea-freight was slow and uncertain, and airfreight did not exist at all. Even international telephone calls had to be booked in advance and were fairly unreliable. The situation now exists where documents and other information can be reliably transmitted to anywhere in the world almost instantaneously and at negligible cost. Containerization has rendered sea-freight far more efficient and reliable, while airfreight, although relatively expensive, is a simple and rapid method of moving low volume, high value material. The barriers to manufacturing and selling goods anywhere in the world are now largely cultural and political. Trade barriers rather than cost and time are the main obstacles to full globalization.

Technological development continues to accelerate, with a substantial amount of evidence to suggest that the growth of technology is exponential rather than linear. This is partly the cause of the rapid development of globalization. Without the rapid development of microelectronics, global communication would not be the facility it is today. Technology, however, influences all areas of operations, from the demands of the marketplace for more sophisticated and reliable products, to the availability of low cost, automated processes. Technological development in unrelated fields can also have a dramatic effect upon established technologies. Of course, local developments rapidly become global.

Case Study

Genetic engineering has been publicized mainly in terms of increased food yields with reduced dependence upon pesticides. In this form it has little implication for operations management – crops are still grown, harvested and processed. The same technology is being used to develop plants/animals that generate pharmaceuticals and even vaccines. The ultimate aim is that a dish of genetically modified food will actually confer immunity to the specified disease when eaten.

Exercise

Consider the implications of this for the operation of a traditional pharmaceutical manufacturer.

The impact on operations

We have moved, in a little over forty years, from a situation characterized by high levels of stability and little competition to a situation characterized by intense global competition, rapid technological change, and increasingly informed and demanding markets. The pressure on operations has been intense, since, at the end of the day, it is operations that must deliver a competitive product in this turbulent environment.

Figure 12.1 represents the traditional manufacturing situation, seen throughout most of the nineteenth century, and up to about 1960 in the twentieth century (and still seen today in many manufacturing organizations that are still living in the past).

The aim of this approach is to maximize efficiency through maximum utilization. Many suppliers are used to trying to minimize cost. As suppliers are being played off against each other, the relationship is characterized by a lack of trust – it is adversarial. Stock is therefore essential to preserve the production schedule against late, or wrong, deliveries. Customers do not matter much either, since there is little competition. They are supplied from stock, with limited choice, or they will wait. As Henry Ford famously said of

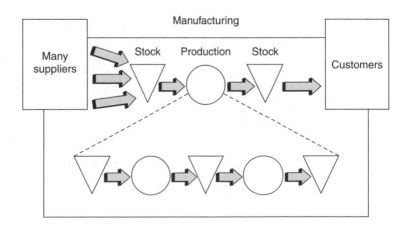

Figure 12.1 Historic manufacturing model

the model T, 'You can have any colour as long as its black'. This allows long runs with the consequent reduction in set-up cost. To ensure that nothing interrupts manufacture, interstage buffer stocks are also held. The net result of all this stock is very slow response times. It may take a year or more for raw material stocks to be converted to finished product and sold. This does not really matter when demand is stable.

To thrive now, as we enter the twenty-first century, a manufacturer must follow a model more like that shown in Figure 12.2.

The production process is run on JIT principles, with little stock and possibly no stock as a goal. This both minimizes cost and maximizes responsiveness. For this to work effectively partnership with suppliers is essential, so few suppliers are used and the relationship is characterized by trust. Suppliers will know the master production schedule and will be kept up to date on changes. With simultaneous engineering, suppliers may even be involved in the design of new products, thus shortening the time to market. On the customer side, the main emphasis is on beating the competition. It is not enough to supply superior products; the customer must be helped to maximize the benefits of these products. Again partnership encourages this and also raises barriers to entry for competitors. Overall the barriers between firms are much less pronounced and more permeable.

Within the organization the emphasis is on maximizing value rather than minimizing cost. All aspects of available resources are recognized and the traditional divisions between labour and management are relaxed. Delayering and the use of empowered teams harness all the human resource of the organization.

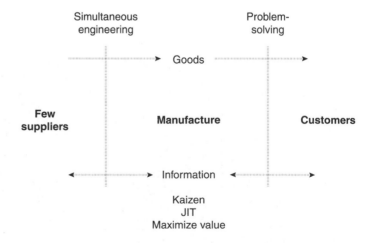

Figure 12.2 Emerging manufacturing model

A manufacturer of dust extraction equipment uses several hundred different fasteners (nuts, bolts, screws, clips, etc.) in the assembly process. These items are of little intrinsic value, but are still essential to the smooth running of the assembly process. They present a major task to both purchasing and stock control. The company subcontracts the whole process of supply of fasteners to a specialist supplier. This supplier sources components, delivers them to stock points on the shopfloor (which it maintains), monitors stock usage and arranges replenishment. Instead of having to deal with several hundred stock lines and several dozen suppliers, purchasing only has one annual contract to manage.

Much of the traditional, hierarchical division-of-labour basis of the traditional scientific management approach has been superseded. The operations function remains the core of the organization, but is now leaner and more responsive. It is still this competence which the organization is selling, but this is now much more explicit. As markets, competition and technology change, so operations must keep pace if a firm is to be successful. If a firm wishes to lead, then operations must anticipate and drive change rather than merely respond to it.

And services

While the emphasis of the preceding section was on manufacturing, where the changes have been most dramatic, the service sector faces the same pressures. Services used, in many ways, to be even more local than manufacturing. Most services were delivered face to face and so had to be within reach of the customer.

Customers are now much more mobile, and the communications infrastructure has developed to the point where many services can be delivered by telephone or computer, possibly with some support from postal and parcels services. Services no longer need to be physically proximate to the customer, which opens the whole market to potentially global competition.

CDs are substantially cheaper in the USA than in Britain. Many purchasers find it convenient to order CDs from American retailers via the Internet. Even with postage and duty charges, this can be significantly cheaper if sufficient numbers are bought.

The effect of globalization on many services has been to increase the back shop content of the service. Front office is no longer so important when the customer is not physically present. It has been replaced by printed material, a computer interface or staff on the other end of a telephone. As in manufacturing, however, there has been increasing pressure on responsiveness and quality. Global services are competing globally and must be comparable with the best. Internet services must have sufficient capacity, and the interfaces must be friendly, relevant and accurate. With telephone services the same applies. Not every service has reached this goal yet, but globalization is far more recent in services.

Improved communications also means that services can be located almost anywhere. The availability of suitable labour is the main criterion, with cost being a frequent secondary consideration.

At the time of writing a number of major bookmakers in the UK are seriously considering relocating their telephone betting services off shore. Gibraltar is a favoured location because its people are English-speaking. This will avoid the tax imposed upon betting by the UK government. Since the tax is paid by the customer rather than the bookmaker, the relocation is mainly for competitive advantage rather than cost reduction.

It might appear that globalization is only a threat to certain services. Services that must be delivered locally – restaurants or hairdressers, for example – may only compete locally, but even here there is the threat from global branding, for example McDonald's in the restaurant trade and Walmart in retail distribution. Monopoly services, for example, public health, welfare, education, might seem to be immune to competitive pressure. The overall increase in the public awareness of quality as an issue has had an impact even on these services. Customers simply have higher expectations and are more willing to express their dissatisfaction if they are not met. In the public sector, government has reacted by seeking to impose surrogate private sector pressures. Charters are published outlining customer rights and league tables are published showing relative performance in education, health care and other public services. Whether these have any real effect upon genuine issues of quality is not proven, but they certainly expose public sector providers to the same sorts of pressure as are found in the private sector.

The product/service dichotomy

Manufacturing has traditionally been seen as concerned with the production of goods. Services were seen as peripheral and economically unimportant. This is certainly no longer true, if it ever was. Services are responsible for the generation of ever-increasing proportions of global wealth as Figure 12.3 shows. In many ways it can be argued that the boundaries between manufacture and service are becoming increasingly blurred.

The response of manufacturing to the environmental changes outlined above has been, in part, to greatly increase the service component of the package. It is not enough to produce goods that

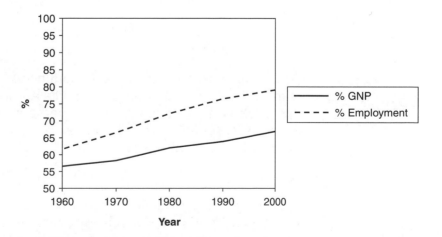

Figure 12.3 Contribution of the service sector to US economy

are of excellent quality and competitive price. Real success requires that the customer is helped to maximize the benefit they gain from the goods. The ultimate TQM aim of maximizing customer benefit, coupled with the problem-solving/partnership approach shown in Figure 12.2, means that service is often as important an element of the transaction as the product.

At the same time, the reverse trend can be seen in many services. Financial services and many retail services are now delivered remotely by telephone or computer. The front office component is reduced to a communications interface, and the back shop element becomes increasingly more dominant. The process of producing an insurance document or packing and dispatching a book order is manufacturing rather than service in operations terms. Perhaps one effect of these trends is that manufacture and service will genuinely merge.

The following brief case studies illustrate some of the developments in book distribution. Similar developments are seen in recorded music. At the extreme, the final stages of manufacture are actually carried out by the customer.

Amazon is a successful Internet-based bookseller. The book buyer may browse the online catalogues by author, title or subject, get an immediate price quotation and even read reviews. Delivery is immediate, by post, if the book is in stock.

The local bookshop offers the opportunity to browse, and actually handle the books. Delivery is immediate if the book is in stock. If the book is not in stock it cannot be seen, and it may not even be easy to identify – the customer is not usually allowed direct access to the catalogues.

A number of publishers are experimenting with direct downloading of books via the Internet. Samples may be read free of charge, but not saved or printed. On payment the whole text may be downloaded and saved, and printed at leisure if required.

Productivity, responsiveness and quality

The new competition has highlighted these three aspects above all others. Maximizing productivity is an essential prerequisite to minimizing cost. While price competition is not necessarily dominant in many markets, competing on other issues usually requires healthy profit margins. In the public sector, the increasing public expectation and scrutiny, and the forced application of private sector methods, has led to similar pressure.

Responsiveness is important on two levels. In terms of existing products/services, maintaining a competitive position requires that customers are not kept waiting. If the demand pattern is variable then the operation must be able to cope with this. In terms of new products/services responsiveness is perhaps even more important. The successful organization leads rather than follows, but must always be prepared to follow on the occasions when they are beaten. Even leading, time to market is increasingly critical. The organization must be able to recover the development and launch costs before the competition catches up.

When Dyson introduced the bagless vacuum cleaner, the major manufacturers first dismissed the idea, but as Dyson sales increased they very rapidly introduced their own versions.

Quality is the other issue upon which competition can obviously be based, and there are few areas where it is not important. The successful organization will compete on all three.

Just in time is sometimes described as 'Producing whatever the customer wants, at minimum cost, with perfect quality, instantly'. This is self-evidently impossible, but it is used as a target to drive the process of continuous improvement. It is precisely this condition which an organization which perfects productivity, responsiveness and quality will achieve. Once a number of organizations approach this, how will they compete? It is difficult to envisage other dimensions for competition, although perhaps social and/or environmental awareness might become significant.

What becomes of those organizations which fail to achieve these rarefied heights of perfection? The evidence is that many consumers are not so discriminating. The overpriced still sells, and many consumers neither expect, nor apparently particularly want, perfect quality. The mediocre will continue to survive, and perhaps even flourish.

Case Study

For the past ten years or more the major UK retail banks have all, at one time or another, stressed quality of service. Despite this, customer satisfaction as measured by independent surveys (for example, the Consumers Association) has shown little or no improvement. Is this because the banks have failed, they have addressed issues that do not matter to their customers or that improving quality of service is not really that important?

Summary

The operations environment

Operations is the core activity of any organization. In the past it has been relatively stable, largely due to a slow-moving and uncompetitive environment. The recent developments of globalization, accelerating technological change, and overcapacity, have subjected organizations in general and operations in particular to ever increasing pressure. The result has been the development of lean and responsive operations structures giving increasing attention to value rather than cost and to maximizing customer satisfaction as a means of resisting competition. Traditional boundaries, both within and outside the organization, are eroding.

The product/service dichotomy

As manufacture strives to achieve greater customer loyalty through maximizing customer satisfaction, service becomes a much more important element of the product/service mix. Meanwhile technology leads a revolution in many areas of the service sector, allowing services to be accessed remotely. The service provider is increasingly finding that the back shop, quasi-manufacturing activities are becoming dominant.

Productivity, responsiveness and quality

These are the main elements of any really competitive package. World-class organizations will strive to maximize all three. If this is ever attained, then competition must move on to other issues, perhaps social or environmental. Meanwhile the evidence to date suggests that there will always be a market for the second division.

Self Assessment

1 Historically markets have been characterized by:
   (a) undercapacity
   (b) overcapacity
   (c) neither of these?
2 Competition in most markets is now:
   (a) greater than in the past
   (b) less than in the past
   (c) about the same?
3 Competition has increased because of:
   (a) globalization
   (b) increased capacity
   (c) more discerning customers
   (d) all of these?
4 In the past operations was most concerned about:
   (a) efficiency
   (b) customer satisfaction?
5 At present operations is most concerned about:
   (a) efficiency
   (b) customer satisfaction?
6 Supply partnerships are designed to:
   (a) keep out the competition
   (b) reduce costs
   (c) maximize benefits to all parties
   (d) all of these?
7 Name four of the main characteristics of the historic manufacturing model.

8 Name four of the main characteristics of the 'world-class' manufacturing model.
9 The front office content of services is reducing because:
   (a) customers are no longer interested in service.
   (b) customers don't have time
   (c) remote access to services is now available
   (d) it is cheaper?

Further reading

Cole, W. E. and Mogab, J. W. (1995). *The Economics of Total Quality Management*. Blackwell.
Hill, T. (1993). *Manufacturing Strategy*. Macmillan.
Harrison, M. (1993). *Operations Management Strategy*. Pitman.
Kanter, R. M. (1989). *When Giants Learn to Dance*. Routledge.
Vandermerwe, S. (1993). *From Tin Soldiers to Russian Dolls*. Butterworth-Heinemann.

Case studies

The following case studies allow some of the issues in the book to be developed in more depth than the examples and exercises in the individual chapters. While they have been linked with specific topic areas, these are by no means exclusive and most cases will involve several aspects of the book.

The majority of cases are based on real situations, though in most cases the organization has been disguised. In common with most case studies, these are not intended to demonstrate good or bad management practice, but are designed to promote discussion of the issues.

The cases are:

P. T. Dresswel International (Chapters 1, 2, 3, 10 and 11)
High Performance Pumps (Chapter 3)
The library (Chapter 4)
Alton Towers Limited (Chapter 5)
A day at the Tunnel (Chapters 3 and 11)
Capacity planning in the technical services department of Advantage Textiles Limited (Chapters 4 and 6)
Midtown General Hospital (Chapter 6)
Security Products Limited (Chapters 7 and 8)
Oldborough development plan (Chapter 9).

Case Study

P. T. Dresswel International

P. T. Dresswel is a well-established garment manufacturer (founded 1976) based in Indonesia. The company is entirely export oriented, and specializes in the manufacture of a range of woven garments for a variety of internationally known customers. It operates from a single location within a free trade zone. The free trade zone allows the company to import and re-export materials with minimal delay and without payment of local import taxes. A typical customs throughput time in Indonesia is 15–20 days, however, goods are released within 1–2 days in the free trade zone.

The company has a workforce of 3000, operating 1500 sewing machines, and has a capacity of 25 000 dozen garments per month. The turnover in 1992 was $24 million. The company currently concentrates on the production of shirts, blouses and Bermuda shorts.

The production facility

The production unit is located on two floors of a two-storey building. The basement contains preparation (cutting, fusing, accessories) and finishing (ironing, folding, packing), while the first floor consists of eleven lines of 135 powered sewing machines each. The layout of the two floors is shown in Figures CS.1 and CS.2.

Production operates on a minimum batch size of 500 dozen, which, at an average throughput of ninety-five dozen per line per day gives one week's work for one line. After a batch, the line(s) have to be cleaned, serviced and reconfigured for the next batch, a process which typically takes two days.

The forward schedule is generally set four weeks in advance and, given the relatively standard process, day to day scheduling presents few problems. Fabric is inspected, cut and, if necessary fused, for the next day's assembly, and held in the fabric ready store until required. Likewise accessories are assembled in the accessory ready store.

Fabric cutting is carried out manually using a powered band-knife. A paper pattern is laid upon a stack of 90–100 layers of fabric 30 metres long. To ensure a good colour match on assembly, each piece is then labelled with the layer number so that fabric from the same layer is matched. This process can take a team of forty workers one and a half days.

Assembly operates on a manual flow process basis. Between one and six lines may be devoted to a single batch at any one time depending upon the order size.

Completed garments are returned to the basement for ironing, again a manual operation, and packing.

Where washed garments are required, the batch has to be shipped to a subcontractor, since P. T. Dresswel does not have in-house washing facilities. Delivery lead times from the subcontractor are unreliable which leads to problems with the scheduling of ironing and packing.

Trained inspectors are employed to control quality throughout the process. Fabric is inspected before cutting, continuous sample

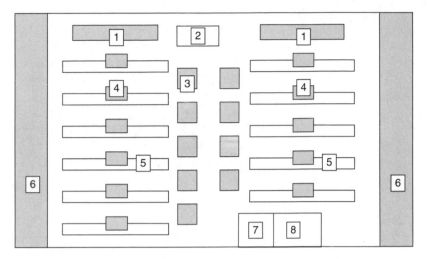

PRODUCTION FLOOR

1   Quality Control table
2   Lift
3   Trimming Table
4   In-Line Inspector
5   Sewing Line
6   Preparation Table
7   Production Manager
8   Administration

A SEWING LINE

135 machines/two per table

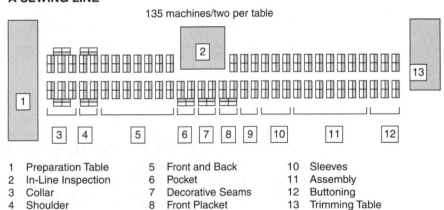

1   Preparation Table
2   In-Line Inspection
3   Collar
4   Shoulder
5   Front and Back
6   Pocket
7   Decorative Seams
8   Front Placket
9   Cuffs
10 Sleeves
11 Assembly
12 Buttoning
13 Trimming Table

Note: this sewing line is set up for making blouses. The number and disposition of machines will vary with the garment.

Figure CS.1 Sewing floor layout

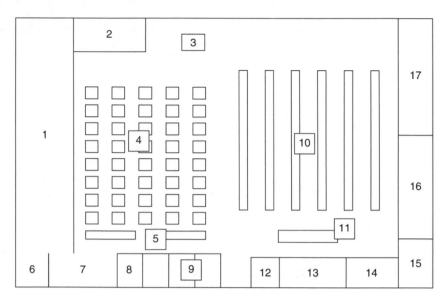

1	Packed goods store	2	Packing store	3	Lift
4	Ironing tables	5	Packing tables	6	Container stuffing
7	Packing section	8	Carton store	9	QC rooms
10	Cutting tables	11	Fabric inspection	12	QC manager
13	Accessories ready store	14	Fabric ready store	15	Reception
16	Incoming fabric	17	Incoming accessories		

Figure CS.2 Basement layout

inspection takes place during assembly, and a sample of finished garments is checked before and after ironing/packing. Despite this, problems do arise, partly because there is no rigorous system of sampling in place on assembly. Typically nine inspectors per line take random samples from various stages during the shift, however, given that twenty-eight or more operators may be carrying out the same operation, this does not guarantee that every operator is sampled. The result is that defects are frequently detected at final inspection and, on occasion, the production manager has over-ruled quality control in order to meet shipping deadlines. (Dispatch is usually by sea. The use of airfreight could add a safety margin, but at a prohibitive cost.)

Labour costs are governed in part by statute, and the minimum wage at present is $2 per day. To this can be added a food and transport allowance of $0.75. Trained workers will earn substantially more than this, with a skilled sewing machine operator earning as much as $80 per month, and a skilled cutter $100. The average wage including allowances is $70 per month.

The market

The main products are shirts, blouses and Bermuda shorts, made from woven fabric.

The main customers include: in the USA – Levis, J. C. Penney, Chorus Line, Lee, Gap, Charming Shoppers; and in the European Community – Marks & Spencer, BHS, Primark, Karstadt, Naf Naf, Tchibo.

Until 1992, customers would approach P. T. Dresswel (and other Indonesian suppliers) with design and fabric specifications, so all the supplier was required to do was source the fabric, often locally (some customers specified the fabric supplier in the contract), and make the order. Indonesia was, in general, competitive on price with other Far Eastern countries, and superior in quality. No marketing or promotion was required, nor any significant purchasing skills.

Unfortunately, since 1992, the market has changed. Competitive countries have improved their quality and their productivity, and Indonesia is no longer a low labour cost economy. Table CS.1 gives some comparative figures.

Furthermore, the maturing market is demanding greater control and greater service.

Fabric specifications are becoming ever tighter, with a requirement for certification of shrinkage, colour fastness etc., and written guarantees that the fabrics are produced without the use of carcinogens and other potential poisons (formaldehyde, DDT, PCB, AZO dyes). This is causing particular problems with locally sourced fabrics, since the Indonesian fabric manufacturers are, in the main, unable to provide acceptable certification.

Table CS.1

Country	Output/Machine/Day	Cost/Dozen ($)
Indonesia	8.2	23
China	16	16
Myanmar	12	12
Bangladesh	10	8

Increasingly, customers are requiring suppliers to bid for contracts. This not only requires a sales force, but also samples, and successful bids increasingly depend on collections being produced by the manufacturer. Even when the contract has been awarded, customers are demanding pre-production samples and shipping samples as quality checks. Customers are delegating a greater degree of design and supply work to the manufacturer, but demanding more stringent control, with documentary and physical evidence, of quality.

The effect of these changes on Indonesian exports as a whole is shown in Figure CS.3. The trend has been more marked with knitted garments, but woven garments are following the same pattern.

The organization

P. T. Dresswel is still organized on the basis of a purely production-driven organization. While it has the necessary finance and HRM functions, almost all other functions, with the exception of marketing, report to the production manager. Even the marketing function is relatively small, consisting of a Marketing Manager, three Contracts Managers, each of whom oversee a group of clients, and six salesmen, whose real role is more of a client liaison role.

The present management structure is shown in Figure CS.4.

Questions

P. T. Dresswel is a successful company struggling to come to terms with a changing market. It has already gone some way towards addressing the new concerns of the market by obtaining ISO 9000 accreditation, but this is unlikely to be enough to ensure survival.

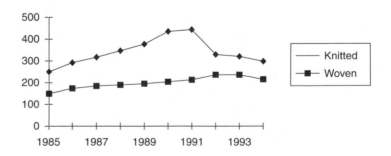

Figure CS.3 Garment exports: Indonesia

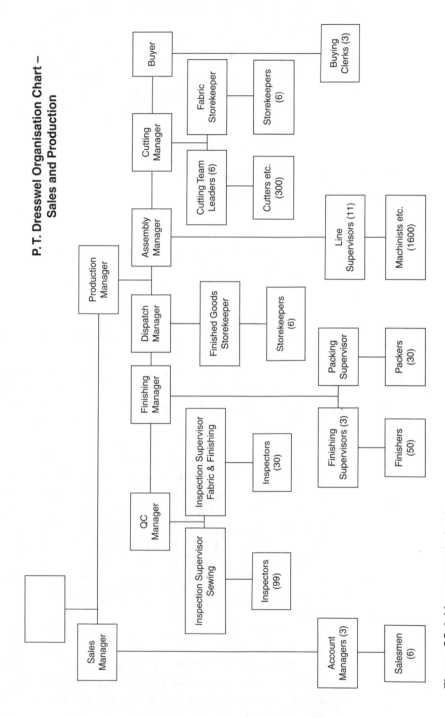

P. T. Dresswel Organisation Chart – Sales and Production

Figure CS.4 Management structure

1 What are the key changes, for operations, in the market requirements?
2 How should P. T. Dresswel change its operations strategy to accommodate these?
3 What changes in the structure, layout and processes of operations would you recommend?

Case Study

High Performance Pumps

A small business venture producing high performance pumps for 'off highway' equipment had establish itself as a successful and profitable manufacturer in what was essentially a specialized market. The product specification was very demanding in terms of performance, quality and reliability. These together with providing an effective backup service, were in fact the key order-winning criteria. The products range from relatively small 3-inch (diameter) pumps to large standalone specials, some 12 inches in diameter, The smaller pumps were produced in batches of 100 while the large specials were produced in small batches of five, but generally utilizing the same equipment in the production process.

All pumps had a camshaft that was a major component. The size of the camshaft was determined by the pump size. The business developed a high level of production and process 'skills' relating to the operations tasks for producing camshafts. The production process was also (apparently) cost-effective when compared with competitors. So successful was the camshaft business that the other companies that used camshafts as a component in their own products began enquiring about design, costs and delivery of camshafts. Over a period of time (some six years) the production of camshafts increased four times. Virtually all the increase was for customers asking for a 'special' to be produced in a variety of volumes. The high-and low-volume camshafts were produced approximately following the same process plan and machine routing.

However, over the same six-year period, as camshaft production increased profits slumped. Work in progress increased by a factor of three, and the trend was towards a major cash flow crisis. On the surface it appeared that all three major products (small pumps, large special pumps and the camshafts) should be profitable. The problems were discussed in detail at a special meeting. The production manager came under very severe pressure during the meeting to come up with ways of reducing costs. He argued that major problems had been created by sales and product design. These included:

1 Sales had over the previous two years 'chased orders' to fill the gaps in the order books following a general downturn in the industry, when volumes for standard pumps dropped by 10 per cent.
2 The effect had been that the new orders, won against 'tough competition', were mainly for non-standard pumps and camshafts where volumes tended to be smaller.
3 Product design had carried out a value analysis programme with the objective of reducing the costs of 'standard products' by a target figure of 10 per cent.
4 The value analysis changes had been introduced into production at the time as variety was increasing and volume generally was reducing. New jigs and fixtures had to be made to accommodate the newly designed components and assemblies.
5 Production had been disrupted through both the value analysis exercise and increased the number of set-ups to cope with the variety increase and volume drop. The result was that delivery performance had suffered, priorities kept changing in response to customer pressure, and the work in progress was at an all-time high.

The production manager, therefore, argued that he could not achieve cost savings without a great deal of collaboration with sales and design. Both these functional managers, however, refused to accept any 'blames' for poor production performance and suggested the factory required a new planning system and a great deal more discipline on the shopfloor. The managing director's response to what had become an acrimonious and increasingly emotional debate was to appoint a young planning analyst to report on the problem and suggest solutions.

The analyst was a highly qualified production engineer, well respected by the shop floor supervision. They gave him a great deal of co-operation in identifying key problems, bottlenecks and all the major process 'excesses'. The main problem, however, occurred when the analyst came to identifying product costs. Many components used common processes, irrespective of values. Because the management accounting system could not provide detailed component and process costs, engineers worked to estimate cycle times and applied 'blanket' overhead rates on the major production processes. The analyst discovered that standards and 'specials' were costed using the same 'standard costs'. Further investigation showed:

1 The larger (12 inch plus) pumps were generally given high priority because:
   (a) they took up so much floor space that production tried to push them through quickly
   (b) the major customers tended to press hard for delivery.
2 An average six weeks in-progress production time was recorded for small, standard pumps as well as large, non-standard pumps. The estimators, however, are working on lead times of one to two weeks for small pumps.
3 Camshaft production had more than doubled since subcontracted work had been undertaken. This had required the purchase of additional grinding machines and necessitated a reorganization of the pump, machine and assembly shops. This, in turn, had put pressure on the available assembly floor space.
4 Labour tended to be shifted to the camshaft production from the general machine shop whenever there was a 'big order' of subcontract work in the belief that fast delivery meant more profitable business.

The engineer reported his findings verbally to the managing director, together with his own conclusions. He said that in his view the major problem was the failure to recognize that within one factory were three separate businesses, each competing in different markets, against different order-winning criteria, and making different and conflicting demands on the same production processes. His proposal was more fully to investigate the issues based on the concept of separating the three businesses (small pumps, large pumps and camshafts) by rearranging production on to an autonomous product basis and building walls physically to separate the plant, and managing them totally independently. This would require a relatively high investment in the new plant in order to create the three separate units.

Questions
1 Identify the problems faced by the company.
2 Is the particular view of the planning analyst justified?
3 Demonstrate how the proposal made by the planning analyst can be implemented. Evaluate its benefits to the company and its possible disadvantages.

Case Study

The library

A university library serves a number of different functions for a number of different client groups with different needs. These range from the researcher requiring up-to-date access, to the latest publications in the field, to the first year undergraduate wanting somewhere quiet (and warm) to work. It thus provides both space and information, and, of course, through its skilled staff, advice. Despite the growth of electronic data sources and remote access, university libraries are still primarily sources of printed information, in the form of books and periodicals. This case concerns the physical book stock of the library and is not concerned with issues of study space, access or electronic information.

It is a common complaint of library users that the books they require are either not in stock, or are already out on loan. Given the finite nature of space and funds, there will always be a high probability that a book will be out on loan when required, and various ways of reducing the inconvenience this causes are used, for example, reservation, recall, short loan.

The issue of books not being in stock is more complex. Librarians are not clairvoyant, and need requests from users in order to add new books to stock. There is thus an inevitable time lag between the need arising and the book being available (this lag may be extended by the need to await funding, given the annual budget system, but that is hardly an operations issue).

Library structure

The library is physically divided into different subject areas, each the responsibility of a subject team. The subject team is responsible for the maintenance of the book and periodical stock in their area, dealing with user requests and queries, and offering training to users.

The purchase order and cataloguing section is a centralized back office function responsible for order processing, progress chasing, and the inspection and cataloguing of books received.

Ordering procedure

The majority of new books are ordered to satisfy taught course requirements. Since all courses provide reading lists for their students, the reading list is used as the driver for this process. Module leaders are required to submit reading lists for their modules and the majority of the lists are received in June and

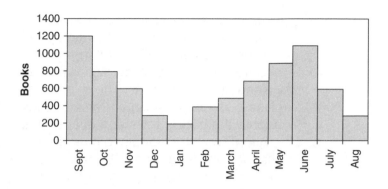

Figure CS.5 Orders received for input

Questions
1 Identify the factors that are important in determining quality of service in a university/college library. How important is availability of books in this?
2 Chart the process for adding to the book stock of the library.
3 Critically appraise the process and chart a revised process based upon this.
4 What steps are needed to implement your revised process?

Case Study

Alton Towers Limited

Alton Towers is Britain's number one theme park. It occupies an 800-acre site, which belonged to the earls of Shrewsbury, near Stoke-on-Trent. The land was developed by the fifteenth and sixteenthth earls into one of the most famous English mansions with spectacular gardens. The gardens were first opened to the public in 1860. Thirty years later the twentieth earl, Charles Henry John Talbot, initiated the leisure park tradition and held the first of a series of August fetes.

However, towards the end of the nineteenth century, the fortunes of the Talbots had declined and the gardens deteriorated. In 1924 the estate was purchased by Alton Towers Limited. During the war the house was requisitioned by the army and was returned to the company in poor conditioned. The company has since restored the gardens and much of the hall and now the gardens are open to the public along with the rest of the grounds, which have been used to create the largest theme park in Britain. Its service concept is to provide an inclusive package of magnificent surroundings, historic heritage, fun and fantasy to suit all ages and tastes.

There are over 125 'rides' in the park, of which more than third is covered. The latest attractions include Oblivion, the Nemesis, Ugland and Energizer. There are also a wide range of eating places, shops, amusement arcades, live entertainments and exhibitions, the nature trails and over 500 acres of gardens to explore.

Alton Towers entertained over three million visitors in 1998. The cost of entry was then £19 for an adult or a child, with reductions for senior citizens and organized parties. The entry price includes unlimited use of all the rides. In the peak season, Alton Towers Limited employs over 1800 people to staff the park. The staff includes ride operators, caterers, cleaners, shop assistants, supervisors and security personnel.

The company hopes to increase its annual volume of visitors. To achieve this goal, the company has been introducing new rides and attractions that hold particular appeal for families. Such additions include the Ugland, Runaway Mine Train, the Land of Make Believe and the haunted house. In recent years, Alton Towers uncovered the awesome new ride challenge of Oblivion, Nemesis and attractions such as Toyland Tours, an enchanted new dark ride which takes one on a magical journey through a toy factory, where the toys make themselves. These rides represented a £20 million investment at Alton Towers, which is part of a continuing ten-year development programme of the park. Cable cars and an air-guided train are installed to help visitors to get to different areas of the park. As Alton Towers grows, it takes more than one day to do everything. The magical Alton Towers Hotel was opened in 1996, and gives one the opportunity to extend the magical days into nights.

During the year, demand peaks at about 40 000 on Easter Bank Holiday Monday, and runs at about 30 000 throughout the summer. The park is closed during November and February. The busiest times are usually during the week. Fridays and Saturdays during the peak season tend to be relatively quiet. At the gate peak time is 10.30–11.00 a.m., the peak time for the fast food restaurant is 12.30–1.00 p.m. The major rides such as Oblivion, are busy all day, but queues reach a peak in the early afternoon. The likely volume of visitors for any day is difficult to predict. But estimates are based on last year's figures and the weather forecast. The operations staff are updated each hour via their mobile phones of the number of visitors in the park.

The park caters for a large age range, from toddlers to pensioners. Special toddler play areas are available with height restriction boards limiting the size of the entrants. Also, in close proximity to all the main rides are rides for the younger visitor to play on whilst other members of the family are using the rides which have a minimum height requirement. The elderly are also catered for with the gardens and floral displays, shops, restaurants and frequent seating areas, and old fashioned amusements. The need for the variety of activities is also created by the weather, so about a third of all the rides are either indoors or in covered areas. In managing customer satisfaction through the provision of entertainment and recreation facilities for a wide age group, the need for productivity, in a potentially price-sensitive market, could militate against client satisfaction.

Questions

1 Identify the strategic determinants of service productivity at Alton Towers.
2 Suggest actions that may be taken by the company management to enhance the overall service productivity.

A day at the Tunnel

The Brown family was looking forward to their holiday in France. They had experienced more than their fair share of difficulties during the year, and felt ready for a relaxing fortnight.

They usually crossed the channel by hovercraft but, impressed by the stories of several friends and acquaintances telling of a smooth and trouble-free crossing not in any way influenced by the weather, they had decided to use the Shuttle. Armed with a prebooked ticket for the 2.54 train on a Wednesday afternoon they set out in plenty of time.

They arrived early, joining the queue for admission at 1.35 p.m. They were surprised to find that, despite having a prepaid and booked ticket, it still took them fifteen minutes to reach a check-in booth. Here their ticket was checked, and they were given a piece of card with the letter R on it to hang from their rear view mirror.

'That's fine,' said the check-in operator, 'you are on the 2.54. We are boarding from the terminal today, so just wait in the terminal until your letter is called.'

After parking their car they bought some duty free goods and then waited. Video screens were calling letters M and N. At 2.45 screens were showing N and O, so Mr Brown approach the enquiries desk to find out what was happening. 'Oh, we had a problem this morning so we are running an hour late', said the receptionist, 'but we are running three trains an hour'.

While queuing for a coffee, letters P and Q were called, and a little later letter R. It was now 3.15 p.m. As the Browns made their way out to their car, they were surprised to hear the public address system call letters S and T.

The car park was chaotic. It looked as though almost all the cars were trying to get out at once, and it took the Browns almost thirty minutes to get to passport control and security.

Finally, half way up lane three in the marshalling area, they waited to embark. Lane 1 was embarked first and seemed endless. It became apparent that cars still on the access road were been ushered down lane one and on to the train, presumably to clear congestion. Eventually this stopped and lane 2 was embarked, followed by the first few cars in lane 3. The Browns were now five from the front of the queue and the next train was in twenty minutes. It was 3.55 p.m..

Background

The Shuttle
The Shuttle carries cars and their passengers between England and France by train through the Channel Tunnel. Services run frequently with a thirty-minute crossing time. Since it is underground, the crossing is not affected by adverse weather, which can make sea crossings uncomfortable or even impossible. Cars are driven on to the train, on two levels, and drivers and passengers remain with their cars throughout he journey. Tickets may be bought in advance, but it is also possible to turn up on spec and buy a ticket on arrival.

Figure CS.6 shows an approximate schematic of the terminal area.

It is the policy of Eurotunnel in the event of difficulty to 'recover the timetable as quickly as possible and minimize disruption. Keeping our customers informed of the progress of this process is . . . difficult to manage'.

Alternatives
There are several alternatives for motorists crossing the channel. All are surface vessels and therefore more or less influenced by inclement weather. This can vary from mild discomfort, particularly for those prone to seasickness, through to cancellation of services

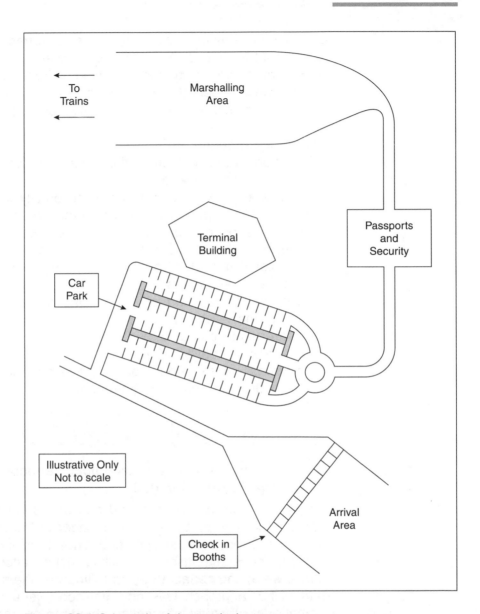

Figure CS.6 Schematic of the terminal area

in extreme conditions. All methods provide terminal buildings with duty free shopping facilities and refreshment facilities. They are:

1 Ferries. There are a number of alternative routes, but the 'short' crossings have a crossing time of about ninety minutes, with a typical check-in time of one hour. Passengers are not allowed to remain with their cars. The ferries provide restaurants, bars, snack bars and duty free shopping.

2 Fastcraft. Similar in many respects to ferries, but crossing the Channel in only forty-five to fifty minutes.

3 Hovercraft. A thirty-minute check-in and thirty-five minute crossing. Passengers sit in coach-style seats with little opportunity to move around. Limited duty free goods for sale.

Issues for discussion

1 What does quality mean in this situation? List examples of poor quality in the scenario.

2 What are the key drivers of service quality likely to be in this operation? In the event of problems, what sort of customer service recovery procedures would you recommend?

3 How does the layout of the terminal area interact with service provision? In the light of the Browns experience, what changes would you recommend?

4 Produce a flow chart of the Browns process and use this to identify the following:
   (a) areas of operational inefficiency
   (b) areas of quality failure
   (c) areas where operational efficiency requirements might conflict with quality requirements.

Case Study

Capacity planning in the technical services department of Advantage Textiles Limited

Kally Patel had just experienced one of the worst periods in her career. She took on the role of manager of the technical services department four months ago, and since then she felt as though she had never stood still. Unwilling just to accept the way that things were, she set about trying to improve the situation. The first part of her approach was now finished – she had managed to gather a lot of useful information about the operation. Now all that remained was to understand what it all meant and take some positive actions for the future.

The role of technical services

Advantage Textiles is a large manufacturer of sportswear, supplying leading high street retailers in the UK. The role of technical services is to support the design and sales teams by making sample garments and fully costing them. Design and sales require commercial standard samples from technical services. These are then used for presentations to the retailers. During the negotiation process with the retailers, revised designs and costing may be requested and even new designs introduced.

The technical services department consists of the following areas:

- The sample machine room. Seven operators and a range of machines provide the full range of manufacturing capabilities available in the whole production unit of Advantage.
- Computer design. One operator runs a computerized design system that provides detailed cutting instructions to make best use of the lengths of fabric and information on the company's standard times for each operation in the make-up of a garment.
- Computerized costing. In this area four operators produce computerized data on the standard minutes for each operation involved in manufacturing a garment, and the associated labour, material and overhead costs.

Each section works from 9.00 a.m. to 5.00 p.m. The flow of work through the department is indicated in Figure CS.7.

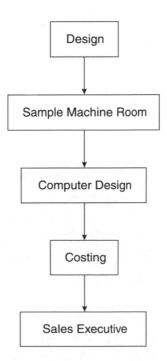

Figure CS.7 Outline process diagram

Kally's experience of managing technical services

Kally had spent a lot of time trying to explain to the design and sales staff why her department could not provide the necessary samples in time. Her case lacked convincing information and she felt uncomfortable about this. Usually, senior management resolved the situation by drawing up a list of priorities reflecting the business interests surrounding each case. Such interventions, however, only resulted in other jobs being delayed and then these, too, became the subjects of heated debate over lateness.

The results of Kally's fact finding

At Kally's request the industrial engineering department had provided her with a list of how long each type of activity should take (Table CS.3).

Kally took the opportunity of this relatively quiet time to talk to the design and sales teams. She found out that samples and costings are required within two days of them being presented to the sample machine room. In the case of 'fast track' developments this lead time is reduced to one day. Owing to the dynamic nature of the market and the demands of the retailers, fast track developments and revisions seem likely to increase in the future. In addition, Kally also used the discussions to compile an estimate of the forthcoming demands from all of the design and sales teams (Table CS.4).

Table CS.3

	Computer design	Sample machine room	Computerized costing
New shorts	0.75	1.0	2.0
New jerseys	0.75	1.5	2.0
New tracksuits	0.75	2.0	2.5
Revised shorts	0.75	0.5	1.25
Revised jerseys	0.5	1.0	1.25
Revised tracksuits	0.5	1.5	1.5

Table CS.4

	Jan	Feb	Mar	Apr	May	Jun	Jul	Aug	Sep	Oct	Nov	Dec
New shorts	23	23	35	184	184	184	30	30	95	171	166	110
New jerseys	45	45	80	139	134	125	71	71	78	103	128	99
New tracksuits	45	50	50	60	96	121	121	107	65	56	87	96
Fast track	6	6	6	6	6	6	6	6	6	6	6	6

Note: All the figures are actual numbers of sample designs required.

Questions

1 Produce a graph showing the capacity of the technical services department against the estimated demand. What problems does it show?

2 Recommend a staffing schedule for the next twelve months and suggest how it might be achieved.

Case Study

Midtown General Hospital

Midtown General Hospital is a 300-bed hospital providing a range of services, including surgical care. The operating suite for surgical care consists of three theatres. Bev Greening is the Theatre Manager, reporting to the Director of Nursing. She has responsibility for providing the non-consultant staff for the theatres and to schedule their usage. The overall aim of the staff is to provide a safe environment for surgery, provide total patient care during the pre-, intra- and post-operative phases, and to guard the patient's safety and dignity during periods of unconsciousness. Ten consultant surgeons use the theatres, covering general, orthopaedic, gynaecology, oral, plastic and bronchoscopy. At present the theatres offer twenty-four sessions per week. The pattern of use is shown in Table CS.5.

The morning list runs from 8.30 a.m. to 1.00 p.m. and the afternoon list from 1.30 p.m. to 6.00 p.m. The current nursing staffing requirements to meet this pattern are shown in Table CS.6.

Table CS.5

Day	Time	Theatre	Use
Monday	Morning	1	Occupied
		2	Occupied
		3	Free
	Afternoon	1	Occupied
		2	Occupied
		3	Free
Tuesday	Morning	1	Occupied
		2	Occupied
		3	Occupied
	Afternoon	1	Occupied
		2	Occupied
		3	Occupied
Wednesday	Morning	1	Occupied
		2	Occupied
		3	Occupied
	Afternoon	1	Occupied
		2	Occupied
		3	Free
Thursday	Morning	1	Occupied
		2	Occupied
		3	Free
	Afternoon	1	Occupied
		2	Occupied
		3	Free
Friday	Morning	1	Occupied
		2	Occupied
		3	Free
	Afternoon	1	Occupied

In addition, three Grade A auxiliary staff and three porters are required for the whole week. The average normal-time pay for these positions is estimated by Bev to be:

E	£19 000
D	£16 000
A	£11 000
Porters	£8000

Table CS.6

Day	Time	Theatre	Theatre staff *	Floor control Staff	Recovery staff
Monday	Morning	1	D, E	E	2.5D
		2	D, E		
		3	–		
	Afternoon	1	D, E	E	2.5D
			D, E		
			–		
Tuesday	Morning	1	D, E	E	3D
		2	D, E		
		3	D, E		
	Afternoon	1	D, E	E	3D
		2	D, E		
		3	D, E		
Wednesday	Morning	1	D, E	E	3D
		2	D, E		
		3	D, E		
	Afternoon	1	D, E	E	2.5D
		2	D, E		
		3	–		
Thursday	Morning	1	D, E	E	2.5D
		2	D, E		
		3	–		
	Afternoon	1	D, E	E	2.5D
		2	D, E		
		3	–		
Friday	Morning	1	D, E	E	2.5D
		2	D, E		
		3	–		
	Afternoon	1	D, E	E	3D
		2	D, E		
		3	D, E		

Note: * The letter indicates the salary grade of the staff and the number indicates the number of staff of this grade. Where there is simply a letter this means that only one member of staff with this grade is required. The grade D and E requirements are minima and in fact staff on higher grades (up to G) may be employed in these roles.

These staffing levels are increased by 20 per cent to allow for annual leave, sickness and other absences. There is a small bank of theatre nurses who are available for temporary employment over short periods. The standard working week for all theatre staff is thirty-seven and a half hours. All time over this limit is paid as overtime, at rates one and a half times greater than those paid for normal working hours. Maintenance takes place outside current operating hours. It is estimated that the total time of this maintenance amounts to one session per week.

Bev Greening now faces a problem. Her director has asked her to look into ways of increasing the usage of the theatres. Performance measures show that the hospital's waiting times for surgery are growing longer and that they are cancelling more scheduled operations at short notice. Recently, patients have been contacted by phone on the day of their admissions to be told that their planned surgery has been cancelled. These cases have attracted adverse publicity in the local and national media and the hospital directors are keen to stop a reoccurrence and to reassure the public.

Questions

1 Generate a list of the options open to Bev to increase usage of the theatres.
2 For each of the options identify the costs and other likely problems.

Case Study

Security Products Limited

Jim Baxendale's redundancy had proven to be a golden opportunity. Pooling his redundancy payments and modest borrowings with those of a few friends, Jim had been instrumental in starting Security Products Limited (known as SPL). Drawing upon their own experiences of the trade, they specialized in electronic security products for both domestic and business consumers. Today they employed around 200 people in design, manufacturing, sales, installation and finance functions. Now, however, the situation looked less happy. A meeting of the senior managers had just reviewed a gloomy scenario. For the second consecutive year the company had made a loss. A marketing survey had shown them to be less well thought of than they had imagined. The conclusion of the meeting was that the control of materials was at the heart of the problem. Jim resolved to get some facts and to get them fast.

At the end of the week Jim told his secretary that he was not to be disturbed whilst he reviewed what he had found in the relative calm of his office. First he returned to the customer survey. A sample of buyers from both sectors had been asked to rate the company against its competitors on a scale where -5 represented very bad and $+5$ signified very good. In summary, the results were as shown in Table CS.7.

Next, Jim turned to the financial reports. The company accountant had provided a concise set of figures. With this year shown as Year 0, last year as Year -1 and so on the key figures were as shown in table CS.8.

The company accountant had explained that the main current asset was materials.

The production planning manager reported a fairly chaotic situation. Plans for each week were often altered at short notice to try to give sales what they wanted. This upset production management, who tried their best to meet such changes but who also complained about the disruption caused. Sales and production planning worked together to produce sales forecasts to an established cycle. The first forecast for a quarter's (i.e., three months') production is made thirteen weeks before the quarter begins. Revisions are made nine and five weeks before the quarter. When

Table CS.7

	SPL	Company A	Company B	Company C	Company D
Reputation	+1	+5	+4	+5	+3
Quality	+2	+5	+4	+5	+2
Delivery	0	+4	+4	+5	+3
Cost	+1	+3	+3	+4	+2
Responsiveness	0	+4	+4	+4	+3

Table CS.8

Year	Current assets	Sales	Profit before tax
	£ (000)	£ (000)	(%)
0	6 504	11 535	−3
−1	4 531	9 436	−3
−2	4 090	8 700	1
−3	2 985	7 600	4

the quarter arrives a new forecast is issued, and this is updated at four weeks and nine weeks into the quarter. Production planning attempt to follow each updated version of the forecast. The production planning manager felt that on some items the degree of forecasting accuracy was not good enough.

The warehouse manager had delivered a representative sample of the many items held as raw materials (Table CS.9).

All the items have an approximate lead time of four weeks and the average monthly usage is thought to have a standard deviation of around fifty.

The warehouse manager also provided a spot check sample of dispatches (Table CS.10).

The manufacturing manager traced thirty-three orders on the factory floor and found that fifteen were held up waiting for raw materials to be delivered.

By now Jim was satisfied that materials management was indeed a major concern.

Table CS.9

Item code	Stock (units)	Purchase price (£ per unit)	Average monthly usage (units)	Reorder level (units)
163	665	16.30	205	400
55	3 760	0.56	1 180	2 000
225	0	23.29	9 580	6 500
41	14 600	3.66	41 400	10 000
45	10 714	4.13	3 225	5 000
330	3 505	24.44	655	2 000
32	1 198	8.63	410	1 000
147	0	11.58	975	1 000
41	1 470	1.15	7 205	7 000
237	5 745	3.51	2 520	2 000
33	14 854	24.61	13 550	10 000
542	0	21.69	150	500
144	12 211	23.82	310	1 500
22	10 251	11.52	5 830	5 500
556	0	15.54	675	500
61	11 743	19.98	930	1 000

Table CS.10

Order number	Requested delivery week	Promised delivery week	Actual delivery week
7790	30	33	34
7791	32	34	34
7795	35	35	36
7800	36	36	36
7801	31	33	34
7803	32	32	35
7810	34	34	33
7812	35	35	35
7815	32	32	36
7816	33	33	36
7822	35	36	37
7824	32	34	34
7839	34	35	35
7840	31	32	33
7841	33	34	34
7842	34	34	34

Questions

1 Analyse how effective the materials control system is at Security Products Limited.
2 Recommend improvements for Jim to consider.

Case Study

Oldborough development plan

(This case is reproduced from Principles of Operations Management by Les Galloway, published by International Thompson Business Press. Reproduced with the permission of the author and publisher.)

Oldborough Council is about to embark on a substantial redevelopment plan, involving both the city centre and the southern fringes of the town. The new University of Nether Whitton has reduced the student numbers at Oldborough Technical College to the point where the college is no longer viable. The college is next to the police station, which is no longer adequate to meet the needs of an expanding community, and the opportunity has arisen to sell both to a developer for the building of a new shopping centre. The shopping centre will require a new traffic plan for the city centre. The money released from this sale will enable the council to purchase the disused railway station from BR [British Rail] and build a swimming pool and leisure centre to replace the facilities in the technical college. A legacy of £500 000 has been left to the council but a covenant requires that it be spent, within three years, upon measures to improve the fitness of the community, but not upon buildings. The council proposes to use this legacy to equip the new leisure centre. A long-standing commitment to build a new southern relief road will allow the building of the new police station and new council offices on the southern outskirts of the town. The sale of council land near the proposed road for a private housing development will help defray the cost of the scheme. The developer will also be required to provide a new school.

New pollution control regulations require the sewage treatment plant to be upgraded before any occupation of the new housing development. It is unlikely that a developer would buy the land until the sewage upgrading work had already started.

In summary the activities are as Table CS.11.

Table CS.11

Activity	Duration (Months)	Cost (£ million)
Build relief road	14	
Sell development land	3	−4
Upgrade sewage works phase 1	1	3
Upgrade sewage works phase 2	2	18
Build new police station and council offices	12	18
Move into new police station	1	
Sell college and police station	3	−14
Buy station	1	2
Demolish station	2	0.5
Build leisure centre	14	16
Equip leisure centre	2	1.2
Develop new traffic plan	6	0.2
Install new traffic plan	3	0.5
Developer builds shopping centre	18	
Developer builds estate	9 (to first occupation)	

Questions

1 Determine the earliest that the whole project can be completed and identify the critical path.
2 The borough treasurer has insisted that borrowing must be kept below £22 million. Prepare a schedule to satisfy this constraint without putting out the overall completion time. For the sake of simplicity assume that all moneys become due immediately the activity finishes. The contractors will not pay for the college, police station or new building land earlier than they need to.
3 What implication does the answer to question 2 have for the legacy?
4 The project has commenced under the schedule developed in question 2 and it is now month 14. A change of government has led to a resurgence of interest in rail travel, and BR has indicated that they may wish to reopen the railway station. What do you do?

Answers to self-assessment questions

Chapter 1

1 Inputs, processes, outputs
2 False
3 (d)
4 False
5 Quality, speed, dependability, flexibility, cost
6 Control
7 (d)
8 (b)
9 False
10 (d)
11 False
12 (b) and (d)
13 Increases profit and defends against foreign competition in the commercial sector. In the public sector, productivity gives a greater return for the money invested.
14 (c)
15 Agriculture, manufacturing, service.
16 (b)
17 True
18 (e)
19 Description should mention the ideas of measurement, comparison and action to change linked by a feedback communication loop.
20 Hard systems methodology and soft systems methodology.

Chapter 2

1 A macro operating system refers to the business as a whole. For example, a manufacturing or service organization. A micro operating system is a part of the total business. For example, the marketing department in a manufacturing or service organization.
2 Finance, marketing, operations, sales
3 Marks & Spencer, De Montfort University, IBM
4 (a)
5 (e)
6 True
7 False
8 (b)
9 (b)
10 (a)
11 Interest rates, inflation rates, growth rates
12 'Transformed resources are those whose status will change as the result of the conversion process. For example, materials or information. 'Transforming' resources are those whose status will not change as the result of the conversion process. For example, facilities such as a building.
13 (a)
14 (d)
15 Changes in law, innovation by competitors, supplier problems
16 Identification of the range of inputs and an indication of the more dominant one, identification of the mismatches and areas for adjustment, identification of the alternative methods or processes available, identification of the labour skills and determination of training needs.
17 People that are used to collect data, instruments that are used to collect data, supervisors and managers who compare the results against objectives
18 (e)
19 Corporate strategy – how the organization as a whole should fulfil its long-term objectives; business strategy – how the individual functions in the business should compete in the marketplace; functional strategy – how the individual operations should manage their resources in order to contribute to the achievement of a firm's objectives.
20 (c)
21 The content of an operations strategy is an outline of the operation's policies and principles. The process of an operations

strategy shows the way in which the above policies and plans are decided/resources.

22 Quality, cost, flexibility, speed, dependability
23 False
24 True
25 (d)
26 Structural decisions are those which are related to the operating environment. For example, facilities decisions or technology decisions. Infrastructure decisions are those which are concerned with the day to day planning, control and improvement activities. For example, capacity decisions, or inventory decisions.
27 True
28 False
29 (b)
30 (a)

Chapter 3

1 (d)
2 (a)
3 (d)
4 Effectiveness – clarity of function, resolve conflict between different groups of 'customers', improve efficiency by focusing on core activities; efficiency – avoid waste, maximize service.
5 Respond to changes in demand pattern, in product/service characteristics, in technology, in political/social/environmental climate.
6 Variety, volume, availability/response requirement, stability/variability
7 (a) and (d)
8 (a) and (c)
9 (b)
10 (c)
11 (c)
12 (b)
13 (c)
14 In services: production and consumption are simultaneous, stock-holding impossible, high variability of demand, subjectivity of criteria
15 (b)
16 (c)
17 (b)

18 Minimize process subject to variability, subjective. Maximize utilization of resources through scheduling, stockholding.
19 Reduction in choice through standardisation, interpersonal interaction, responsiveness.
20 Near market, labour availability, infrastructure, transport facilities, political factors
21 Economies of scale, smoothes demand variation, simpler communication, better facilities/resources
22 (a)
23 Locate near source of labour/material etc., simpler operation, specialization (greater skill), preserves economies of scale.

Chapter 4

1 (c)
2 Select, record, examine, develop, install, maintain
3 (e)
4 (b)
5 Operation, inspection, transport, storage, delay
6 Operator, material, two-handed, customer
7 Purpose, place, sequence, person, means
8 (b)
9 (e)
10 (c), (d) and (e)
11 (b)
12 (b)
13 (d)
14 (c)
15 (c)
16 (a)
17 (e)
18 (c)
19 Capacity planning, payment systems, productivity monitoring
20 Select, record, measure, publish, maintain
21 (c)
22 Observed time, rate, basic time, add allowance to give standard time
23 Relaxation, contingency, unoccupied time
24 (c)
25 (b).

Chapter 5

1 National productivity, industry productivity, organizational productivity

2 Industrial productivity: the productivity of different industrial sectors is measured and compared to the industry average. It is often expressed in terms of output per employee per hour. Organizational productivity: the productivity of an organization is measured, usually in monetary terms. It is expressed as the ratio of output sold to the costs of inputs used to produce the output.

3 Increasing the working speed, improving the working methods, reducing cost and wastage

4 People, equipment, space

5 Materials, people, machines, space, money

6 (e)

7 (d)

8 (e)

9 (e)

10 (c)

11 (c)

12 (b)

13 (c)

14 (b)

15 (d)

16 False

17 True

18 (d)

19 (e)

20 True

21 False

22 Are customer focused, are well motivated, set measurable milestones

23 (c)

24 (a)

25 (b)

26 (c)

27 An investigative approach in which workers are trained to trace every fault to its ultimate cause by asking 'why' as each level of the problem is uncovered, and then think of a solution.

28 False

29 Management cycle, business structure, management resources, management design, corporate culture, management performance

30 (e)

31 (d)
32 (a)

Chapter 6

1 Ability, work, users
2 (c) and (e)
3 False
4 True
5 Should include the notion of regular cyclical movements around the trend.
6 False
7 (a)
8 Lowest
9 Expressed in clear units of capacity, accurate and issued in sufficient time.
10 (d)
11 Make or buy, focusing on the core business, compulsory competitive tendering
12 Overtime, subcontracting, recruit an extra shift, employ part-time labour
13 Changing shift patterns, part-time work, multiskilling, scheduling appointments
14 (b)
15 False
16 By modifying the demand. Pricing and promotion are two important tools in this respect.
17 (c)
18 Operations scheduling
19 (a)
20 (c)
21 Cost, inventory, investment, customer needs, staff morale
22 The outline should show a time horizon on the top of the diagram and activities listed down the left column.

Chapter 7

1 False
2 (c)
3 Buffer stocks
4 (c)

5 Undermines product or service, costs of idleness, stoppage costs, expediting costs
6 Brake on cash flow; exposure to risks; deters improvement
7 (d)
8 Turn or turnover
9 (c)
10 Approximately 80 per cent, 15 per cent and 5 per cent
11 (b)
12 (e)
13 (b)
14 False
15 (a) and (d)
16 True
17 Demand constant, lead time constant, independent replenishment, costs constant, supplier compliance
18 (c)
19 True
20 True
21 (a)
22 (b)
23 True

Chapter 8

1 False
2 (c)
3 (d)
4 (b)
5 Effective use of resources, level of customer service, cash-flow effects
6 (d)
7 Materials requirement planning
8 On-site stock, supplier order quantities, lead times, safety stock levels
9 (a)
10 Bill, materials
11 True
12 (c)
13 Manufacturing resources planning
14 Master scheduling, capacity planning, purchasing, finished goods delivery schedules, cash flow forecasting, personnel requirements
15 Enterprise resource planning

16 Information system
17 Optimized production technology
18 Bottleneck
19 Please refer to the chapter for the full ten
20 Just in time
21 (e)
22 Kanban
23 (c)
24 False
25 Early
26 (a)

Chapter 9

1 A set of activities with definable start and definable end
2 Construction of channel tunnel, relocating a factory, developing a new software, building a new bridge
3 Plan, schedule, budget, and control the activities involved in a project in order to meet the project specifications in terms of time, cost and quality.
4 A well-defined objective, temporary nature of the project, different phases that all projects have to go through
5 (b)
6 (a)
7 Suppliers' reliability, other projects, local laws, political instability
8 (c)
9 (d)
10 (e)
11 Gantt chart; critical path method (CPM), programme evaluation and review technique (PERT)
12 A full arrow represents an activity that carries resources. A dummy arrow represents a dummy activity that does not carry resources in terms of labour, materials, time, etc. It is only there to demonstrate dependency or time constraint.
13 In an activity on arrow network, activities are represented by arrows. Rectangular boxes or 'nodes' are used to draw the activity on node diagrams.
14 (a)
15 Earliest start time, latest finish time, duration
16 Total float is the amount of time a non-critical activity may expand without extending the project completion time. Free float is the amount of time an activity can be extended without

rescheduling other activities or extending the completion time. Total float is normally found at the end of a non-critical path.

17 The optimistic time, the most likely time, the pessimistic time

18 False

19 False

20 True

21 Critical activities are those where any delays will result in the whole project being late. Hence, critical activities carry no spare time or float. Non-critical activities are those with float. Therefore, delays may not affect the project completion.

22 (a) The arrow diagram is shown in Figure SAQ.1; (b) The activity on node diagram is shown in Figure SAQ.2.

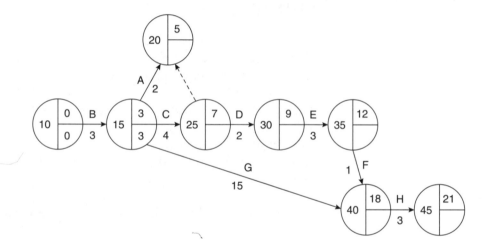

Figure SAQ.1 Arrow diagram

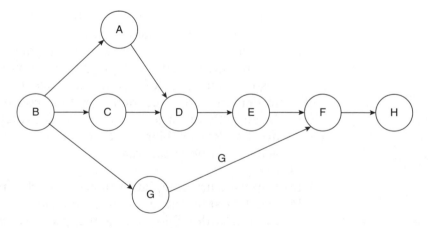

Figure SAQ.2 Arrow on node diagram

Chapter 10

1 The cost of materials purchased is usually a large proportion of business spending. Operationally, the quality of input materials and products can affect the quality of operations outputs. Reworks and delays can result if suppliers frequently fail to meet the purchase specifications

2 Design, production, marketing, finance

3 Quality, delivery, flexibility, cost

4 The product expected life, serviceability, maintenance cost

5 (d)

6 (a)

7 (b)

8 Single-sourcing, multi-sourcing

9 (d)

10 (c)

11 Design, marketing, production, finance

12 What is the function of the product? Is the function necessary? Are all of its features necessary? What else will perform equivalent function?

13 Could we buy the item from outside at less cost but in similar or greater quality? Could we buy the item from outside and maintain or improve our flexibility and responsiveness? What are the future trends in technology and investment implications – if we go for an outside supplier now will we be able to buy it easily in five years time?

14 True

15 False

16 (b)

17 (a)

18 False

19 False

20 False

21 (d)

22 (e)

23 List the quality expected from a supplier, record supplier's performance against a maximum weighting, take the necessary actions

24 (b)

25 (c)

26 True

27 The past and current company performance in the key markets,

the plans for new markets and investments, the target for the
year ahead
28 (c)
29 True
30 (a)
31 (e)

Chapter 11

1 Competitive advantage, survival, influence on cost, influence on
image
2 Influence on cost, influence on image, influence on paymasters,
social responsibility
3 Same as answer 2
4 (b)
5 (a)
6 (c)
7 Prevention costs – training, components, plant, design; appraisal
costs – inspection, testing, stock
8 Internal – scrap, rework, stock, idle capacity, damage to plant,
motivation; external – goodwill, compensation, rectification,
administrative costs
9 (b)
10 (b)
11 (c)
12 (c)
13 (b)
14 (e), but (d) is a stage
15 (b)
16 (c), but (d) acceptable
17 (d), but (c) acceptable
18 (c)
19 (b)
20 (b)
21 (b)
22 Actual experience; expectation, influenced by prior experience,
publicity, word of mouth, general appearance
23 Tangibles, reliability, responsiveness, assurance, empathy
24 (b)

Chapter 12

1 (a)
2 (a)
3 (d)
4 (a)
5 (b)
6 (d)
7 Many suppliers, raw material and finished goods stock, work in progress stock, strong functional divisions, adversarial relationships, unresponsive, stress on utilization
8 Partnership, lean production, little stock, communication and trust, teamwork, stress on satisfaction and effectiveness
9 (c)

Index

July. This is at the end of the financial year and the beginning of the holiday period. The lists are submitted to the subject team for that particular subject area. Because these are part of student handouts, they contain a great deal of material which is not necessarily relevant, i.e. journal articles, books already in stock. They are also not necessarily complete and up to date. The subject team is responsible for checking that the books are not already in stock, that they actually exist, that the details are correct and that they are in print. This leads to a list of proposed purchases, which is authorized by the senior librarian responsible for the subject team. The request is then sent to the acquisitions section. Acquisitions first check the requested books for completeness and availability, then enter the order on to the computer system. The system generates printed orders for dispatch to suppliers on a daily basis.

When books are received, they are checked against the order, and the order file is updated. The books are physically inspected and then entered into the library catalogue, labelled with class marking and security coded. They are then sent to the library.

The subject team checks the books on receipt and then puts them on the shelves or the new book display as appropriate.

Over a twelve-month period it was found that the process times were as shown in Table CS.2.

The pattern is very seasonal as mentioned above.

The orders received for input in the year in question followed the pattern in Figure CS.5.

Table CS.2 Process times

Process	Time (days)		
	Mean	Minimum	Maximum
Subject team checking	60	1	140
Order approval	8	2	14
Acquisitions checking	60	2	170
Order processing	1	1	2
Supplier delivery time	47	4	70
Checking and cataloguing	19	1	30
Unpack and display	2	2	4

Foundations of Primary Teaching

Fourth edition

The need to achieve the latest Qualified Teacher Status (QTS) standards for teaching must be used as a vehicle to liberate innovative and reflective thinking and action. Written specifically for student teachers on PGCE and BEd courses, as well as students on education studies courses, this textbook provides a comprehensive introduction to all aspects of teaching within the primary school. It will encourage those working towards QTS and all studying for education qualifications to develop a fuller understanding and appreciation of teaching as professional practice through an emphasis on:

- Promoting relationships and motivation in the classroom
- Employing a range of teaching and assessment strategies
- Encouraging creativity and transferable teaching skills
- Highlighting personalised learning.

Incorporating new material on Higher Level Teaching Assistants, learning styles and the Every Child matters agenda, as well as updated further reading, including references to QTS standards and National Literacy/Numeracy, this fully-updated fourth edition remains essential reading for all student teachers on initial teacher training courses at the primary level, newly qualified teachers and more experienced teachers wishing to update their practice.

Denis Hayes is a Professor of Education at the Faculty of Education, University of Plymouth, UK.